PRIVATE EYE ANNUAL 2020

THE COVID YEAR

EDITED BY IAN HISLOP

"Well, if that's not flouting the rules, I don't know what is!"

Published in Great Britain by
Private Eye Productions Ltd
6 Carlisle Street, London W1D 3BN
www.private-eye.co.uk

© 2020 Pressdram Ltd
ISBN 978-1-901784-68-8
Designed by Bridget Tisdall
Printed and bound in Italy
by L.E.G.O. S.p.A

2 4 6 8 10 9 7 5 3 1

PRIVATE EYE
THE COVID YEAR
ANNUAL 2020

EDITED BY IAN HISLOP

2020 B.C.
(Before Coronavirus)

IN/OUT CRISIS DEEPENS

A LIKELY TORY

"I need some technology lessons"

"Floppy disk or hard drive?"

SURRENDER ACT

"Fancy a laptop dance?"

"This'll give Boris a pole boost"

VOTE OF CONFIDENCE

"I love a British mug"

"Here's £126,000"

"It's the trade missionary position!"

Tax paid by Facebook shoots up to 'negligible'

by Our Fiscal Staff **Penny Pinching**

IN A huge step forward, the amount of tax paid by Facebook has soared from an "insulting" amount, all the way up to a "pathetic" sum.

The company made clear that it was delighted to be paying "as much as it could legally get away with and nothing more", and that it hoped that paying £28m of tax on £1.6bn of income was roughly in line with the rates paid by normal people across the country.

The "derisory" £28m was, Facebook said, a step towards showing that the firm was "serious about your pathetic country and its feeble attempts to get us to cough up". But they also clarified the sum was probably just a one-off, and next year they hoped to double their UK income while simultaneously making sure the tax paid was "barely visible to the naked eye".

TV HIGHLIGHTS

New gritty nuclear eco-drama. Following the success of Chernobyl, the BBC presents:

Hinkley
9pm (BBC94)

The clock's ticking and Britain's new nuclear reactor is about to go bust before it's even been built. Tense scenes, as accountants desperately try to stem the flow of money that is leaking out at an alarming rate.

Can they stop it before it's too late? No, it's already 15 months late and £94 billion over budget. But will anyone dare admit it to the government, and who will deal with the fall-out? Don't miss the scene when one of the accountants turns green and starts vomiting.

Starring Emily Watson as Theresa May and Jared Harris as Phil Hammond.

EYE RATING: *Not as toxic as it might have been if it had ever been built.*

What the press thinks a Twitterstorm looks like

What it actually looks like

Daily Telegraph Friday 4 October 2019

Letters to the Editor

SIR – Once again I was incredibly disappointed in the BBC, with its lamentably inaccurate portrayal of Sir Winston Churchill in the concluding episode of "Peaky Blinders".

In the scene in which the future Prime Minister met the gangland hoodlum-turned-Labour MP and anti-fascist government informer, a number of grotesque historical errors made their way onto the screen.

For example, Sir Winston Churchill expressed his approval of the planned assassination of Sir Oswald Mosley by Birmingham gypsy criminals! Fair enough, but whilst doing so he was smoking a cigar that was two inches longer than any brand that Sir Winston Churchill could conceivably have purchased in the 1930s. A travesty!

Do the BBC have no specialist advisers on this programme? This dismally slack approach to historical verisimilitude has the effect of undermining the entire production.

If the BBC cannot get something as simple as the length of a Cuban Romeo y Beckhamista (7.5 inches in Imperial measures!) correct, then the viewer is left wondering whether the meeting between Mr Shelby, the leader of the razor gang, and our greatest war-time Prime Minister ever took place at all?!

I do hope that the forthcoming episode of "Call the Midwife", featuring Neville Chamberlain, pays a bit more attention to the facts and less to cheap visual cigar-style gimmicks!
Yours faithfully,
Sir Herbert Gussett
*The Old Humidor,
Cillian St Murphy,
Dorset.*

POETRY CORNER

Lines in celebration of the exhumation of the late General Franco

So. Hello
Again General Franco.

You are being
Dug up.

Perhaps we should
Not be surprised
To see you,
As dictators are
Popping up everywhere
Nowadays.

E.J. Thribb
(17½ feet under)

Ms Priti Patel
AN APOLOGY FROM THE BBC

WE would like to apologise for The Andrew Marr Show, but more particularly for the one which featured an interview with the Home Secretary, Ms Priti Patel.

In the course of the interview, Mr Marr accused Ms Patel of laughing at the plight of various businesses who might suffer due to the uncertainties over the nature of the Brexit Withdrawal agreement.

We now accept that Ms Patel was not laughing, and her face has a natural look of smugness and amused superiority which does not in any way reflect on the serious of her commitment to British business. Nor is it the smirk of someone who is massively out of their depth and only hangs onto her job because her boss has behaved even more appallingly on foreign trips than she did.

We now accept that when Mr Marr consulted his notes and said, "I can't see why you're laughing", he made a grave error as he should have said: "I can't see why you're Home Secretary." We apologise unreservedly to Ms Priti Pathetic.

NEXT WEEK: Andrew Graham Dixon apologises to The Laughing Cavalier.

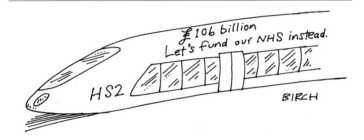

£106 billion
Let's fund our NHS instead.
HS2
BIRCH

WAS SHE SMIRKING?

by Our Smirking Correspondent
Renny Sance

After an appearance by the Mona Lisa on 'The Andrew Da Marr' show this week, there was much discussion in the press about whether she was seen to be smirking during a serious debate about Renaissance Art.

"I was not smirking," said the enigmatic lady. "People are always analysing my expression and wondering what I mean by it, but there's really less to it than meets the eye.

"I'm not very bright, and when I try to look like I care about the threatened jobs of struggling Italian artists my face just falls into that position naturally.

"People seem to forget that even though I'm a public figure, I'm really just two-dimensional when all is said and done."

SHOCK AT SUPREME COURT'S UNANIMOUS VERDICT

We're the only bit of the UK that's not divided

 🔍 Boris Johnson

Home   Create   👥 ⊘ 🔔 ❓

Boris Johnson MP
● Live

People's Prime Minister's Question Time – Live on Fakebook

385,000,000 Views

👍 Like   💬 Comment

0 people **like this**

Hello to the people!
And this is the Question Time that doesn't involve **Parliament**, which is the type I like. Instead, **you** the people, ask **me**, the People's Prime Minister, the sort of questions that **Dom**, the People's Prime Minister's Chief Adviser, has made up on the People's behalf. So, without further ado or die, let's have the **first** question from Miss Carriage, of Justiss, who asks:

> How wrong were those biased left-wing judges in the Supreme Court when they said you'd broken the law, which you hadn't, obviously?

Good question. No one has more respect for those senile old remoaners than yours truly, but the fact is they were **wrong**. It's no business of the judiciary to decide on the law of the land. The whole point of **Brexit** is to give Parliament sovereignty and to give **British** judges power to decide on **British** laws, rather than European judges – oh hang on, Dom's miming hanging himself, so either he wants me to stop or Priti Patel's just come in. The point I'm **making**, and that the Supreme Court Jesters didn't understand, is that the proroguing of Parliament was **nothing** to do with Brexit. So by disallowing it, they're trying to stymie Brexit, which it's nothing to do with – oh hang on, now Dom's out on the window ledge. Either he's getting some fresh air or he's pretending to be the **pound**. Don't do it, Dom! Only kidding, folks.

That Spectator Lunch Menu In Full
(Finger Buffet)

Cheese Fondle
– ✳ –
Old Goat
Spring Chicken Thigh with a squeeze of Johnson
– ✳ –
Grapple Charlotte
or
Bunch of Gropes
– ✳ –
To drink
#TooMuch

"So, it's a stile... get over it"

7

BORIS'S WOMEN PROBLEMS CONTINUE

Just keep your hands where I can see them

SPINELESS BBC CENSORED MY THOUGHT FOR THE DAY

by Chief Jedi **Grand Master Yoda**

ENJOYED my time even though have I presenting For the Day Thought, time it is to leave because censored have I been by Corporation British Broadcasting the Feeble.

Fearful were they that honest a Jedi might controversially tell Evil Empire the history of and Darth Vader his crimes the Rebellion against by Luke Skywalker and Princess Leia led.

"Mention don't the Death Star," told was I. Instead talk only of "on the hand one and other on the" or "in a sense very real that is to say" or "relative it all is when to think about it you come".

But no said I. Protest I will. Be silent will I not. And fired was I.

Shipping forecast handing over no more I will. The Force 10 over Rockall be with you. *(That's enough. Ed.)*

A Doctor Writes

AS A doctor, I am often asked, "Have they just found a breakthrough cure for Alzheimer's?" The simple answer is: "You asked me that last week."

What you are suffering from is repetitive Alzheimer's Breakthrough Syndrome or *Pharmaceuticus Industrius Publicitas*, to give it its full Latin name.

What happens is an International Pharmaceutical Company release a press statement which raises hope for a cure and more importantly raises its share price on the stock exchange, safe in the knowledge that we will forget the last time a

breakthrough of this nature was reported.

The conditions which lead to such outbreaks of optimism spreading through the papers are: Brexit Fatigue, a serious news deficiency, and the Editor forgetting he's already run the story. If you suffer from Alzheimer's Breakthrough Syndrome the best treatment to calm yourself down is to remind yourself that the miracle drugs will be far too expensive for the NHS or will not be available due to Brexit.

© *A doctor*.

THEY WON'T BE TOGETHER LONG

TONY KELLY

Nursery Times

Friday, Once-upon-a-time

ANGER AT FAILURE TO BUILD STARTER HOMES

by Our Political Staff **Little Boy Tory Blue**

THERE was fury at the revelation by the NAO (Nurseryland Audit Office) that the government's promised 200,000 starter homes had not been built.

One old woman, living in a crowded shoe, was furious, exclaiming, "I don't want this many children living with me forever, and they're all in their bloody thirties now! I don't know what to do."

The plan to build thousands of Start-rite first home sandals simply hasn't materialised, leaving many grown-up children without a shoe they can call their own.

Elsewhere, three little pigs were also angry at the inability of the authorities to fulfil their housing promise, resorting to building houses of straw and sticks which failed to keep the wolf from the door.

The crisis in Nurseryland housing has been highlighted by the three bears who went out to the woods to

do whatever it is they do in the woods, only to return to find a squatter had taken up residence.

Said Daddy Bear, "Obviously we are angry about the damage she did to our furniture, but

we do have some sympathy for young girls like Goldilocks who have nowhere else to stay."

Meanwhile in the dark forest, one wicked witch was found to be renting a house made of gingerbread which was well past its sell-by date.

"Look at the mould on the walls," she said, "and it's so cold in here. That's why I had to put these two children in the oven. Honestly officer, that's my story and I'm sticking to it."

The Nurseryland Housing Minister, a Mr Pinocchio, denied there was any problem at all with regard to the government's previous election promise, adding, "You can have 400,000 new starter homes if you just vote for us."

'INCREDIBLE AND UNTRUE' – KNACKER SLAMS 'NICK' ENQUIRY JUDGE

by Our Crime Staff **Tim Vic** and **Vic Tim**

VETERAN police chief inspector "Knacker of the Yard" Knacker hit out today at retired judge Sir Richard Henriques, describing his 994-page report on convicted fantasist Carl Beech (aka "Nick") as "incredible and untrue".

Knacker later admitted to reporters that he had not had time to read the report, but claimed he had seen a photograph of the judge in a copy of the Sun newspaper.

"It was enough for me to entertain grave doubts with regard to the bona fides of this individual," he told the *Eye*.

"Apart from his shifty-looking demeanour, he had attempted to conceal his identity by wearing a

large, old-fashioned wig. But an experienced copper is not going to be taken in by that old trick.

"I am no racist," he added. "However, Henriques is a foreign name and that is entirely consistent with this gentleman's conspicuous failure to relate to British policing methods in the 21st century."

● Inspector Knacker, who is understood to have played a key role in "Operation Ballsup", which led to armed police raids on several innocent pensioners, has since been promoted to head the Met's Office of Independent Police Exoneration Unit, for an annual salary of £899,000.

D I A R Y

L A D Y
G L E N C O N N E R

My maternal grandfather was Lord Crumble, whose great-great-great, I forget how many greats, grandfather, the 1st Lord Crumble, had amassed a fortune with the invention of Apple Crumble. Tipsy in the kitchen one day, he had accidentally dropped some butter into a passing bowl of flour and sugar. Infuriated, he took out his temper on them by beating them up with a wooden spoon then hurling them at some stewed apples. The dish caught on like wildfire, and he was soon wealthy enough to purchase 30,000 acres of prime agricultural land upon which he erected Crumbleton Hall, where I spent much of my idyllic childhood.

My father was what I suppose in these egalitarian days might now be termed a "snob". He owned the whole of Manchester, which he insisted on pronouncing "Manster", even though he didn't know where on earth it was.

Daddy always regarded the Queen Mother as a tradesman; it was only under great pressure that he let her use the front door. I'm afraid it didn't go down at all well with the Royal Family when, after a barbecue at Balmoral, he tried to tip the Duke of Edinburgh, which he insisted on pronouncing Eurgh.

At the tender age of seventeen, I was sent to finishing school so as to perfect my conversation. They taught us skills to last a lifetime. We learnt that when talking to a man at dinner, you should let him speak first, and then, when you are quite sure he has finished, you say, "How absolutely marvellous!" Or, in the case of a bereavement, "How dreadfully sad!" Then you turn to the man on your right, and repeat the process.

They also gave us a thorough grounding in practical matters, such as how to put one's shoes on. A lot of people who have never been to finishing school are in the most frightful pain because they have squeezed a left shoe onto their right foot, or vice versa. Sadly, they have only themselves to blame.

We were also taught flower arranging, which I have enjoyed ever since. The trick of it is actually quite simple. You ask your gardener to cut you some flowers. And then you ask your housekeeper to arrange them for you. Frankly, I don't know why everyone makes such a dreadful fuss about it!

Daddy wanted me to marry his old friend The Earl of Hiccough (pronounced Hiccup), who could trace his family all the way back to Ethel the Unready, the second wife of the famous monarch. Reggie Hiccough had represented Great Britain in the backseat driving event at the 1928 Olympics. Competitors were driven in Bentleys and had to bark instructions at their chauffeurs. But soon after the starting pistol was fired, Reggie dozed off and so scored poorly. Sadly, he lost heart and never married. I would love to have helped him, but by then he was well into his nineties, and, with his snuff and his ear-trumpet was not really "my type".

One thing is for sure: my husband Colin was never boring.

In fact, he was full of surprises. During one memorable meal he held his fork in his right hand and his knife in his left hand! Of course, it became the most tremendous talking-point, and many of our friends still remember that dinner party as one of the most amusing they ever attended.

Colin was deliciously eccentric. On another occasion, he wore his jersey back-to-front all morning, even though we had some very important guests to stay, including Archie Hellmann of mayonnaise fame. Honestly, it was all I could do to keep a straight face!

But he was highly strung and, under pressure, his temper was prone to surface. When the Archbishop asked him on our wedding day if he would take me as his lawfully wedded wife he said, "Mind your own bloody business, you bloody little oik" and delivered a punch to the Rt Rev's tummy.

Our honeymoon night was scarcely any better. I had had a sheltered upbringing. To be honest, I hadn't the foggiest clue about what was beneath my clothes. A few days before the big day, my mother had tried to warn me of what would be expected of me.

"Have you ever observed common people dipping the end of a biscuit into a cup of tea?" she said.

"No," I said.

"Well, they do," she said. "And it's a bit like that."

So on the night of our honeymoon when Colin took me to our suite and took off his trousers I swiftly boiled myself a cup of tea. But the digestives were nowhere to be found and I burst into tears.

Of course, Colin was furious, and stormed off to seek refuge in the arms of the famous society beauty Cruella de Vil, who was later to become a very dear friend. Despite what they say, Cruella had a warm heart and was always very kind to animals.

I will never forget the day Her Majesty the Queen arrived on Mustique.

What happened was this.

Her Majesty the Queen arrived on Mustique.

Certainly a day to remember!

The proudest day of my life was the day Princess Margaret asked me to be her Lady-in-Waiting.

She phrased it so sweetly. "You'll do," she said. "You've only got five children. The least you can do is look after me."

I had barely had a chance to thank her, before she said, "You can start now," and gave an endearing flick of her ash. I hurried across the room for an ashtray. I felt I had passed my first test. "Provide your own shoes, meals extra, any breakages will be paid for."

Then she glanced at the grandfather clock. "Is that the time? For heaven's sake, where's my drinkie-winkie?"

People say she could be spoilt and ill-mannered, but that was far from my experience. In fact, she loved nothing more than "mucking in". I'll never forget the day she picked up a small pile of magazines in Kensington Palace and moved it slightly to one side without ringing the bell for her footman. And, relaxing in the free and easy atmosphere of Mustique, I once witnessed her pouring her own drink, something she had taught herself to do. She then honoured us with a spirited rendition of "Chattanoogie Shoe Shine Boy" before collapsing graciously onto her sofa. Happy days!

As told to
C R A I G   B R O W N

Exclusive to all tabloids
GRETA GARBAGE!

GRETA LOOKS AT TRUMP

by **GLENDA HARTLEY-SLAGGER**

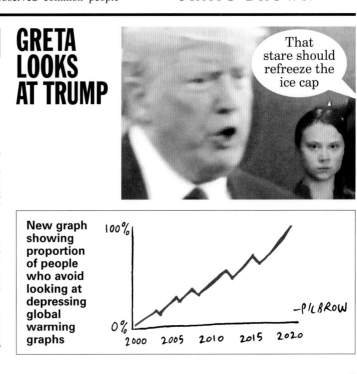

That stare should refreeze the ice cap

LOOK love, no offence, but we've had enough now. OK, the world's going to end and we're all going to die – tell us something new!

And in the meantime, here's a thought for saving energy: why don't we all turn off the telly whenever Greta appears? That way, we minimise energy consumption, reduce fossil fuel dependence, save the planet and stop starving polar bears from eating penguins. (*Is this right? Ed.*)

It's simple! Just grab the remote and turn the TV off!! Sorted! It may be a drop in the ocean, but then with sea levels rising, that won't help anyway! (*Are you sure about this? Ed.*)

So with all due respect, Ms Iceberg, go back to Sweden on your floating yurt and cool off!?

Now excuse me while I book my well-earned holiday somewhere hot (ie the South Pole) – I hear it's lovwely down there and they've got sandy beaches and new vineyards to die for... literally!!

Byeeeeeee!

New graph showing proportion of people who avoid looking at depressing global warming graphs

100%

0%

2000 2005 2010 2015 2020

–PICBROW

THE DONALD TRUMP GUIDE TO GREAT AMERICAN BATTLES THROUGH HISTORY

NORMANDY
The Allied invasion of Western Europe was launched on June 6, 1944, when the US forces from the combined Saving Private Ryan Battalions stormed the beaches of France with the help of British and Canadian troops, but with no help from those cowardly losers, the Kurds.

AMERICAN WAR OF INDEPENDENCE
The American War of Independence (1775-1783) was a brutal and bloody battle between the American freedom fighters, led by George Washington, against the oppressive British rulers, where the cowardly Kurds failed to offer the air support Washington so desperately needed, with none of their planes flying bombing missions after he rammed the ramparts and took over the airports in 1779.

CUSTER'S LAST STAND
Custer's Last Stand, or the Battle of the Little Bighorn, on 25 June 1876 was a fierce battle between the Lakota, Northern Cheyenne, and Alpacino tribes and the 7th Cavalry Regiment of the United States, where General Custer's defeat is blamed by all bigly historians on the cowardly Kurds not killing all the scary Red Indians.

THE ALAMO
The Battle of the Alamo in February 1836 was a 13-day siege when Mexican troops, under President Old El Paso, overran the American fort manned by Davy Crockett and John Wayne after their desperate pleas for help from the cowardly Kurds for assistance in the form of a Trojan Horse fell on deaf ears. (That's quite enough Trump Great American battles. Ed.)

THAT ALL-PURPOSE PRESS RESPONSE TO PRINCE HARRY'S FORTHCOMING LEGAL ACTIONS AGAINST THE FOURTH ESTATE

WITH all due respect to His Royal Highness, and bearing fully in mind the sad history of relations between the Prince's mother, the late Princess of Wales, and of course recognising the Prince's understandable

desire to protect his wife and family from unwarranted intrusion, we do, however, feel that our response to the Duke of Sussex must, by necessity, be as follows: SHUT IT, BEARDY, YOU GINGER WHINGER, BECAUSE IF YOU THINK IT'S BEEN BAD SO FAR, YOU AIN'T SEE NOTHING YET! WE KNOW WHERE YOU LIVE, MR WHINEY WINDSOR, YOU HYPOCRITICAL, HEN-PECKED HUMBUG, WITH YOUR PAMPERED, PETULANT PRINCESS, AND WE'RE COMING ROUND TO SHOVE A TELE-PHOTO LENS UP YOUR JACKSIE!

So, whilst we bow to no one in our admiration of the Royal Family and its constitutional role in the fabric of British public life, we have to consider the vital importance of freedom of speech and the freedom of the press, particularly at this troubled juncture in our island history, and conclude, albeit reluctantly, that: YOU'VE REALLY COCKED UP THIS TIME. DON'T MESS WITH US, SONNY, OR YOU MIGHT FIND YOURSELF ON A ONE-WAY TRIP TO THE GUILLOTINE. NO OFFENCE.

© *All newspapers.*

Kurds   **Turds**

GLENDA WAGG
The gal that Fleet Street calls Slagatha Christie (Geddit??!!)

■ COLEEN??!! Dontchaluvher??! Hats off to the supersleuthin' supermum turned detective who solved the crime of the century, ie, which fellow WAG was a-leakin' and a-sneakin' to the red tops – or should I say rude tops (Geddit!!??!!) Move over Inspector Morse, Hercule Poirot, Sherlock Holmes, Brother Cadfael *(who he? Ed.)*, our Coleen has proved herself the finest private investigator the world has ever known!!!???! I say La Rooney should be solving all the world's problems, including Brexit, global warming, the war in Syria and why Fleabag is so great!!??!! Come on Popey, forget dreary old Cardinal Newman, make it St Coleen of Rooney – patron saint of the soccer sisterhood.

■ COLEEN?! Arentchasickofher??!! Who does she think she is!??!!! Miss Marple in a bikini??!! So you found out that one of your fellow witless WAGs was spillin' the Instagram beans and sellin' tales of your boring life!!??! No sh**, Sherlock!!?! If you're such a great detective, "Columbo" Coleen, how come you can't solve the mystery of what your hubbie, Wayward Wayne, aka Mr Spudface, gets up to with mystery blondes in hotel rooms when he's playing away??!?! No offence, darling, just sayin' it like it is!!?!!

■ SHED a tear for poor Rebekah Vardy!??!! Named and shamed in the red tops – or should I say the roo-tops??!! (Geddit??!!!? Talk about a kanga-Roo court!!?!) Bullied Becky is getting a right old kicking from the snooty soccer sisterhood!!? Just cos she's a nooo-girl and doesn't suck up to old timers like Crabby Coleen, everyone gangs up and calls her a sneaky, snaky slapper!?!!!! Leave La Vardy alone, all of you!!?? She's with *child*, for gawd's sake – as is Coleen!?! ie, the man-baby Wayne!!?! Geddit??!!

■ REBEKAH Vardy!??!!!! What a disgrace!!?? How dare she betray the confidence of the blameless leader of the Wagnificent Seven, Queen Coleen of Bee!!!?? Lock her up, Mr Policeman, she's to blame for everything, including climate change, war in Syria and Brexit!!!?!

■ SEE the celebs at Extinction Rebellion!!!?? Not tryin' to save the planet, more their careers!!?? It's you I'm talkin' about, Juliet Stevenson, Benedict Cumberbatch and some other people, I expect!!?? Talk about an eco-trip!!?! Why don't you just put a sock in it, luvs, and leave the complex subject of man-made global warming to the experts, ie ME!!?!?!

Bye-bye, or should I say Dubai-bai??!!

SWAMPY   SWAMPY'S TREES

Then   Now   Then   Now

SYRIA LATEST: RUSSIA AND TURKEY IN HISTORIC DEAL

We've agreed to share control of the US president

"This is fun!"

Haven't we cared enough now?

by Our Extinction Rebellion Correspondent **Paula Icecap**

There was widespread surprise today right across London, as a fresh wave of Extinction Rebellion protests once again brought Central London to a standstill.

"We thought we'd all done our bit worrying about life on earth ending, when we vaguely supported the Extinction Rebellion protests last time – despite it leading to some

heated arguments down the pub," grumbled all Londoners.

"If we'd have known we'd have to go on worrying about life on earth ending beyond those two weeks, then we'd never have supported the protests in the first place.

"If these ongoing Extinction Rebellion protests mean we're going to be late for work and have to catch a tube five minutes later than we intended, then, on balance, the planet can burn."

School news

St Rice Cakes (formerly St Cakes) Independent School for Girls

Trafficking Term begins today. There were 394 Vietnamese pupils in the school but now there are none and we don't know where they are. The Headmistress, Ms Nell Bar, is taking a sabbatical to help the police with their enquiries. The bursar,

Colonel Pimp, cannot be contacted as he is abroad doing a sponsored runner throughout the Far East. There will be no performance of the school play "The Lady Vanishes" as the cast have disappeared. Exeats have obviously already taken place. Prize-giving will be on 23 November. The guest speaker will be Detective Superintendent Ian Terpol (O.C.) and he will be offering a prize for anyone who can tell him the whereabouts of any of the school.

Notes&queries

I was listening to the radio with my good lady husband when we/they heard the Prime Minister use the phrase: 'Ignoratio elenchi'. What on earth does this mean?
The Reverend Corby Trouser-Dress, The Old/Young Vicarage, Womanchester.

● Come on Rev, this is an easy one. "Ignoratio Elenchi" is the famous Lebanese chef whose Christmas cookbook *1001 Uses of an Aubergine* we all have on our shelves and will no doubt be in yours or your lady husband's stockings or socks this Yuletide or Winterval. Famed for his ingenious use of the eggplant, Ignoratio has changed British Lebanese fusion cooking forever, as many kitchens throughout the land have adopted his use of obscure if frighteningly expensive spices and exotic culinary utensils such as the Elenchi-zestometer which measures the degree of zestiness of your citrus fruit to the nearest pip.
Heston Services, The Fat Duckhouse, Bray.

● Oh dear, Mr Services has got the wrong end of the ladle entirely. Anyone who has read any literature will recognise immediately that Ignoratio Elenchi is a character in *The Merchant of Venice* who provides the

light relief during the pound of flesh scene (often cut). The Elenchi were a famous Venetian family related to the Doge, and Ignoratio, his second cousin, is famous for his Shakespearean one-liner, "Beware of the Doge!," which at the time was considered hugely amusing. In a recent Young Vic version of the play Ignoratio was reimagined as a Nazi and played by Daniel Radcliffe entirely naked apart from an armband.
Gordon Ramsay MacDonald, Duncookin', Isle of Eigg.

● In the words of the Bard himself, Mr MacDonald is talking "Frippleweights and Pipplekins". As anyone with the humblest of education will know, "Ignoratio Elenchi" is the Eton school motto, first inscribed on the buttocks of Sir Edward Pantaloon, the first of the school's Headmasters – or "Skullywags" as they are known to this day. Roughly translated it means, "The stupid will succeed" and is chanted during the Eton Wally Game by the short-trousered Squiblings in Pop on the twelfth minute of every hour on Bullying Sunday. Mr Johnson's use of the motto indicates that he is, in Eton terms, a "Lucnius Magnius" – or, in plain English, a fagglebucket of the first order.
Jo and Rachel Johnson, 'Siblings', Port Stanley FU2 B0J0

DOES HEADING A FOOTBALL GIVE YOU BRAIN DAMAGE? NEW EVIDENCE EMERGES

TITANIC NEWS

Announcement From Captain

LET'S GET THE ICEBERG DONE

I know some people have expressed concern about the fact that there is an iceberg in our path. But what I say to you is this: we have to get on with it. It's ahead of us, we're moving towards it, that's all there is to say on the matter. Anyone who thinks differently has to just get over it. And the great news is that the sooner we hit the iceberg, the sooner we'll be able to get on with attending to so many other things that need fixing on this ship:

- The sanatorium needs to be cleaned out
- One of the violinists in the band has broken a string
- The kitchens need to get on with preparing tomorrow's breakfast
- The Irish below decks are being a bit boisterous

But we can only solve these pressing problems once we've dealt with the iceberg that sits in our path. So I say this to you: we are going to hit the iceberg in a controlled and safe way, cross that off the list, and then – once that is done – we can deal with all the other problems of life on board the ship.

The Beatles – the early years

CANADIAN ELECTION LATEST

LIBERAL PARTY MPs RALLY IN SUPPORT OF JUSTIN TRUDEAU

BREXIT RIOTS LATEST

by Our Political Staff
Clare Monger

BRITAIN was rocked to the core today by the extent of Brexit riots which an unnamed cabinet minister assured this newspaper would take place if parliament blocked Brexit on October 31st.

"At the time, I warned of disturbances on the level of the gilets jaunes riots in France or the Compton riots in LA, saying there would be tens of thousands of people on the streets," said the minister. "And just look at this picture, with its terrifying scenes of pro-Brexit riots right across Britain today after parliament voted in favour of a Brexit extension."

What You Will Hear

John Humphrys

Classic FM

Humphrys: And now it's Beethoven's "Ode to Joy".

(Music begins to play)

Humphrys *(interrupting)*: Yes, that's all very well, Beethoven, but in the interest of balance I think we need some misery here. Let's bring in Mozart with his "Requiem".

(Music begins to play)

Humphrys *(interrupting again)*: I think you've made your point, Mr Mozart, and perhaps a period of silence might be welcome. John Cage has something to say on that.

(Cage's 4'33" begins to play. It is then interrupted by Beethoven and Mozart resulting in cacophony)

Humphrys: Please, gentlemen, let Mr Cage have his say. *He* didn't interrupt you…

(Barrage of noise continues)

Humphrys: I'm sorry, I'm going to have to cut you off there. Thank you very much. Now it's time for Schubert's Symphony Number 8 in B Minor. *(Music begins to play)* No, I'm afraid that's all we've got time for, Mr Schubert, and don't complain that it's my fault your symphony was unfinished…

(Humphrys is fired.)

Film highlights

When Harry Met Silly

Classic sweet/sour rom-com which asks the age-old question: can a Royal be just friends with the press without getting screwed? No.

Enjoy the banter as Harry (a moody Damien Lewis) and Silly (an in-form Meghan Markle) fall in and out of love with the press (but mostly out), as their relationship takes a rollercoaster ride from bad to terrible.

Includes the infamous scene where Harry asks Silly if they should sue the Mail on Sunday for a technical copyright infringement and she replies, "Yes, yes, yes, yes, oh *yesss!*"

The scene finishes with a whip-smart wisecrack from the old lady who is watching her (the Queen, portrayed perfectly by Helen Mirren), who says, "Whatever she is doing, I'll have none of it."

You'll laugh, you'll cry, you'll start thinking Wills and Kate aren't that boring after all.

EYE RATING: Hysterical.

YES — IT'S ELECTION FEVER!

TORY FLOOD OF PROMISES

Only we can sort out the mess that we created

LABOUR SPENDING SPREE

What'll it cost us?

The election?

BREXIT PARTY DEAL

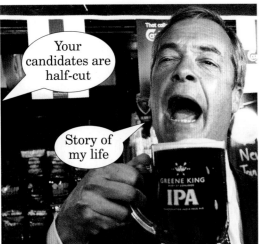

Your candidates are half-cut

Story of my life

LIB DEM PLEDGE

I'm going to be Prime Minister

I wasn't born yesterday

Disastrous first week for Tories sees poll lead collapse to a new high

Boris Johnson's Tory party paid the price for a shambolic start to their election campaign, with disastrous gaffes by Jacob Rees-Mogg over Grenfell, James Cleverly being empty chaired by Kay Burley and a video emerging of a drunken Boris Johnson contradicting his own Brexit deal on Irish border checks, as opinion polls punished them with a two-point increase over Labour.

"This should be a salutary lesson to us all as to how we must conduct ourselves throughout this campaign, yes, stupidly," Boris Johnson told senior Tories whilst leading a conga around Number 10. "That means Matt Hancock body-slamming Peston, Liz Truss chucking potatoes at the Irish embassy and Chris Grayling... being Chris Grayling."

Empty chair row

Conservative Party insiders have described the interview given by the empty chair to Kay Burley on Sky Breakfast as "impressive".

"You have to say, when compared to the shambolic performances of James Cleverly on *Good Morning Britain* or Rees-Mogg on Talk Radio, this was impressive stuff, with no gaffes or embarrassing soundbites going viral.

"The empty chair has certainly leapfrogged the likes of Gove, Raab and Hunt as favourite to be the next Tory leader if Boris messes up the election."

THAT TOP SECRET RUSSIAN PROBE DOCUMENT – WHAT YOU WILL READ

After months of painstaking investigation into possible Russian involvement in Britain's democratic process, we have reached the following conclusions:

1. Do Russians have access to British government computer systems? Nyet

2. Do Russians want to hurt their good friends, the British? Nyet

3. Is Mr Putin very nice man? Da!

4. Do we want to throw people who suggest otherwise off the top of that magnificent and much visited 123-metre-high Salisbury Cathedral? Nyetski!

5. Simples!

Key finding

BREXIT MEANS BREⱭIT

End of report.

The Sad End Of The Apostrophe Society

IT'S OVER, but it's legacy lives on. And we at the Daily Gnome will never forget the Apostrophe Societys role in keeping the use of apostrophe's strictly correct in a society who's grammatical education is not as good as it's predecessor's and who'se standard's are s'adly *(cont. p94)*

"If you'd just allow me to finish evading your question!"

THAT ALL-PURPOSE CANDIDATE'S SOCIAL MEDIA APOLOGY

I WOULD like to say how much I regret the **tweet/selfie/Facebook post** in which I expressed views which could be construed as **anti-Semitic/Islamophobic/misogynistic**. I would like to point out that this was **a long time ago/yesterday/earlier this afternoon** and it should be taken into consideration that I was much **younger/drunker/more unpleasant** back in those days. Nowadays, my older self would never refer to someone as **Zionist whore/Jihadi lookalike/fat old bag**. And I would certainly not threaten to **murder/murder/murder** anybody simply because I disagree with one or two of their views on **Brexit/Climate Change/Strictly**. So, I hope this clears the air and I look forward to standing as your MP for the next **5 years/3 months/1 day**.

Lib Dem poll shock

A stunning new poll* commissioned for the Liberal Democrats has revealed that the Lib Dems are on course for an HISTORIC General Election victory which will propel Jo Swinson into No 10.

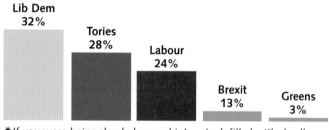

Lib Dem 32%
Tories 28%
Labour 24%
Brexit 13%
Greens 3%

If you were being slowly lowered into a tank filled with deadly piranha fish and ravenous man-eating sharks and the only way to stop you from dying, screaming in agony, was to vote Liberal Democrat in the General Election, who would you vote for?

> My wife thinks I'm totally insane
>
> She's right you don't have a wife

The 30th Anniversary of the Wall

by Our History Staff
Dominic Sandbag

No one will ever forget where they were when they heard the incredible news about the wall, which for so long had been a symbol of division and hostility.

Now, suddenly after 30 months, Donald Trump's wall is still not up.

Scenes of people happily crossing the border marked a weekend of anniversary celebrations, as people all over the world remembered what it was like before and after the wall was built, ie exactly the same.

President Trump himself led the 30th anniversary celebrations, saying, "It was a historic moment when the world really did shift and Colorado moved from the middle of the US to the border with Mexico."

Trump then repeated his promise to the huge crowds who had failed to turn up to the White House.

"The Cold Wall is over!" he shouted, and repeated the words of President Kennedy: "Ich loony bin ein Hamburger!"

WHAT TO DO IN A DISASTER

A guide from our wealth and safety expert JACOB REES-MOGG

THE TITANIC Well, obviously the common sense thing to do in any ocean-going liner versus iceberg situation is to avoid the ship all together. No offence to the poor fools who drowned, but their big mistake was to get on board and to accept the authorities' assurances that the vessel was unsinkable. I would have stayed at home or, if the journey had been truly necessary, caught the Hindenburg airship instead.

THE HINDENBURG Well, obviously the common sense thing to do in any gas-filled and highly combustible air balloon situation is not to let it catch fire. No offence to the poor victims of the tragedy, but what I would have done is loll across three seats at the back and ignore the authorities' advice not to light a candle to read the safety instructions. After the ensuing explosion, I would have headed straight for the exit door and stepped out. Finding myself 300 feet above the ground, common sense would have prevailed, and I would have held my top hat above my head as a makeshift parachute, before drifting gently to the ground and safety.

BREXIT Well, obviously the sensible course of action is to ignore the advice of the so-called experts and take a blind leap over a cliff edge into the unknown, having first of all guaranteed one's safety by setting up a branch of one's business in Dublin. It's common sense.

GRENFELL FIRE CHIEF REFUSES TO RESIGN

> I've been advised to stay put

POETRY CORNER

In Memoriam Terry O'Neill, photographer (1938-2019)

So. Farewell
Then
Terry O'Neill.

You were famous
For many
Photos of legendary
Celebrities.

But only one
Will last as
Your enduring
Legacy.
(see below)

E.J. Thribb (F17½)

Mr Brill O'Pad and friend captured by the late Andrew O'Neill

SAME-SEX COUPLE DANCING ROUTINE PROVOKES 200 COMPLAINTS TO BBC

From the BBC Duty Log

LIKE many other angry BBC viewers I was astonished and appalled to discover that there were gay people on Strictly Come Dancing.

Last week I was enjoying a wholesome Sunday night in with my wife and family and was shocked when suddenly there were two men dancing together on the box.

May I make it clear that we don't watch Strictly for this gay propaganda. We watch it for the sort of honest heterosexuality that only Bruno Tonioli and Craig Revel Horwood can provide.

I hope that literally tens of other brave, anonymous complainers like myself, have rung in to Auntie Beeb, to make it clear that she has fallen well below the standard that we have come to expect. What was wrong with the good old days when the BBC provided wholesome entertainment with the likes of Frankie Howerd and Jon Inman?

Name and address withheld

AN EYE SPOT-THE-TOFF QUIZ!

Which Old Etonian do you think is doing the most to undermine his party / government / church / institution / country?

MOTHERCARE TO CLOSE, DESPITE BEST EFFORTS OF PM

by Our Retail Staff **Tony Broke**

THE once giant maternity goods chain, Mothercare, is on the brink of bankruptcy, recording huge losses in the UK sector.

The potential failure of this iconic high-street colossus is a huge embarrassment to the government and, in particular, to the new Prime Minister.

A spokesman for Number Ten (Dominic Cummings, obviously) said, "Listen, fuckwit, Boris has done everything he can to keep Mothercare in business. You can't blame him for not trying. Now fuck off."

Retail analysts agree that the Prime Minister has, over the

last few decades, single-handedly propped up the ailing baby behemoth.

Said one, "Sales of rattles, dummies and toys to throw out of the pram have all boomed thanks to Boris. And his production of babies has been very helpful too."

Jeremy Corbyn WRITES

HELLO! It's me again. Did you see Boris Johnson at the Cenotaph last Sunday? What a terrible performance! He missed his cue! He had his wreath upside down! Oh, for goodness sake!

That's what happens when you leave wreath-laying to a complete amateur! If Britain does vote for me, it can rest assured it will be getting an Olympic-standard wreath-layer as PM. Many's the time I have been congratulated for my wreath-laying and I wasn't even involved, merely present. That's how expert I am! I even keep a foldaway wreath in my suitcase in case there's a deceased terrorist who needs to be honoured while I'm on my hols!

But that's by the by. I'm in too much of a good mood to get picky about Boris's wreath laying. It's election time! Hurray! It's my favourite bit of politics, because it's like a month-long sabbatical; no paperwork or boring meetings, you just hand out leaflets, sing about the red flag, stand on stages with other old grey-bearded people and shout incoherently into cheap microphones – all of which happen to be my favourite hobbies! And to make it even better, everywhere I'm campaigning is completely flooded, so I don't even have to change out of my gardening Wellingtons!

There are concerns that this election is going to be difficult for us. I'm sure you also saw all that stuff about Russian money suddenly flooding into the Conservative Party coffers. I would be tempted to be angry about that, but, thankfully, I've trained for many years not to be angry about anything the Russians do, so that's one less thing to worry about!

All the same, I do feel a bit of a twinge of annoyance. Here I am, the biggest Russian fan ever; I've read the book and bought the T-shirt (literally!) but, come our moment of triumph, they're funding the enemy! One almost might suspect that Putin and his comrades are just mafia-style oligarchs rather than principled proponents of Socialism! But that's hardly likely! I bet it's all a subtle and farsighted plan to stick it to George Soros. That's what I think!

Got to go, plenty to do now that Tom Watson has sadly decided to go. Tom promised me that his departure was not political, but "personal". He said, "I just really hate you, Jeremy". So that was a relief.

Meanwhile, there is some silly talk of having TWO Labour leaders after the election. Really? So what's new?
Cheers,
Jeremy and Seumas

PS. Now that schools are going to be used for polling stations, they have had to cancel all the nativity plays and no one will be singing *O Come All Ye Faithful*. This is apparently what they will be singing instead...!

"I didn't expect that reaction. Normally, people like it when you show off your new baby at work..."

Maitlis

Mateless

Nursery Times

·········· Friday, Once-upon-a-time ··········

GRAND OLD DUKE OF YORK RELIEVED OF DUTIES

by Our Royal Correspondent **Nicholas Wicked Witchell**

THE not-so-Grand Duke of York was today ruing his disastrous TV interview on Newsnightynight, which has been described by everyone on Nurseryland as a massive pumpkin coach crash.

The Duke of York had 10,000 men sponsoring his various charity and business activities, and they are all now distancing themselves from him after his disastrous fall from grace. Said one, "When he was up he was up, and it was great to be associated with him, but now he's down, he's down, and we don't want to have anything to do with him."

Said another, "The Duke is not even half-way up or half-way down – he's completely over the hill." It's widely acknowledged in court circles that the Duke's image problem stemmed from the fact that the Grand Old Duke had had 10,000 women, when what he actually needed was 10,000 PR men.

Top Royal insider, Pussycat Pussycat, revealed, after a visit to look at the Queen, that the Grand Old Duke's big mistake in the ill-fated interview was not that he was "Old", or a "Duke" but that he had simply been too "Grand".

The Queen who has been in her parlour eating bread and honey, has finally given the Duke his marching orders, and he may now face questioning from the FBI, the Fairyland Bureau of Investigation.

Royal Lodge, Windsor
November 29th

10am His Royal Highness Prince Andrew will be awoken by his alarm clock. He will turn it off and go back to sleep in the company of himself.

10:30am His Royal Highness will attend a breakfast event in the staff quarters, attended by himself. The breakfast will comprise one bowl of "just-add-hot-water" porridge served in a Tupperware container from the Queen's own collection. Cold coffee will then be served by himself.

10:45am His Royal Highness will attend the turning on of the television set by HRH Prince Andrew. He will be entertained during the course of the morning by the following celebrities: Ms Lorraine Kelly, Mr David Dickenson, Mr Bargain Hunt and Mr Eamonn Holmes-Under-The-Hammer.

12 noon His Royal Highness will mark the passing of midday with a minute's silence in which he contemplates whether he can be bothered to have a shave or not. He will conclude that there is little point.

1:00pm Luncheon. HRH will attend the grand opening of a can of beans, by a member of the royal family (himself).

1:15pm He will receive a phone call from a Mr Patel from a Coventry call centre asking him if he's had an accident at work. Prince Andrew will reply in the affirmative. But on taking his details, Mr Patel will tell HRH to stop bothering him and ring off.

2:00pm His Royal Highness will oversee the reception of a package from Amazon for his neighbour and will officially sign his name with his finger on the electronic delivery device.

2:05pm His Royal Highness will attend a screening in his bedroom of *The Treasure of Sierra Madre* on the Turner Movie cable channel.

4:00pm Prince Andrew will set the alarm for *Pointless*, before an official visit to the Land of Nod.

5:05pm On returning from a successful tour of Nod, HRH will wake to the sound of his alarm and then welcome Messrs Alexander Armstrong and Richard Osman into his living room, along with several members of the public. He has no further engagements.

PRINCE ANDREW INTERVIEW

It was a car crash

That's my boy!

Late News

ROBERT NO LONGER THE WORST MAXWELL

FERGIE NO LONGER THE MOST EMBARRASSING YORK

Russia 'relaxed about sporting ban'

by Our Moscow Correspondent
Anna Bollix-Steroid

Kremlin sources insist Russia will shrug off the four-year ban handed down by the World Anti-Doping Agency, as they will be able to continue competing in their favourite sport: fixing foreign elections.

"We are very proud of our highly trained Russian team running rings round the Facebook regulators as they propel our preferred candidates to victory," said a clearly relaxed President Putin.

"From our triumph at the 2016 US Presidential election to the murky politics of the 2020 British General Election, Russia is once again winning around the globe. We're Number One!

"Democracy has been out-paced, out-thought and played off the pitch. They think it's all over. It is now."

Boris Johnson PM
● Live

People's Prime Minister's Special Election People's Question Time Leader's Questions – Live on Fakcheck

385,000,000 Views

👍 Like   💬 Comment

0 people **like this**

Hello Fakefolks!

This is me. **Fact**. Tick. **Correct**. It is me. Proof there, that you can trust the Conservatives to tell you the truth. **Fact**. Tick. Tock. So, time for some questions and with the election just days away or weeks or whatever it is, details, details, let's have some questions as filtered by **Dominic Cummings** who's back, helping us out with a few of the sort of questions he imagines the people might ask, were they real. Which they are. **Fact**. Tick. Dominic looking as well as ever, after the heart implant. Sorry Dominic, you've gone pale, well paler. So, first question, from Vic Titious, who asks:

> Has there ever been anything more brilliant than your election video?

Simple answer, **no**. Our amazing slice of life, non-scripted non-reality TV-style, fly-on-the-trousers documentary about five minutes in the life of yours truly is already **wowing** the punters and has over 85 billion likes. **Fact**. Tick. It's going gang-bangers, I mean gang-busters, or perhaps ghost-busters, anyway, in case you missed it, here it is.

SCENE 1: INTERIOR TORY HQ

We see Boris walking down the corridor with nothing better to do than make a cup of tea. We hear Barry Geezer asking in-depth questions in a relatable working class voice…

GEEZER: Watcha, Bozza!

BORIS: What ho, Mr Geezer! Fancy seeing you and your camera crew here. First relatable question please.

GEEZER: How does your day begin?

BORIS: Usually I say "What's your name, darling?", then I look for my trousers and — oh, since I became Prime Minister? I go out, with my new dog, to do his business. Get it done, I say to him, get this ghastly smelly business over with.

GEEZER: Great normal-bloke story, Normal Boz.

Boris walks down corridor as though he's in the West Wing, past hastily blu-tacked poster reading: "20,000 more police, 50,000 more nurses, 100,000 more posters".

GEEZER: Here's a tough question for any Prime Minister to have to answer: Fish and chips or Sunday roast?

BORIS: Obviously fish and chips, wearing a Kiss-Me-Quick hat, with Blackpool rock for pud, on the end of the pier, with lots of other geezers like your good self, before going down the Rub-a-dub-dub for a pint of apples and pears. Not an elitist posh roast pheasant, cooked by the staff and washed down with a nice bottle of claret — yuck!

GEEZER: Good answer Bozster! And cue Mr Bame…

A well-turned out person of BAME extraction appears from doorway. Boris gives him a friendly pat on shoulder.

BORIS: Hello, Bamey! Fancy seeing you here. I mean in this office, not this country. On your way now.

GEEZER: Wow, you're so relatable. What's your favourite band?

BORIS: Marmite, definitely.

GEEZER: Nice one, but a bit early. That one's coming up next.

BORIS: Oh good point, yes, sorry. Fish and chips.

Boris makes tea by putting mug and teabag in dishwasher and pressing button.

BORIS: There we go, cup of cha, oven-ready. Like Brexit.

GEEZER: Talking of which — The Clash or Rolling Stones?

BORIS: Well, I'm very much a Let's Spend the Night Together kind of Prime Minister and I can't get no Brexit satisfaction, without an election, and London Calling will probably be a summons from the police. So, Sunday Roast it is.

Boris walks past poster saying "20,000 more policemen are after me" and heads off down corridor. He then opens door and exits into broom cupboard.

ENDS

Hope you enjoyed that kitchen sink drama. Eat your **heart** out, Ken Loach! Time for another question from Olly Garch:

> What's all this nonsense that the media are trying to drum up, about you changing the name of the Tory Twitter page to Factcheck UK?

Well, I'm afraid Olly, you **haven't** checked your facts. I **have**. And what happened was that **we**, in a spirit of transparency, changed the name of the Tory Party to **FatCheque**, reflecting our open-door policy to all those who'd like to invest in a go-getting, forward-looking party that **believes** in the freedom of movement from Russia to Conservative Party Headquarters, or FactCheck Central as it's now known. **Fact**. Tick. Cheque! That's all we've got time for. **Fact**. Tick. Tock. Mouse. Clock. Dickery.

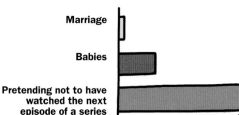

"He was that needy, he actually asked me for a second date"

Cordell

Challenging times in a relationship

Marriage

Babies

Pretending not to have watched the next episode of a series

MAX ELLIS

DIARY
CARLY SIMON

WHO IS THE 'YOU' IN "YOU'RE SO VAIN"?

JEFFREY ARCHER: I salute Carly for refusing to reveal my identity. She must have known it would embarrass me if the news got out!

Strictly between these four walls, Carly and I go back a very, very long way.

We were young and carefree and determined to make our ways in the world.

Ah, memories, memories! All the clues are there in the song. The apricot scarf. The clouds in her coffee. The truly unforgettable total eclipse of the sun after I'd flown my Lear jet up to Nova Scotia. And Carly begging me to autograph her first editions of Cain and Abel and Not a Penny More, comparing them – bless her! – to those veritable masters of the written word, Dickens and Tolstoy.

JULIAN FELLOWES: I may or may not have dallied with Miss Simon in my youth. That must remain between myself and Miss Simon. But let me make something perfectly clear. One should never ever EVER walk into a party wearing a hat, unless, of course, one is attending an open-air gathering, eg Royal Ascot, at which hats are obligatory – though, even then, it is dreadfully common to dip one's hat "below one eye". Furthermore, I would ask Miss Simon to withdraw her allegation that

"your scarf, it was apricot". As we both know, white scarves are permissible at the opera, and scarves of sober colouring may be worn at shooting parties (though then only *en plein air*). The very idea that one would have worn an apricot scarf AND a hat to Miss Simon's party is really too ghastly. One hates to say this about any woman of "a certain age", but I'm afraid to say that Miss Simon lacks breeding.

GERMAINE GREER: For Chrissake, everybody who was around at the time was agreed that Carly Simon was the poor plug-ugly fat-lipped tub of lard who no one in their right mind wanted to talk to, let alone go to bed with. Guys like Mick and Warren would see her coming and run a mile rather than go through the intensely tedious and frankly soul-destroying process of having to snog her. So it frankly makes me hopping mad when I hear her trying to make out that they had it off with her. Cut it out, Carly! I was there at that party, and for what it's worth, Mick and Warren and Kris and Jack Nicholson were all gathered around me, and let's face it, when YOU walked into the party you were so grotesquely unattractive that all the guys rushed out the back door with me, and that's a fact.

MARY BEARD: I had Carly Simon on the show, so I put the question to her that has been on everybody's mind these past 46 years.

"So, Carly," I said, "wonderful to have you 'on the show', as it were, and great that I should now have what I might call the 'golden' opportunity to 'put to you' the question that has been at the root of 'public discourse', if I might call it that, for what is getting on for half a century now, and that question, if one can

call it a question, which, on reflection, I think one can, is this, and this alone: to what extent is the 'true identity' of the person you are addressing in 'You're So Vain', which is, I might add, a song that is a personal favourite of mine, to what extent is the 'true identity' of that person – though obviously we'll have to examine in some detail, whether any one of us can ever really have what can be called a 'true identity' – so, as I say, to what extent is the 'true' or 'real' identity of the person in question a valid subject for speculation, given the confines of what one might call the 'popular song', and, if it is a valid subject for speculation – that is to say, if the question may be asked in any remotely legitimate or 'proper' way, then I would very much like to ask it of you, notwithstanding any objections, personal or otherwise, you may have to my so doing? But, very sadly, we're out of time, so let's move 'swiftly on' to the fascinating exhibition of Spode Tableware we've all been to see at the Anstruther Gallery in Bath…"

RACHEL CUSK: Why does she say I'm so vain? What right has she? We've never even met, but the hatred in her song screams out at me. It makes me want to scream back, "Why me? Why are you telling everyone I'm so vain? Why do you want me dead? I am blameless!"

It's my former husband who has put her up to it, of that I am certain. I can't take this any more. I pick up her record and hurl it across the room. It hits a priceless vase and smashes it into a thousand little pieces, jagged and the shards stare back at me, bent on a revenge I don't deserve.

As told to
CRAIG BROWN

Game of Thrones actress 'pressured over nudity'

by Our Game of Thrones Correspondent
George X.X.X. Martin

A Game of Thrones actress has revealed that after considerable pressure from the producers she relented and agreed to appear in a scene fully clothed.

"They kept insisting that wearing some clothes was integral to my character, but I was understandably reluctant and in the end felt pressured not to disrobe," said the actress.

"I looked around the set and everyone else had their tits out for no obvious reason

and I thought, why am I being singled out? Why do I have clothes on? It means none of the fan boys will be fantasising about me and making me an internet sensation.

"After a few weeks of appearing on screen fully clothed, I knew I would have to leave the show – and that none of the viewers would notice as they would be staring at all the tits on display."

Bañana – the banana that never comes

POETRY CORNER

**In Memoriam
Bob Willis,
England cricketer**

So. Farewell
Then Bob Willis,
Hero of Headingly,
You have gone from
Ashes to ashes.

You will be missed,
Much like your
Better deliveries.

You reached 70,
A good innings for
A fast bowler.
But now, alas,
It is "over".

E.J. Thribb
(17½ runs per wicket)

*(Sorry this is a
Bit short, which,
As a Sky pundit,
Was your complaint
About a lot of
England's bowling.)*

EXCLUSIVE TO ALL NEWSPAPERS

ME AND MY SPOON

THIS WEEK

JENNIFER ARCURI

Do you have a favourite spoon?

I'm not going to answer that question. It's a private matter and I don't see why I should become collateral damage.

But that is the only reason we are doing this interview. To talk about spoons.

Look, I've been heartbroken and I have been tossed away as if I were an old spoon…

So you will talk about spoons?

What I will say is this. I've had a special relationship with a particular spoon. Not just a one night spoon, and I've kept that spoon affair secret, and I've been loyal and discreet which is why I'm going on national television to say nothing about it.

Ok, if you won't answer questions about spoons, may I ask you a more general question as a technology entrepreneur and business guru?

Yes, certainly.

Did you shag Boris?

Can I tell you about something amusing that happened to me in connection with a spoon?

No!

NEXT WEEK: *Boris Johnson, "Me and my Johnson"*

"He cast me aside! You'd think I was his wife!"

THE RISE OF THE 'PRESIDENTIAL' ELECTION IN THE UK

WHAT exactly is a 'presidential' election? Here are six ways elections have become more 'presidential' in the last few years:

- The man who'll end up winning is a priapic, tubby, straw-haired truth-dodger
- The principal opposition figures are either an enormously unelectable octogenarian left-winger (Bernie Sanders) or an enormously unelectable septuagenarian left-winger (Jeremy Corbyn)
- Unrealistic promises being thrown around (2000-mile wall) matched only by even more unlikely promises (20,000 police officers)
- Everyone hates everyone else
- Strong chance of impeachment within the year
- Whoever comes first, Russia wins

NEW ON TV!

Jeremy Clarkson's Reverse Gear

Amazon Dave Prime

TV's favourite motormouth *(surely "petrolhead"? Ed)* performs an incredible U-turn as he suddenly notices all the damage that he has done to the environment over the years!

Join Jeremy on a white-knuckle ride down a dried-up river bed to a puddle that used to be Lake Titicacrash!

Special guest, Greta Thunberg, is the star in a Reasonably Priced Yacht! Watch as she and Jeremy banter about the dire effects of global warming, carbon emissions and how much they *love* lycra-wearing vegetarian cyclists!

From The Message Boards

Members of the online community respond to the major issues of the day…

Trans controversy

Guys, is it me or is it hard to keep up with gender etiquette? My teenage daughter Charlotte calls me Gammonosaurus (!) and informs me that current causes célèbres include: trans awareness in primary schools; removing the female symbol from sanitary products; the deputy chief constable of Cheshire asking her Twitter followers to observe National Pronouns Day and 'respect those who are transgender or gender non-conforming'; and Humberside Police's 'hate crime' investigation into a man who declined to employ a trans model as a female porn actress because she has a penis! – *Bogbrush*

I am a Reader in Gender Studies with a particular interest in LGBT+ education for young children. To illustrate the progress we have made, in 1985 a small co-operative published 'A Sock Is A Shoe That Doesn't Know What To Do' (a simple allegory about gay identity in a heterocentric society) and it was roundly condemned by the establishment. This year, the book was updated for schools with the assistance of the Ministry of Justice and the National Police Chiefs' Council and retitled 'A Sock and a Shoe, Woo-hoo!' (One sock identifies as a sock, the other as a shoe.) – *Dr Sarah Reeves*

I was a hospital radio DJ for 50 years, until I had a 'PC' complaint about my jingle, 'It's Simon Smith and he's amazing dancing bare!' (a saucy pun on 'Simon Smith And His Amazing Dancing Bear'). ☹ . Life was so innocent when I started, and a 'tranny' was a transistor radio! I remember Noel Edmonds telling a delightful story from a listener who had a glazier at her house. When the man used the loo, she heard her young son call out, 'Remember the three things: trousers down, winky out, and hold still!' Edmonds had been unsure whether 'winky' was an acceptable Radio 1 word, but they told him, 'Of course it's OK, you're talking about a little boy!' 😄 Nowadays all sorts of silly conclusions would be drawn. – *Simon 'Sunshine' Smith*

So true! Kinks, Beatles, Floyd, Who, etc all had "trans" hits and no one took offence. The BBC's only objection was that one song mentioned Coca-Cola! – *Sweet Loretta Martin*

Is your username a reference to Sweet Loretta Modern [NOT 'Martin' as widely misquoted on the internet] who, in the song 'Get Back', 'thought she was a woman, but she was another man'? If so, you misattribute the recording to 'Beatles'. The label clearly states: THE BEATLES with Billy Preston. – *PCS 3042*

If the Beeb bring back The Old Grey Whistle Test, they'll probably call it The Senior Gay Sexual Health Clinic Test. ☹ – *Rupert*

Great stuff guys! – *Bogbrush*

WHERE'S WALLY?

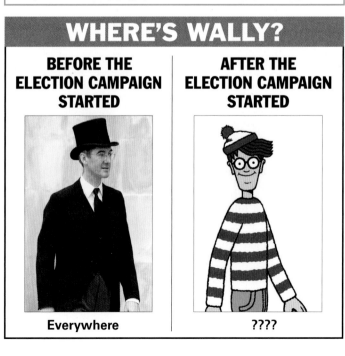

BEFORE THE ELECTION CAMPAIGN STARTED

Everywhere

AFTER THE ELECTION CAMPAIGN STARTED

????

19

ELECTION WEEK IN PICTURES

BORIS FORGETS WORDS OF SONG

The lies on the bus go round and round ♪ ♫♫ ♪

BREXIT PARTY CANDIDATES BRIBED

The Tories offered me a major role

Widow Twankey?

LIB DEMS TO LEGALISE MIND-ALTERING DRUGS

Go on! Change your mind! Vote for me

Twitter embraces left-wing firebrand Andrew Neil

by Our Social Media Correspondent **Nia Eve**

Twitter today embraced left-wing firebrand Andrew Neil as a folk hero, after prime minister Boris Johnson was seen to be running scared from the BBC interviewer.

"How could anyone doubt that Neil was one of us? I bet that right through the 80s he was on the picket line with the miners organising Red Wedge concerts with Billy Bragg and not editing Rupert Murdoch's *Sunday Times* where he hired Britain's foremost Holocaust denier, Nazi apologist David Irving," tweeted BORISOUT-JEZZARULES2345#FBPE to his 72 followers.

"Andrew Neil is one of us!

He's anti-Tory, anti-austerity and anti-Boris from the soles of his shoes to the Adam Smith Institute tie he wore on the Daily Politics show in 2017," agreed TORIESCUMOUT9834#FBPE.

"Andrew Neil is a hero of the left, with his denouncing of the scientific consensus on climate change and chairmanship of *The Spectator,* which gives a voice to such dedicated left-wing opponents of the Tories and Johnson as Fraser Nelson, Toby Young and Brendon O'Neill," tweeted 0JEREMYCORBYNFORPM8325

The BBC has defended having such a left-wing firebrand as Twitter hero Andrew Neil carrying out their interviews, saying it balances out the extreme right-wing views of the host of their *Andrew Neil Show.*

HOW THE ELECTION COVERAGE WILL LOOK FOR THE NEXT THREE WEEKS

THE ☒ TIMES
Corbyn: I will send World War II veterans to Middle East to liberate Palestine

Sun
COMRADE CORB TO REPLACE NELSON'S COLUMN WITH INFLATABLE STALIN

The Daily Telegraph
Corbyn: My First Act As PM Will Be To Rip Off Queen's Head And Vomit Down Her Throat

DAILY EXPRESS
CORBYN TO HUNT DOWN SAD GHOST OF DIANA AND SUCK HER UP WITH A HOOVER

i HAS ANTI-CORBYN HYSTERIA IN RIGHT- WING PRESS PEAKED TOO EARLY?

theguardian
No. We hate him too

The Eye presents the new amazon corporate adverts

20

WHO TO VOTE FOR
The ultimate tactical voting guide

IF you're a SOUTHERN REMAIN voter in a CONSERVATIVE seat and you're not happy you should vote BREXIT to suck votes away from the CONSERVATIVES unless you live in a MIDLANDS LIB DEM seat in which case you should vote CONSERVATIVE to punish the Libs for their revocation policy and because you didn't like Jo Swinson's photoshoot, but then again if you're a NORTHERN LEAVE voter in a LABOUR seat you should vote GREEN to punish the TORIES for what they did to your entire community and to punish LABOUR for paying you zero attention while they were flashing their ankles at the IRA, unless you are a NORTHERN REMAIN voter in a TORY seat when you should vote for the SNP to show your opinion on regional independence, although if you're a LABOUR voter in the WELSH LEAVE HEARTLANDS you should vote BREXIT if you want Labour and TORY if you want Brexit but vote PLAID if you like dragons but then again if you live in SURREY you should vote LABOUR to send a message about BIN COLLECTION yet then again if you are a WEST COUNTRY CIDER-FANATIC you should vote LIB DEM for their apple policy but LABOUR if you like the delicate rouge of autumn leaves and CONSERVATIVE if Jacob Rees-Mogg once employed you as a nanny but also if you are a PRO-INDEPENDENCE ANTI-BREXIT SCOT you should vote for the DUP to show you're serious about messing everything up for everyone else and finally if you're in a GREEN seat you live in Brighton and you can do what you like really.

'STOP POLITICISING THIS TRAGEDY' SAY ALL POLITICIANS

by Our Politicising Staff **Ronnie Jerk**

IN AN immediate response to the terrorist murders on London Bridge, members of all political parties accused each other of trying to make political capital out of a personal tragedy.

Said one Conservative spokesperson, "We didn't politicise these events, Labour did. They're the ones responsible for changing the rules on sentencing, which, let's face it, allowed this murderer out onto the streets."

A Labour spokesperson immediately replied, "We're not in the business of finger pointing, but you have to point the finger at the Conservatives. After ten years of Tory austerity and cuts to policing and parole services, the Tories might as well have killed everyone themselves."

Not to be outdone, a spokesperson for the Lib Dems said, "This is typical of the two main parties, to use any event, however unpolitical, as a political football. The Lib Dems wouldn't do this, which is why you should vote for us, because we are not responsible for murder, or indeed politicising it, unlike Labour and the Conservatives." She added, "Back of the net!"

Said one witness to the crime, "I don't see what this has to do with the General Election. I think the person who murdered them was an Islamic terrorist."

To which all the parties responded, "Shut up! That's completely irrelevant and won't win us any votes."

POLICE ATTEMPT TO DISARM MACHETE-WIELDING YOUTHS AT FROZEN 2 SCREENING

Let it go, Let it go!!!

REES-MOGG SAVES SELF IN SWIFT EXIT FROM DISASTER

Farage told me to stay put, but it was common sense to get out

FAMOUS SUCCESSFUL THREE-WORD POLITICAL SLOGANS

- Get Brexit Done.
- Take Back Control.
- Build A Wall.
- Make America Great.
- Liberté, Egalité, Fraternité.
- Veni, Vidi, Vici.
- Our Neutral Position On Brexit Is Perfectly Clear And We'll Get A New Deal Then Campaign Either For Or Against It. *(Not sure about this one. Ed.)*

THAT HISTORIC MADRID CLIMATE CHANGE AGREEMENT IN FULL

1 Countries should reduce their emissions to fight Climate Change
2 Unless they don't want to
3 Oh, and China, America and Russia take no notice of these conferences anyway
4 Er... see you in November 2020 in Glasgow
5 That's it (for the planet)

Jacob no longer silliest Rees-Mogg

by Our Political Correspondent
Irma Fruitcake

IN an extraordinary moment for British politics, Annunziata Rees-Mogg made a dramatic intervention in the election campaign, where she clearly made a pitch to be considered the silliest Rees-Mogg yet.

Formerly sidelined by her more famous and more idiotic brother, Annunziata blazed into the public consciousness with her dramatic announcement that she now backs Boris Johnson and thinks Nigel Farage is a disaster.

This monumental U-turn on the part of Annunziata, who only 25 minutes ago was the poster girl for the Brexit Party, has now left her brother trailing badly in the silliness stakes.

Even his desperate ploy, to appear standing in front of some prehistoric stones and still look more outdated than them, has flopped, compared with Annunziata's display of opportunism and disloyalty.

Pack your Gladstone bags, Jacob, there's a new Mogg in town!

"I'm here to be seriously offended on behalf of someone I've never met"

CONFUSION AS FORMER POLITICAL LEADERS SPEAK OUT

DON'T VOTE LABOUR

DON'T VOTE TORY

VOTE WHICHEVER WAY YOU LIKE AS LONG AS FACEBOOK MAKES MONEY

A Doctor Van Helsing Writes

AS A Doctor I am often asked "Is Dracula gay?"

The simple answer is that vampires tend to suffer from low blood pressure due to not having sucked enough blood out of their victims. This requires them to seek further infusions and, to be honest, they're not too bothered what gender their victim is.

The fact there is no Countess Dracula does not make the Count homosexual, and there is some evidence – Bride of Dracula 1, Bride of Dracula 2, Bride of Dracula 3, Bride of Dracula 4, Bride of Dracula 5, not to mention 6, 7 and 8 – that

he has contemplated marriage on a number of occasions.

However, accounts of the Count's blood count do vary, and in some sources there are male as well as female victims.

So, without definitive evidence, it's perfectly all right for, say, the creators of the modern Dr Who to take a few liberties with the traditional narrative and portray Vlad as a bi-vampirical non-binary impaler.

No doubt, in future Christmases, we can look forward to even more modern accounts, involving a trans-Transylvanian aristocrat who identifies as a bat. If you're worried about Dracula being gay, you really should decorate your room with garlic and arm yourself with holy water, a stake, a mallet, a silver sword and maybe even a sun lamp.
© *A Doctor Van Helsing*

KEY

"WE'RE RECRUITING FOR THE ARMY... MIGHT THAT BE OF INTEREST?"

"NOT REALLY – I'M AN EX-MARINE"

POETRY CORNER

In Memoriam lots of people, including Clive James, Gary Rhodes and Dr Jonathan Miller

So. Farewell
Then Clive James,
I must admit
That I wrote this
Ten years ago
And just got it
Out the drawer,
But as a fellow
Poet, I'm sure you
Would sympathise.

And. Farewell
Also Gary Rhodes,
Spikey-haired star
Of such TV cookery
Classics as:
*Rhodes Around Britain,
More Rhodes
Around Britain,
Rhodes Across Italy*
And *Rhodes Across China.*
Now, sadly, it is
The End of the Rhodes.

And. Farewell
Also Dr Jonathan Miller,
Satirist, author, actor,
Neurologist, TV presenter,
Theatre and opera director,
In short – a polymath.

But, sadly, your
Passing didn't get
As much coverage
As the other two.

If only you'd
Made jokes about
Japanese TV or been
A celebrity chef.

E.J. Thribb (17½)

POPE AND EX-POPE IN DOCTRINAL DISPUTE

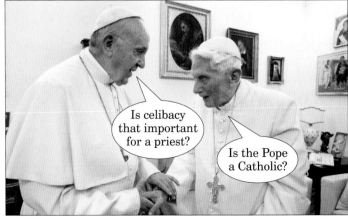

Is celibacy that important for a priest?

Is the Pope a Catholic?

BEARDED OLD MAN HANDS BORIS CHRISTMAS PRESENT

Happy Christmas, here's a landslide

Thanks, Jeremy!

Labour and Tory parties join in historic agreement

by Our Political Staff **Fi Licence**

The healing has begun after the two main political parties issued a joint statement about the election. Both the Labour and Conservative leaders had no doubt that the BBC had behaved appallingly and should be closed down.

A spokesperson for The Conservatives said, "The conduct of the Bolshevik Broadcasting Collective was so biased against the Conservatives that we only got a landslide majority. If it hadn't been for Laura Kuenssberg and Andrew Neil, we would definitely have won every seat in England and Wales and would probably have broken down the yellow wall and won all the seats in Scotland as well. The BBC bias was undeniable and inexcusable."

The Labour spokesperson agreed, "The conduct of the Boris Broadcasting Cheerleaders was so biased against the Labour party that we were deprived of a triumphant hung parliament. If it hadn't been for Laura Kuenssberg and Andrew Neil, we would this minute be arguing with the SNP and the Lib Dems and indeed ourselves over how to form a government. With its constant mentioning of our anti-Semitism, our disunity and in particular our Leader, the BBC deliberately made us lose."

Former Lib Dem leader Jo Swinson was also available for comment but no one could be bothered to contact her.

Labour and Tory leaders agreed: "The BBC has forgotten its prime duty as a state broadcaster, which is to deliver uncritical propaganda on behalf of ourselves. We have no option but to abolish it, and leave broadcasting in the capable hands of Channel 4. Oh no, hang on – we're going to close them down as well. Fox News it is then, and Russia Today."

GOOOOO JEREMY CORBYN
GOOOOO JEREMY CORBYN

Wild scenes of celebration across the country

by Our Election Correspondent
Ida Entickle

Joy was unbounded across the North of England Friday as the size of Boris Johnson's Conservatives landslide victory became apparent.

"Finally, the hated Conservatives, who have presided over a decade of savage cuts to our public services, the decimation of the NHS and the demonisation of the poor through Universal Credit, have been swept away by a Conservative party promising to bolster public services, increase NHS spending and care for the poor," said a group of cheering first-time Tory voters.

"We couldn't have survived another decade of Tory rule, so the Tories sweeping them from office hasn't happened a moment too soon," said another.

"Tonight is the night we told the Tories enough is enough by re-electing the Tories to rule for another five years," said voters celebrating in Sedgefield. (*That's enough. Ed.*)

TORIES APPEAL TO WORKING CLASSES

THIS WEEK

THE PRIME MINISTER'S FATHER, STANLEY JOHNSON

What is Boris's favourite spoon?

I'm not here to talk about Boris, I'm here to talk about me, Stanley Johnson, founder of the Johnson dynasty, the man whose DNA runs through all the Johnsons. Let's talk about me.

But I don't think the British public are terribly interested in your spoons...

I don't think the British public could even spell "spoons".

That's a bit snobbish, isn't it?

I don't suppose they could spell "snobbish" either.

Did spoons feature strongly in Boris's upbringing?

I have no idea, I wasn't there much.

So why are you here to talk about Boris?

I'm not – I'm here to talk about me. I thought this feature was called "Me and My Me", which is my sort of feature. Nobody's interested in spoons. A burka-wearing fighter pilot wouldn't be able to get a spoon into her mouth, would she?

Not only is that a mad reference to the Second World War for no reason, but it's actually rather offensive!

You see – I should be Prime Minister, not Boris! The Prime Minister's my son, you know. He wouldn't be there if it wasn't for me. Me, Stanley Johnson. Me, me, me!

Has anything interesting ever happened to you in connection with a spoon?

Well, there was that very funny time in 1979 when I was in Brussels as an MEP and...

So that's a "no".

NEXT WEEK: *Stanley Johnson tries to come on again*

Boris Johnson MP
● Live

The People's Prime Minister
An Election Message

385,000,000 Views

👍 Like   💬 Comment

0 people **like this**

I would like to thank the people of this **great** country of ours for putting their trust in me. The **sceptics** and the **naysayers** and the **doomsters** and **gloomsters** didn't believe that we would triumph, but as we say oop North, in the Tory heartlands, there's **nowt** so queer as bumboys. This really is a new Jennifer – sorry, Dawn. Or is it Hope? Never very good on details. **Anyway**, **whatever** her name is, it's a new day, a new beginning and a new government. Well, **newish**, we've only been in power for ten years, which is just a fraction of the time that I intend to be **World King**, or is it Prime Minister? Details, details. So may I

thank in particular the good people of **Oop North** and indeed those in the constituency of **Oop South**, not to mention **Oop Central**, who, though not natural Tories, decided to lend me their vote. As **tripe** lovers, they saw something in me that they liked the look of. And the **key** to this election is that we didn't patronise them. Those blunt-speaking, no-nonsense Workington class men and women voted with their **clogs**, chained up their whippets outside t'polling station, and put t'cross in t'box, then went **home** and tucked ferrets into t'trousers. (Is this right Dominic? I sound like I've got a bloody stutter. You've got a castle in Durham – you know how those black pudding munchers speak, don't you?) **Anyway**, when the results came out and they saw that a down-to-earth former head of **Pop** at Eton had won, they all said at once "O.E. bah gum!" which is Yorkshire for "We hate Corbyn".

So, I'm truly humbled by my **stonking** victory outside the liberal metropolitan elitist bubble where I've always lived, a win which **spaffed** Comrade Jezza up against the Red Wall **big** time. I'm humbled to think this is the biggest win since the great Mrs Thatcher, a heroine to us all, who **crushed** the Northern mining industry and signed up for the European Single Market. (Dom? I thought we cut this bit? Oh "get on with the constituencies", yes! Right...) So, specific **thanks** to the cloth-capped matchstick men of Lowryland **and** their lady wives – we don't want to be **stereotypical** here – in their hairnets, slippers and

rolling pins. So, flat caps **off** to the constituents of... Sedge Valley, Blyth Spirit, Don Revie, **Bassett Hound**, Wheelbarrow and Furnace, Bishop's Finger, **Bolshyover**, Grimnorthsby, Outofworkington, Bluecar, Wuthering Heights, and **Nora Batty**. Hope I haven't forgotten anyone there. It was a **privilege** to come and visit you and I can't wait to do it again in five years' time.

So as you can see, this is a time for healing the **divisions** in our country. North and South, Leave and Remain, Rich and Poor, Husbands and Wives, Cats and Dogs, Strictly and X-Factor. This is going to be **one** nation. Well, possibly **two** if Mrs Krankie has her way. And maybe three since poor old Dobbsy got the old heave-ho in Northern Arleneland. But not four, hoorah to the song-loving Illleek-Illlovers of the vallllllllleys who came up with the **goods** and shut down comrade Corbyn **faster** than Mrs Thatcher shut down the Welsh pits. So look, you **boyos**, and **girlos** (no stereotypes here, remember!), thank you, or as we say in the Tory Valleys "Cym Baya" which is Welsh for "We hate Rebecca Long-Bailey".

And now a message from Dominic Cummings, The People's PR Man

Happy fuckmas, you liberal fuckwits, you got what was fucking coming to you, so fuck the fuck off.

Twitter users 'stunned'

In the wake of the Conservative election landslide, Twitter users have expressed their astonishment that their carefully curated echo chamber didn't accurately represent the views of the wider world.

"On election day, my feed was full of pictures of young people queueing to vote Corbyn with everyone agreeing that Boris was a mendacious liar who could never be trusted with the keys to No 10," said all Twitter users.

"So, when the results of the exit poll came in, it was almost as if Twitter and what happens on it has zero impact whatsoever on the real world.

"But obviously that can't be true, so we'll instead start re-tweeting a viral conspiracy theory that Laura Kuenssberg conspired with Dominic Cummings to steal the election from Corbyn with the assistance of Steve Bannon, Putin, Ernst Stavros Blofeld and Doctor Evil."

GREAT MOMENTS IN HISTORY WHEN THE ARGUMENT WAS WON   No. 94
The dinosaurs and the meteorite

THE dinosaurs effectively argued that they should not be wiped out and that the meteorite was acting in an entirely destructive manner. The meteorite had no valid counter arguments but merely insisted it was going to "Get Annihilation Done". The result of what we now know as T Rexit, saw the entire dinosaur population obliterated on the grounds that they were literally dinosaurs, and that a new modern form of rapacious lizard *(the Borosaurus)* would take over in the modern era.

Next week:
How the Titanic won the argument with the iceberg, but lost most of its passengers.

TONY BLAIR

The former Labour leader and three-times Prime Minister writes exclusively for Private Eye about Jeremy Corbyn's election defeat

As we reflect on this seminal moment in Labour's history, we are reminded of the state of the Party in 1983 and ha

US President attacks Trump

by Our Washinton Staff
Michael Whitehouse

PRESIDENT TRUMP has furiously condemned himself for his decision to assassinate General Soleimani and drag the US back into the Middle East morass.

"I was elected to end America's involvement in wars in the Middle East, bring our troops home and to let the Arabs fight it out amongst themselves," insisted a furious President Trump.

Trump later took to Twitter to condemn himself again after President Trump vowed to ignore an Iraqi parliament vote demanding that all US troops leave Iraq.

"I don't know who this Donald Trump guy is, but he sounds like an idiot to me," President Trump tweeted to his millions of followers in the early hours of Saturday morning.

"This guy doesn't seem to realise I was elected President to get our boys home and out of Iraq, yet this asshole wants them to stay? Over my dead body. And millions of other dead bodies too. God bless Mushroom Clouds with extra cheese and Pepper-oni."

AMERICAN DRONE ATTACK

Well, we expected a bit more support from the Europeans I mean he was a very evil man and was responsible for thousands of deaths and the pre-emptive strike has saved hundreds of thousands of lives and there was no alternative and the intelligence was absolutely clear and the action was obviously designed to stop the war not start a war and our allies really should stand shoulder to shoulder with us and er…

POETRY CORNER

Lines on the 103rd birthday of legendary actor and star of Spartacus

So. Not Farewell
Then Kirk Douglas,
At time of writing.

In the Old Actors' Home,
When you say:
"I'm Kirk Douglas",
Do all the other actors
Get up from their
Chairs and declare:
"No, I'm Kirk Douglas!"
"I'm Kirk Douglas!"
"No, I'm Kirk Douglas!"?
Just asking.

E.J. Thribb
(85½ years to go)

In Memoriam David Bellamy

So. Farewell
Then David Bellamy,
Environmentalist,
Broadcaster,
Eccentric.

Latterly, you were
Under a cloud
Because of your views
About climate change.

Let us hope you are
Now over a cloud
And your current
Environment is not
Getting any hotter.

E.J. Thribb (17½)

THE TEHRAN TIMES

COMMENT

How dare the Great Satan act like this?

AS the Middle East reels from President Trump's illegal assassination of Iran's General Qasem Soleimani in Baghdad, there is one question above all others which needs to be asked – how dare the Americans act like us!

For years, General Soleimani inflicted a brutal reign of terror across the region, from Lebanon, through Syria, Iraq and into Yemen, ignoring the rule of law and killing anyone he pleased, and then touring the sites of the murders to take selfies like some sort of monster.

We therefore expected the Americans to behave cautiously, act with restraint and conduct themselves with a respect for international law. We hardly imagine that they would instead go into someone else's country and kill people in order to stamp their authority on the region.

This blatant attempt to copy our tactics is an absolute disgrace and demands that we, in Iran, retaliate by firstly taking over Iraq, which we should have done during that long war which we (cont. 2094)

"It's my step-ladder. I never knew my real ladder"

Plans announced for HL2

by Our Westminster Correspondent
Michael White-Elephant

THE government today revealed ambitious plans for the construction of HL2, the new House of Lords, in York.

"HL2 is every bit as exciting and ambitious a project to revitalise the North as HS2," said the Number Ten spokesman.

"HL2 has perhaps even greater potential for ending up being an embarrassingly expensive project which never actually ends up being built. Dominic Cummings has already found the perfect location for HL2 in York, which would require the compulsory purchase and demolition of hundreds of local homes and York Minster.

"Three villages and most of Leeds will be levelled in order that their lordships can travel easily to and from the bathroom, so we don't foresee any delays in construction."

DIARY

THE CROWN: 1977
(With explanatory notes by series adviser Robert Lacey)

PRINCE PHILIP *(Peering through the net curtain of the Principal Bedroom, Buckingham Palace)*: Bloody hell, who the hell's that arriving?

THE QUEEN: It's President and Mrs Ceausescu of Romania[1], over here on a state visit.

PRINCE PHILIP: Nobody tells me a bloody thing! I'll have to cancel my day-trip to Yorkshire![2]

THE QUEEN: We must make sure their visit is a success. The future of our country is dependent upon it. I've hired one of this year's top young musical groups to entertain them after dinner. Remind me of their name, Charles.

PRINCE CHARLES: The Sex Pistols[3], mummy.

THE QUEEN: I knew it was something military.

PRINCE CHARLES: They're said to be frightfully "with-it".

PRINCESS ANNE: You can say that again, Charles! I had a bit of fling with their lead singer, Johnny,[4] last week. Not my type at all... too boisterous... but he might suitable for Auntie Margaret.

THE QUEEN: From what I hear, she's been making a bit of a fool of herself with Mr Moon, the drummer with The Who.

PRINCESS ANNE: Only Keith Moon's just gone and died, the clumsy clot.[5]

THE QUEEN: Oh dear. Margot will be dreadfully upset.[6] Oh well. Chin up.

---

20 buglers deliver a fanfare

PRIVATE SECRETARY: President and Mrs Ceausescu, Your Majesty.

THE QUEEN: Welcome! Oh, how very kind. Do look at what the Ceausescus have brought us, Philip! Ferrero Rocher![7] Our favourite! Oh, and here's the Prime Minister! Come in, Mr Callaghan!

CALLAGHAN: Very kind, Your Majesty. I may be working class, and you may be Royal, but we hold each other in the deepest respect.[8]

THE QUEEN: Get on with it.

CALLAGHAN: Might I have a word, Your Majesty? Between the two of us, our economy's up the spout, your former lover, Jeremy Thorpe, has been arrested on charges of conspiracy to murder and there's a serial killer on the prowl. Goes by the name of the Yorkshire Ripper, and he's leading the police a right merry dance.[9]

THE QUEEN: It never rains but it pours.

CALLAGHAN: I'm sorry to say this, Your Majesty, but your husband-

THE QUEEN: Philip?

CALLAGHAN: ...is under suspicion.[10]

THE QUEEN: Oh, Lord. That's not the way we do things in this family. Dignity. Ceremonial. Tradition. Those are our lynchpins. Not going around stabbing people. *(Looks winsomely into the Louis XIV mirror)* On days like today, one asks oneself, what has one actually achieved?

The Royal Family are getting ready for the State Banquet.
The Prince of Wales adjusts his bow tie and carries on talking

---

PRINCE CHARLES: Nobody understands me, Camilla. Am I listened to in this family, am I seen for who and what I am? And what of the British public? Do they appreciate everything I do for them? What is my purpose? What is my destiny? Oh, woe is me!

Meanwhile Camilla is in the bathroom, secretly on the telephone to Sir Anthony Blunt.[11]

CAMILLA: You mean everything to me, darling Anthony... everything! So what if you're a KGB spy working on behalf of the Ceausescus! Why should we let a little thing like that come between us?

A knock at the door. 30 buglers herald the arrival of a footman, who delivers Prince Charles a letter on a silver salver. The Prince opens the letter with his ceremonial sword.

PRINCE CHARLES: It's from the Duchess of Windsor! *(reads)* "My Dearest Charles, As you surely know by now, my dear friend President Ceausescu has accorded me the singular honour of requesting that I become the new Queen of Great Britain after the Palace coup planned for later this evening, at an agreed sign from Sidney Vicious, Esq. But I would not feel up to the burden of the Crown without you as my King.

Marry me, Charles – and let us usurp your mother's throne together!
Yours ever,
Wallis Windsor (Duchess)
PS: No need to feel guilty. It's what she would want".[12]

CAMILLA *(from bathroom)*: Who was that, Charles?

PRINCE CHARLES: Oh, nothing, darling. *(Prince Charles talks to the mirror)* Aha! With Wallis by my side, I shall be King at last![13]

---

[1] True. Crown scriptwriter Peter Morgan has brilliantly interweaved the visit of the Ceausescus into this episode of the Crown.

[2] True. The Duke of Edinburgh has visited Yorkshire many times.

[3] True. The Sex Pistols were an immensely popular "rock" group of the time. Though there is no record of them ever playing at a state banquet, there is no reason why they might not have.

[4] True. The lead singer of the Sex Pistols was Johnny Rotten. By engaging him in a romance with Princess Anne, Peter Morgan may be using artistic licence, but it points towards a deeper truth.

[5] True. Keith Moon did die that year.

[6] True. Princess Margaret was sometimes very upset.

[7] True. Ferrero Rocher is a luxury chocolate brand often used as gifts between Ambassadors, Presidents and Heads of State.

[8] True. Peter Morgan's researchers uncovered the fact that Prime Minister James Callaghan was born working class, and he has cleverly interweaved this with the narrative.

[9] True. The economy was doing badly in 1977, Liberal Leader Jeremy Thorpe was arrested and the Yorkshire Ripper was at large.

[10] True-ish. Though the Duke of Edinburgh was never formally charged with the murders, there are still many questions to be answered.

[11] True. Sir Anthony Blunt spied for the KGB, and Camilla Parker-Bowles conducted an affair with Prince Charles, so it is surely reasonable to assume that they would have plotted together to bring down the monarchy.

[12] True. The Prince of Wales had met the Duchess of Windsor, and it is known that she felt betrayed by the Royal Family so it is probable that she would have plotted to marry Charles and take over throne.

[13] True. The Prince of Wales is likely to be King. By pairing him with the Duchess of Windsor, Peter Morgan reveals the underlying passions that existed in the Royal Family around this period.

As told to
CRAIG BROWN

MILLENNIAL CHOICES

Products involving deaths of animals

Products involving deaths of young black men

YES, IT'S LADY MORGAN
"Say goodbye to unelected EU bureaucrats – from now on, we're going to be governed by unelected chums of Boris!"

YES, IT'S LORD ZAC
"Say goodbye to unelected EU bureaucrats – from now on, we're going to be governed by OE chums of Boris the electorate actually rejected!!"

Boris Johnson MP
● Live

People's Prime Minister's New Year Message – Live on Fakebook

385,000,000 Views

👍 Like   💬 Comment

0 people like this

Hello to you, the People's People...
The first question comes from Miss Plenty O'Flattery, a young lady from Ireland no doubt... Fire away!

> Well done for coming back so quickly from Mustique, only three days after the international crisis blew up – why didn't you stay longer on your well-earned break with the lovely Carrie?

That's a long question. But a good one. The answer is that I was kept **fully** briefed, by the pool, on the situation in Iran and the chaps at the Foreign Office thought I would be more effective having another piña colada than coming home and putting my **foot** in it re the mad mullahs. But, rest assured, I wasn't in the **dark** at any point, as it was actually very **sunny**. But obviously now I'm back and I'm in complete charge of doing whatever President Trump wants or else we won't get a trade deal. And the next question comes from a Ms Jo Public...

> As the champion of the working classes, why did you spend your holiday in Mustique, rather than in, say, Blackpool?

Good question, and the answer is tripartite, and I won't patronise you by saying, as my dad, Stanley, probably would, that you're too **stupid** to know that that means "in three parts". So the answer is: a) I spent a lot of the election campaign hiding in a **fridge**, so I needed to go somewhere hot to warm up. Where better than the People's Luxury Paradise of Mustique? b) On "Love Island", as I call it, you meet a wide range of **diverse** people including Tory donors, billionaire celebrities and waiters, many of them **black** and smiling broadly and c) Mustique is just like the beautiful island of Britain will be very soon. With years of **constant** sunshine and **blue** skies ahead and a **massive** injection of investment from undisclosed sources keen to avoid unnecessary red tape, ie taxation. The next question comes from a Ms Wheeler, formerly Johnson. That rings a bell, have we met?

> How the hell can you afford to go to Mustique? I thought you didn't have any money?

Oh **cripes**, Marina, it's **you**. Look, I flew economy for a start. And the £20,000-a-week villa was a **gift** from a grateful admirer. I'm not saying who. It could've been my old chum Johnny Hedgefund or my other old chum, Ivan Oilpipe. But it's no one's business, especially not your divorce lawyers. So, let the **healing** begin, by you getting off the line. Last question from Mr Olly Aginous...

> Is the Iranian crisis the first test of your premiership, a challenge you will obviously rise to, proving that you are a great statesman?

Well, that's for future historians to decide but, as a **current** historian, I would have to say "yes". I have already taken **decisive** action by flying home, issuing a statement and despatching no less than **two** warships to the Gulf – HMS Inadequate and HMS Unfeasible – which sends a **clear** message to the Iranians... not that we don't have any other ships, but that they shouldn't mess with the nation that boasts such **glorious** wartime supremos as Admiral Nelson, the Duke of Wellington and Dominic Raab. Dominic has the situation under control, he's worked out where Iran is (quite near Dover) and we're ready at a moment's notice to be attacked by Iran. I hope that reassures you.

> But has President Trump actually spoken to you?

When you have a really **special** relationship with someone, you know what the other person is thinking, and there is no need to talk.

> So he didn't tell you?

Look, I've got to go now because I don't know if you're aware, but there's a **war** on and I'm expecting a call on the secret hotline any minute now. (**Ring**! **Ring**!) That'll be the Donald now, wanting to include **me** in the top-level international decision-making process. So I'd better go. Your Prime Minister (again!)

EVANGELICALS FOR TRUMP

We pray to be delivered from unstable, heavily armed, extremist religious fanatics

Amen!

St Cakes happy to accept philanthropist's controversial donation

by Our Education Staff
Grant Pleaze

THE Headmaster of the independent Midlands fee-paying school, St Cakes, yesterday said he would be delighted to take the £1 million offered by Sir Bryan Thwaites "to help disadvantaged white British boys".

Mr R.G.J. Kipling, long-serving Master of the prestigious educational institution, whose motto *Quis paget entrat* has been an inspiration to generations of old Cakeians, told the Daily Telegraph, "If Dulwich College and Westminster don't want the money, then I definitely do. Many of the pupils at St Cakes are white and suffer the extreme disadvantage of going to public school, so it seems entirely reasonable to me to have a special fund set up for them.

"Many of the boys do relatively badly in exams, due to the high standards of education here, therefore it would be entirely appropriate for St Cakes to have all the money, in order to build new sports, drama and media facilities, which will attract diverse rich Chinese pupils."

Mr Kipling added, "If Mr Stormzy would like to give St Cakes some money as well, that would be excellent. We have many black pupils here who also have the disadvantage of their parents owning large sections of various African countries and *(cont. p94)*

HISTORIC CRISIS

"All you have to do in the Royal Family is wave"

"Goodbye!"

WHAT'S A NEWSPAPER? WHAT'S A LETTER?

MEGHAN SUES NEWSPAPER OVER LETTER

ROBERT THOMPSON

Nursery Times

································ Friday, Once-upon-a-time ································

FROG PRINCE AGREES TO HOP IT

by Our Royal Insider **Tom Thumb Bradby**

IN A historic development that has rocked the Nurseryland monarchy, the Frog Prince has announced that he wants to give up his royal duties and return to life as a normal frog.

In an online statement, the Prince explained, "The Princess and I plan to transition to a new progressive role on the other side of the pond. We are stepping back from our royal duties, such as the grand opening of Old Mother Hubbard's cupboard, launching the *HMS Pea Green Boat* and starting the Gingerbread Man's Charity Marathon Run."

Going forward, the Prince will start life again as a common or garden amphibian, but will have to repay the cost of refurbishing his luxury Frogmore lilypad, which formerly cost the taxpayers of Nurseryland several Golden Goose eggs.

The Nurseryland media, including the Daily Mirror-Mirror-on-the-Wall, and The Sun-Has-Got-His-Hat-On, are blaming the Frog Prince's

decision on his wife, pointing out that she also has amphibian connections, as her father is a toad.

The Prince is hoping he will be photographed less often by the paparazzi once he's a frog, and in future will just stick his tongue out, if only to catch a fly.

The Queen invited the Frog Prince to her parlour for showdown talks over bread and honey, and demanded a solution or she would cut off everyone's heads.

But while the Frog Prince and his bride have polarised Nurseryland, the media are suddenly in agreement that his brother Prince Charmless has magically become rather charming, as he and his charming wife charmingly travel around Nurseryland in a First Class Pumpkin Carriage charmingly charming everyone with their charming charm.

The Grand old Duke of York was not available for comment, but was delighted that for once it wasn't him in the headlines.

JUSTIN TRUDEAU GREETS MIXED-RACE ROYALS

Welcome to Canada! We'll make you feel right at home!

Daily Telegraph Friday 24 January 2020

Meghan: My Advice to Bryony

'Why don't you just pack it in – and stop writing for the Daily Telegraph?'

There she was in my kitchen at Frogmore and I thought, why not give her a bit of sisterly advice?

She was telling me about the terrible pressures of filling up space in the Daily Telegraph and it suddenly struck me – I can help here. I can tell her to take control of her own life. And put a sock in it. Resign.

"Just stop, Bryony," I said. "You don't have to do this. No one will blame you and everyone will be happier."

But Bryony just smiled sadly and *(cont. p94 of 94-page Royal Supplement)*

Your constitutional questions answered No.94

The line of succession

Q *With the removal of Meghan, who is next in line of succession to be slagged off in the Daily Mail?*

A The new line of succession now goes thusly:
1 Greta Thunberg
2 Emma Thompson
3 Daisy Ridley
4 Amal Clooney
5 Anyone vegan
6 Still Meghan Markle

NEW OLD ANTIPODEAN SAYINGS

*"Red sky at night
Whole of Australia alight,
Red sky in the morning
So much for no global warming."*

Daily Mail

Exclusive

Famous Philosopher Dies

ONE of the world's leading philosophers, Sir Roderick Sputum, has died at the age of 76.

Though little-known to anyone, Sputum is acknowledged as a philosopher to rank with the great names of the past – Plato, Aristotle, Sir Herbert Gussett *(shome mishtake, shurely? W.D.)*

Sputum was the author of over 100 books, including *Leftie Bastards* (1974), *More Leftie Bastards* (1975), *With Rod and Gun* (1976), *Commie Scumbags at the New Statesman* (1982), *The Joy of Sex* (1984) *(That's enough books. Ed.)*

MORGAN ON MEGHAN

A fame-obsessed, narcissistic social climber…

…but enough about me

TOP TEN RULES FOR SPIRITUAL PEACE

by Chris Evans

1 **Always have at least six holidays booked in advance. If you can't stretch to that, just try to earn more money until you can.**

2 Every ten days, run a marathon. If you're too slow or fat for a marathon, you can switch to a half-marathon.

3 **Get up at 3am (or 5am at weekends). If you're struggling with this, try having a hugely successful morning radio show, which will really give you the impetus to get out of bed.**

4 Don't have a phone. Make sure, of course, that your PA has a phone so you don't miss out on anything.

5 **Don't drink any juice except beetroot juice strained through 12-gauge gauze, which is sourced from a single temple in the Himalayas.**

6 Eat twenty grams of omega-enriched magnesium each day, sprinkled on a coffee or ground up in your meat (if you are a dog).

7 **Don't worry about failing to achieve things in life, apart from all the things on this list which are very, very important if you ever want to find happiness.**

8 Don't hang out with "sappers" (this is a term for emotionally draining people, NOT engineering experts in the British Army. You can hang out with Sappers, provided they are not also sappers).

9 **Eradicate negativity by saying NO when anyone asks you to do something you don't want to do. You have too many 'NO's in your body and you need to get them out.**

10 Meditate about how brilliant you are (if you're me) or how brilliant I am (if you're you).

Exclusive to all Tory papers
AN APOLOGY

IN RECENT months and years, we may have given the mistaken impression that this newspaper is strongly of the opinion that those in the acting profession should refrain from airing their political views.

Headlines such as "Boldly go and do one, Picard!", "Belt up, Baldrick" and "A-ha-ha-ha! Piss off, Partridge!" may have given our readers the erroneous impression that we think the likes of Patrick Stewart, Tony Robinson and Steve Coogan are naïve luvvies, that they should stick to acting and stop assuming that their simplistic opinions have any more weight than those of proper, serious politicians.

We now realise, in light of Laurence Fox's blistering appearance on Question Time, with his very sensible views on racism and sexism, that nothing could be further from the truth. We have always believed that actors have a vital role in cutting through received political opinion and that they shine a light on the issues of the day, provided that their simplistic and naïve opinions coincide with the editorial line of this newspaper.

We apologise for any confusion caused to our readers, and any confusion in the future, when we say exactly the opposite *(cont. for ever)*

NEW YEAR'S HONOUR SHOCK – New title for Bercow

FORMERLY known as Mr Speaker, John Bercow will henceforth be known as Mr Bercow. In the New Year's Honours List just published, he was rewarded for his staunch obstruction of Brexit with nothing at all.

Mr Bercow was given the highly coveted OBA, The Order of Bugger All, after much discussion between Prime Minister Boris Johnson and his predecessor, Theresa May, who finally agreed on one thing – that he deserved no recognition whatsoever.

The Speaker is traditionally rewarded with a peerage, and has been for the last 230 years, but it was decided to make an exception for Mr Bercow on the grounds of his exceptional services to national irritation.

Said the Chairman of the Parliamentary Committee, "I was only obeying ORRR-DEEERS! ORRRRRRRDDD-EEEEERRRS! This matter is LOCKED! Ha ha ha ha ha!"

Mr Bercow may yet be given a peerage in the forthcoming dissolution honours but in the meantime he said he wished to be known as Baron Hard-Up of Wimbledon Theatre, where he will be appearing in panto. *(Rotters)*

New Year's honours — those highlights in full

Nadiya Hussain will be receiving a GBBO and will, in due course, be given an Order of the Bath Bun

Ben Stokes receives an OBN (Order of the Broken Nose) for services to brawling outside Bristol nightclubs

Sir Elton John will now become a thrice-decorated Member of the Empire, and will henceforth be a ME ME ME

Olivia Newton-John will be an OO-OO-OO, which Her Majesty understands is the one that she wants

The Lady of the Like

POETRY CORNER

In Memoriam Neil Innes, musician, writer, comedian and founding member of the Bonzo Dog Doo-Dah Band

So. Farewell
Then Neil Innes,
Founding member of
The Bonzo Dog
Doo-Dah Band and
A fake Beatle, ie
A Rutle.

You sang that
You were an
Urban Spaceman and
Now you are among
The stars.

And, just like
Half the Beatles,
You are dead.

Oh yes, you were
Also known as the
Seventh Python,
But now you have
Ceased to be,
You are no more,
You are an
Ex-Python.

> E.J. Thribb
> (17½ percent of Spamalot royalties would have been nice, allegedly)

EMILY THORNBERRY DENIES 'STUPID' COMMENTS

I would never call the idiots who voted for Boris "stupid"

LAURENCE FOX

Do you have a favourite spoon?

I don't have any spoons. I lost all my spoons in the bloody divorce, so I am renting my spoon, thanks to the so-called family justice system.

But spoon-wise, do you have a favourite?

Oh God, I suppose you're saying that I was born with a silver spoon and that I am a privileged, white male spoon-owner…

No I just really wanted to know if you have a favourite spoon ?

Oh, that's so boring and racist… well, you're the racist for implying that I have an issue with black spoons, which I don't, and which only a woke spoonatic would believe…

Have spoons played a large part in your career?

Oh, here we go – the Fox dynasty and all its hereditary spoons – well, actually I was brought up in a very poor household where my parents had to work hard for their spoons and then I went to St Cakes public school…

And did you come across many spoons there?

Ok, I was expelled for having sex with Matron in the middle of chapel whilst I was drunk on communion wine and out of my head on coke… is that where your spoon question is leading? Is that the sort of loud-mouthed, middle-class wankery that you're hoping for?

Has anything amusing ever happened to you in relation to a spoon?

Look, do you want to have sex with me or not?

Yes, please.

NEXT WEEK: *Billie Piper, "Me and My Piper".*

D^UMB BRITAIN

Real contestants, real quiz shows, real answers, real dumb!

The Chase, ITV

Bradley Walsh: The name of which former prime minister is an anagram of *Rethatch*?
Contestant: Churchill.

Walsh: Donald Watson left the Vegetarian Society to become co-founder of what society?
Contestant: The Sausage Society.

Walsh: Which chain of coffee shops is named after a Roman Emperor?
Contestant: Is it Costa?

Walsh: Who, in 1930, became the first woman to fly solo from England to Australia?
Contestant: Emily Pankhurst.

Walsh: Which London cathedral is dedicated to St Peter?
Contestant: St Paul's.

Walsh: Which US President is said to have cut down his father's cherry tree?
Contestant: Donald Trump.

The Chase Celebrity Special, ITV

Bradley Walsh: What is the only consonant used in the names of the four major blood groups?
Piers Morgan: O.

Walsh: Which British scientist was born on Christmas Day in 1642?
Carol Decker of T'Pau: Einstein.

The Chase Australia, 7 Network

Andrew O'Keefe: Colloquially, another reader examining something offers a fresh pair of what?
Contestant: Pants.

Mastermind, BBC2

John Humphrys: Which river, which rises in the Black Forest in Germany, runs through or touches the borders of ten counties before flowing into the Black Sea?
Contestant: The Nile.

Celebrity Mastermind, BBC1

John Humphrys: In which battle of 1805 was a French and Spanish fleet commanded by Admiral Villeneuve defeated by a British fleet commanded by Admiral Lord Nelson?
Montana Brown (from *Love Island*): Hastings.

Humphrys: Bogota is the capital of which South American country?
Shaun Ryder of the Happy Mondays: Nigeria.

Humphrys: What traditional gift is given by Norway to London every year early in December?
Jessica Regan: A cuckoo clock.

Humphrys: What is the English equivalent of the Spanish *autopista* and the German *Autobahn*?
Abdullah Afzal: Pistachio.

Humphrys: The 2019 book entitled *No-one is Too Small To Make A Difference* is a collection of speeches made by a Swedish climate change activist. What's her name?
***Casualty* actress Amanda Henderson:** Sharon.

Head Hunters, BBC1

Rob Beckett: What European country uses the top level internet domain ".ch"?
Contestant: I guess I'll just go for a guess and say Portugal. Wait! Is that even in Europe?

The Switch, ITV

Sanjeev Bhaskar: Leo Tolstoy's *War and Peace* was originally written in which language?
Contestant: Latin.

Bradley Walsh: The Caledonian Sleeper is an overnight service on what form of transport?
Contestant: Motorbike.

Walsh: In the Bible, Samson lost his strength after what was cut off?
Contestant: His arm.

Walsh: Which John Bunyan novel features the "Delectable Mountains"?
Contestant: *Brokeback Mountain*.

Walsh: At which board game was Bobby Fischer a grandmaster?
Contestant: Monopoly.

Walsh: Andrew Roberts's biography *Walking With Destiny* is about which UK wartime leader?
Contestant: Napoleon.

Walsh: Who was leader of the Labour party in both the 1974 elections?
Contestant: Margaret Thatcher.

Walsh: The inhabitants of which Scottish city are called Dundonians?
Contestant: Cardiff.

Pointless, BBC1

Alexander Armstrong: Name a team that competed in the 2018 Commonwealth Games.
Contestant 1: Kazakhstan.
Contestant 2: France.
Contestant 3: Greece.

Armstrong: We're looking for British gold medal winners from the 2016 Olympics.
Contestant: Mo Mowlam.

Alexander Armstrong: Who was the author of the 1949 novel *Love in a Cold Climate*, who was one of six famous aristocratic sisters?
Contestant: George Orwell.

Alexander: We're looking for a French revolutionary stabbed in the bath by Charlotte Corday.
Contestant: Joan of Arc.

Tipping Point, ITV

Ben Shephard: In Disney's 1937 animated film, how many dwarves did Snow White share a house with?
Contestant: 101.

Shephard: Bronchitis primarily affects the tubes carrying air to and from which pair of major bodily organs?
Contestant: The ears.

Shephard: Which world leader is estimated to have survived more than 600 CIA assassination attempts, including one with an exploding cigar?
Contestant: Bill Clinton.

Shephard: Woodhouse is the maiden name of which Jane Austen character?
Contestant: I think it's one of the Brontës… Charlotte?

Shephard: Which female American tennis player shares her first name with the Roman goddess of love?
Contestant 1: The only American tennis player I can think of is Steffi Graf, so I'll pass.
Contestant 2: No idea. I was going to say Serena Williams, but I don't think she's American.

Shephard: Which English county is often known by its shortened name of "Hants"?
Contestant: Huddersfield.

Shephard: The cricketing badge of which county features a daffodil?
Contestant: I know daffodils are associated with Wales, so Yorkshire.

Shephard: Keith Moon is best known for playing what percussion instrument in the band The Who?
Contestant: The trumpet.

Shephard: In 1955 which prime minister resigned and was replaced by Anthony Eden?
Contestant: John Major.

Shephard: The Honourable Schoolboy and Smiley's People are sequels to which 1974 John Le Carré novel?
Contestant: Frankenstein.

Shephard: Which American composer wrote the music for the musical *Follies*?
Contestant: Beethoven.

Cash Trapped, ITV

Bradley Walsh: In 2010, which African nation became the first to host the FIFA World Cup Final?
Contestant: Albania.

Walsh: In 2000, Michael Douglas married which Welsh actor?
Contestant: Richard Burton.

Walsh: Known in France as "La Manche", which waterway joins the Atlantic Ocean to the North Sea?
Contestant: The Panama Canal.

Supermarket Sweep, ITV

Rylan Clark-Neal: Who replaced Claire Foy to play the Queen on season 3 of the Netflix series *The Crown?*
Contestant: Beyoncé.

Clark-Neal: What is the name of Sherlock Holmes's sidekick?
Contestant: Inspector Morse.

Tenable, ITV

Warwick Davis*:* Name ten US states with a V or Y in their name.
Contestant: Wisconsin.
Same contestant: New Orleans.
Same contestant: Philadelphia.

Davis: We want the ten Charles Dickens novels with an "O" in the title.
Contestant: I'm going to go for *Pride and Prejudice*.

Radio Clyde

Presenter: What does RNLI stand for?
Caller: In real life.

Ken Bruce's Popmaster, BBC Radio 2

Bruce: Paul McCartney, Linda McCartney and Denny Laine were members of which 1970s group?
Caller: The Beatles.

Fighting Fitz quiz, Radio Devon

David Fitzgerald: A blunderbuss is an obsolete variety of what?
Caller: Butterfly.

Richard Osman's House of Games, BBC2

Osman: In 1931, which famous American gangster was sentenced to 11 years in prison for tax evasion?
Contestant: Al Cappuccino.

The Mail ON SUNDAY

A STYLE GUIDE

WHAT'S THE DIFFERENCE BETWEEN BRILLIANT, GRACEFUL, ELEGANT, SELFLESS KATE AND BRASH, GAUCHE, MISGUIDED, SELFISH MEGHAN?

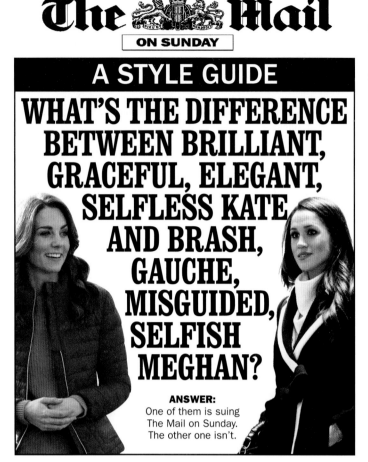

ANSWER:
One of them is suing
The Mail on Sunday.
The other one isn't.

Sarah Vain

Putting the Me in Meghan

LET me tell you, I know a thing or two about being a top glamorous power couple, with a successful man and a beautiful independent career woman.

Everyone hates you. Everyone is jealous of you and your success and your talent. Everyone thinks you have the perfect lifestyle, and so they start sniping from the side-lines, calling you vain and worse.

Some even suggest that you and your husband should leave the country, step down from your public roles and go somewhere very cold, like Siberia.

It's a familiar trope – the feisty, powerful woman is cruelly dubbed Lady Macbeth, simply because she tells her husband what to do, and the man is called weak, feeble and Michael, because he goes along with her. It's a tale as old as time, but that's not going to stop me repeating it yet again.

So that's why I say, as the knives are out for Britain's best-loved couple, leave Sarah and Michael alone. They are a huge national asset and we'll miss them when they're gone.

What You Missed

The scoop of the century

ITN News

Tom Bradby: So, with me tonight is a top royal insider, the man who knows exactly what's going on behind palace doors, and is a personal friend of Wills, Kate, Harry and Meghan. So, Tom, what can you tell us?

Tom Bradby: Nothing at all.

Tom Bradby: That's fascinating. Are you prepared to go on the record with that?

Tom Bradby: I'd rather not say.

Tom Bradby: I quite understand – saying any more than that would jeopardise your unique position of having the ear of the younger royals, and could blow your chance of getting the big interview in Canada.

Tom Bradby: You say Canada, I'm not at liberty to confirm or otherwise.

Tom Bradby: Extraordinary. Can I just end this fascinating interview by asking if you're okay, Tom?

Tom Bradby: Thanks, Tom, nobody ever asks me that.

Tom Bradby: So, are you?

Tom Bradby: No comment.

Tom Bradby: You heard it here first. An ITN Exclusive!

Grenfell Inquiry latest

AS the second phase of the inquiry into the Grenfell disaster began, the cladding contractors and manufacturers gave evidence that they had no idea that their pants would catch fire when they claimed not to know how dangerous the products were.

Said the QC for the guilty parties, "Had they known how quickly the pants would catch fire, my clients would certainly not have chosen to clad their bodies with such inflammable material."

The pants went up in seconds, as soon as they started giving their evidence. As blame spread around the courtroom, it seemed that the truth would not get out in time, but luckily the attempts by the accused to cover their arses went up in smoke.

(Total Rotters)

Who should be the new host of Radio 4's evergreen quiz show? You choose:

**Neil Kinnock
(Just an Hour)**

**Frédéric Chopin
(Just a Minute
Waltz)**

**Roger Bannister
(Just Four
Minutes)**

**Mickey's Girlfriend
(Just a Minnie)**

**Lord Leveson
(Justice a Minute)**

**Martin Jarvis
(Just a William)**

**Kim and Aggie
(Dust a Minute)**

**Nicholas Parsons
(Just a Minute's
Silence)**

FAB FOUR SPLIT UP

by Our Beatles Staff **Penny Lane** and **Eleanor Rigby**

THE world of popular culture was rocked to its foundations with the news that the British group, known around the world as the Fab Four, are "to go their separate ways".

Wills, Harry, Kate and Meghan had become a global phenomenon, being mobbed by enthusiastic crowds and creating hysteria amongst journalists wherever they went.

For a while, it seemed they could do no wrong, with a string of hit tours including Pakistan, South Africa and the Gilbert and Sullivan Islands (now under water).

Frogmore Chorus

But then something happened. Creative differences began to appear and the rivalry between the two foremost members of the band, Will and Harry, erupted into open conflict over who should be the lead singer and what direction the band should go in.

Hard Day's Work

But what really lay behind the split? Fans put the blame squarely on the foreign interloper, Yoko Markle, with whom Harry was besotted and whose every wish he tried to fulfil.

Say top biographer, Hunter Bookdeal, "She wanted the band to modernise, to experiment, to be avant-garde. She was an artist in her own right and had her own ideas about good causes, such as World Peace and Human Rights."

Yesterdailytelegraph

Fab Four historian, Philip Anotherbook, agrees: "Yoko Markle persuaded Harry that he would be a bigger star by quitting and going off with her to stage love-ins and lie in bed all day."

Whatever the truth, it is a sad day for Britain and we can only hope and pray that Harry isn't reduced to trying to make money by churning out *Jealous Guy, Imagine* and *Happy Christmas Fab Four is Over.*

© *All newspapers.*

"It does what it says on the tin"

BORES YOU WITH ITS TIRED OVER-USED CLICHÉ

Fergie – 'I was victim of racism'

by Our Royal Correspondent **Ray Cist**

THE Duchess of York has joined in the furore over the treatment of Meghan Markle, saying that she now realises that she too suffered from racial prejudice: "If only I had been mixed race, then I might not have been treated so appallingly by the British press and the Royal Family, not to mention the British people."

She continued, "I was attacked mercilessly for being pushy, vulgar, publicity-seeking and greedy, and I ended up having to step down from all my royal duties.

"I was stripped of my HRH status and was reduced to promoting the Wazzitup™ Food Processor for Weight Watchers and asking News of the World journalists posing as Arab sheikhs to pay all my bills, so that I could be financially independent."

She went on, "I was given no sympathy, the Royal Family cut me dead and I was forced to go to North America and sell my story to daytime TV in order to make ends meet."

The Duchess of York concluded her heartfelt statement by saying, "This would never have happened to me if I had not been white and posh."

Very Late News (1936)

● Duke and Duchess of Windsor claim they too were driven out of Royal Family by racism. "Britain cannot cope with a ghastly American divorcee," says Duchess.

PRINCE CHARLES MEGXIT FURY

Why would Harry plunge the monarchy into crisis just so he can spend his life with the divorcee he loves?

List of reputable titles with which the Duke and Duchess of Sussex are prepared to co-operate

- Time Magazine
- National Geographic
- British Vogue
- The Daily Telegraph
- Puzzler
- Air Conditioning Today
- What Paperclip
- Cake – The Cranbrook and Sissinghurst Parish Council Magazine
- The Highway Code 2020 Edition
- Luxury Yachts and Yachtsmen

(That's enough. Ed.)

THOSE DISNEY FILMS FOR WHICH MEGHAN WILL BE DOING THE VOICEOVERS

Frozen Out

Frozen Out II

Beauty and the Beastly Press

Woke Beauty

The Not-Quite-a-Princess Diaries

The Lion King's Brother

Snow Flake

(That's enough. Ed.)

THIS WEEK

TONY HALL

Outgoing BBC DG, Lord Hall, gives a no-holds-barred interview about the art of the spoon interview...

Lord Hall, do you have a favourite spoon?

That's a rather aggressive question. But all too typical of BBC spoon interviews these days.

With respect, I think the people have a right to know whether or not you have a favourite spoon...

I would agree, but there are different ways for BBC journalists to get this kind of information out of spoon owners in a less confrontational manner.

Isn't it the duty of a BBC journalist to ask searching questions on behalf of the public about the spoon preferences of prominent people?

Ah, now you're trying to catch me out. I'm a great believer in the long-form spoon interview, where you can explore spoon-related decisions at length, not in soundbites.

But do you have a favourite spoon?

Ah, classic 'Gotcha' spoon journalism. You're a rottweiler trying to trap me into making a major spoon gaffe.

Honestly, I'm not. Please just give me a spoon soundbite...

You're fired!

Thank God for that. And now the news: BBC journalist fired in Spoongate row.

NEXT WEEK: *Simon Rattle, "Me and My Rattle".*

ROYAL NEWS IN BRIEF

Court papers shock revelation

■ Defence papers filed by the Mail on Sunday at the High Court, after it was sued by the Duchess of Sussex, claim Meghan Markle is "money and publicity obsessed".

These claims come from her estranged father, Thomas Markle, who, it emerged, could give evidence against his daughter.

"All Meghan is interested in is publicity and money. I can prove this and I'll happily tell all in an interview with whichever newspaper will pay me massive amounts of cash for my story," said Thomas Markle.

"I can't think where she got this rampant desire for publicity and money from," added her dad.

New Markle list of acceptable publications announced

An announcement has been made by Mr Thomas Markle detailing the publications he deems responsible and with whom he is prepared to co-operate.

That list in full

1. Anyone

2. At all

3. At any time

4. At any price

5. Er...

6. That's it.

"It's diverse casting gone mad"

OLD MONTY PYTHON SKETCHES REVISITED

The Four Yorkshire Men

(Surely Five Labour Leadership Candidates who would like to be Yorkshire Men and Women? Ed.)

Candidate 1: We were so poor when I were growing up that I had to leave school at 12.

Candidate 2: Leave at 12? That's nothing. I had to leave school at 4, every single day.

Candidate 3: School, eh? Luxury. I never went to school. I was taught by my father, scratching on the ground with a stick held in his toes because he lost both his arms in the mine he worked in.

Candidate 4: Coal mine?

Candidate 3: Aye.

Candidate 4: You were lucky. My pa could only get work in a landmine, and he blew up after a week working there, and at his funeral there was so little left of him we had to bury him in a box.

Candidate 5: Wooden box?

Candidate 4: Aye.

Candidate 5: Soft, decadent nonsense. My da was buried in a cardboard supermarket own-brand cereal box and we only got that after everybody at 'mill had a whip-round.

Candidate 3: Flour mill?

Candidate 5: No, it were a pepper mill, and he had to grind the peppercorns wi' his single remaining tooth and we'd all get one peppercorn a year on our birthdays.

Candidate 1: We used to dream of pepper. We only got to have one fleck of salt between nine of us on our raw potato, and once we'd had that we had to lick the inside of the salt cellar

because we were that keen for the kind of exquisite flavours now to be found in a number of restaurants near my North London home.

Candidate 3: North London? That's not North. We grew up so far North we had to climb Blackpool Tower every morning to scrape the algae off it to flavour our whippet soup.

Candidate 4: You're all a bunch of mimsy Southern wazzocks. We were so poor we lived in a hole in the ground so far North we could see the Pole, and we were so cold we would burn our own fingernails to keep warm, and we ate nothing but a lump of mud each month, and we had to stitch our own clothes from each other's dandruff, and it's these formative experiences which gave me my passionate drive to create a fairer Britain and *(continued until early April)*

SMART MOTORWAY LANES
A GUIDE TO THEIR TRAFFIC

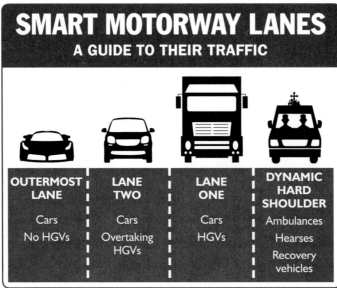

OUTERMOST LANE	LANE TWO	LANE ONE	DYNAMIC HARD SHOULDER
Cars	Cars	Cars	Ambulances
No HGVs	Overtaking HGVs	HGVs	Hearses
			Recovery vehicles

BERCOW IN BULLYING ROW

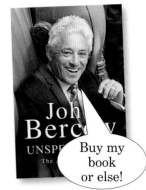

Buy my book or else!

Any Questions

BBC Radio 4
Live from Neasden in North West London

Chris Mason *(for it is who he)*: So, let's have the first question from the audience...

Woman in audience: What the f*** is Stanley Johnson doing on this programme?

Chris Mason: Good question. Anyone on the panel got any ideas? No? Right, next question.

Man in audience: Is it now part of the BBC's charter that every programme has to feature Stanley F***ing Johnson? He's not even an MEP. He's just a reality show contestant who thinks he is entitled to pontificate on current affairs because his son's the f***ing Prime Minister.

Chris Mason: That's not really a question, is it? That's more a statement of fact. So, next question...

Young person in audience: When the Prime Minister abolishes the BBC for being biased during the election, will it at least mean that we don't have to have Stanley F***ing Johnson on every f***ing programme from morning to f***ing night?

Chris Mason: That's all we've got time for. Thanks very much to everyone and that concludes *Any Questions* for tonight. Join us next week, when the panellists will include: Stanley Johnson, Jo Johnson, Rachel Johnson, and Alan Johnson by mistake because we've sacked all our researchers. Goodnight!

We shall fight them on the bleaches

A T LAST, we have broken free from the shackles of Europe, and stand alone on the White Cliffs of Dover, shaking our fists at the rest of the Continent, as blue birds fly over. No longer do we have to toil under the yoke of pettifogging Brussels bureaucracy, and the dread phrase "health and safety", which have held us back for the last 47 years. Now we are free to do as we like with no nit-picking nanny in Nantes to tell us that we can't do what we like, starting with:

1. Drinking bleach Goodbye mollycoddling Hazchem warning on the plastic Domestos bottle, lecturing us about the dangers of drinking it, with a scare-mongering skull and crossbones symbol. Bottoms up, everyone! Mine's a large one.

2. Walking on the electrified lines on the railways Up until last Friday an honest Englishman could have been arrested for going for a walk (as is his right) up and down the Queen's Railway. Now, if we want to go and connect with the national grid without being told off by some Jeux-Sans-Frontières jobsworth, then we will jolly well do so! That should give them a shock!

3. If we want to buy a working buzzsaw for our toddlers to play with, then that's what we're going to do, without a patronising Guy Verhofstadt wagging his Walloon finger in arrogant admonition No more do we have to explain to killjoys from Kortrijk that buzzsaws are character building and the loss of a limb is nothing to whinge about for British children who don't need to be wrapped up in namby-pamby continental cotton wool. Buzz off, Guy.

4. And best of all, the Daily Telegraph now no longer comes with an EU health warning If we bonkers Brits want to expose ourselves to this level of toxic waste, then we bloody well will, starting at Level Janet Daley and moving all the way up to the supposedly lethal Level Allison Pearson. Now, if you don't mind, I'm off to my local railway station for a nice walk on the track, with a hip flask full of bleach, and a buzzsaw to throw for my dog to chase. Goodbye, Madame and Monsieur Snowflake!

© *The Daily Telegraph*

St Cakes fury over Headmaster's seedy texts

by Our Education Staff **David Sext**

THE renowned independent fee-paying Midlands boarding school, St Cakes (Motto: *Quis Paget Entrat*) is at the centre of a scandal involving famous headmaster R.G.J. Kipling.

Kipling, known for his catchphrase "We make exceedingly good Cakeians", was a legend in the world of public schools, and particularly well-known for his strict policy of insisting on taking as much money as possible from all students.

However, he was plunged into controversy when it was revealed he had been secretly sending "flirty texts" to female ex-pupils from the boarding

house (Crumpets) during their first years at university.

The governors of St Cakes have expressed their outrage at Kipling's behaviour.

Said Lord Hobbe-Knobbe, (O.C.) the chairman, "This appalling behaviour is entirely contrary to the ethos of this fine, upstanding institution. A headmaster at a top public school should not be sending suggestive messages to girls. He should be sending them to boys – and certainly not after they have left the school but rather while they are still in the Under-14 Colts Rugby Team."

He concluded, "Mr Kipling is on an indefinite sabbatical and his duties are being taken over by the Chaplain, Canon Peter Phile."

Obvious error appears on Brexit coin

BY OUR NUMISMATICS STAFF
Dee Pockets

THERE was embarrassment at the Royal Mint yesterday when it was pointed out that there was a glaring mistake on the new 50p Brexit coin.

The coin carries the message "Peace, prosperity and friendship with all nations", which has prompted furious letters to the Mint from angry members of the public.

Said one, "I don't mean to be pedantic, but it is clear there has been a cock-up at the proof-reading stage, which should have been spotted long before it ever got to the foundry."

He continued, "Before the comma, the word 'Peace' appears and after the comma the words 'prosperity and friendship with all nations'. This is clearly wrong. Who on earth thought this reflected the toxic, antagonistic atmosphere in which the Brexit talks will be conducted?

"Honestly! The only thing correct on the whole coin is the comma!"

Victoria's Secret suffered 'culture of sexism'

■ It has been revealed that the lingerie giant Victoria's Secret has for years had a litany of complaints made against it by models. Senior executives at the firm, which pays incredibly attractive women to take off almost all their clothes, were astoundingly accused of making lewd comments about the women working for them, sexually harassing them, and behaving inappropriately in the workplace.

"It just goes to show that even the most innocuous business model can have unintended consequences, and that possibly the 70-year-old blokes running it did not have the best interests at heart of the twenty-something underwear models working for them."

"It's a best seller"

New Old Rhymes

❝ Red sky at night, Whirlpool's alight

Red sky in the morning, Check manufacturer's warning ❞

'Crisps should be free' says Lineker

By Our Media Staff
Phil Face

TOP football pundit and crisp expert Gary Vinegar today launched into the controversial crisp-funding row by backing the idea that everyone should have free crisps and only pay "if they felt like it".

Said Gary, "It makes sense to me that if people want crisps, but don't want to pay for them, that's fair enough".

He continued, "I haven't really thought this through, but it seems obvious. If no one pays for crisps, then the crisp manufacturer won't have enough money to give me millions of pounds... oh... hang on... I seem to have scored an own-goal!"

DIARY

REJOICE!

MARK FRANCOIS: If you'll just let me finish. My family and myself celebrated our new-found freedom by tucking into a truly first-class tin of excellent British pork luncheon meat, all washed down with a party-pack of vintage Double Diamond, with Curlywurlys all round for afters. Here's to the future!

Let me tell you this. The people of Essex will have no truck with the vanquished forces of Remain. Why can't they get it into their thick heads that the war is over – and, what's more, they lost!

No more compulsory foreign ballet on our televisions. No more Monsieur This and Signor That clogging up our screens. From now on, we'll be entertained by great British classics like Billy Bunter, Tales from the Riverbank and Hawaii Five-0.

And it's high time we had the great John Noakes back on our screens. Incidentally, whatever happened to Fanny Cradock?

As a newly liberated country, we have so much to look forward to, and I'm not just talking about staging the Eurovision Song Contest on our own terms at last, with no foreign teams to mess around with the scores.

Speaking for myself, I'm already hard at work with my trusty tube of UHU, assembling an Airfix model of a Lancaster Bomber. Anything to avenge the death of the great Nicholas Parsons. I'm sorry, but that's something for which I'll never forgive those Europeans. Rat-a-tat-tat! Rat-a-tat-tat! Achtung! Spitfeuer! Take that, you Jerry bastards!

JACOB REES-MOGG: In dulci jubilo! Oh, how my heart's aglow-o-o!

Nanny and I sing this spirited hymn of freedom together as she bends me over and gives me a jolly good wipe "down there".

"It's high time you took back control, Master Jacob!" she chuckles.

And Nanny is right. At last, all of us are free to do things for ourselves!

Spring is in the air!

From this point forward, ordinary working people can tuck into their delicious "baked beans" and race their trusty whippets, in the full confidence of national renewal! In future, we can shine the bright sunbeam of certainty to put an end to the long night of thunderstorms that has shaken the boats of hope on the blue seas of tranquility beneath the comforting shade of the tree of optimism!

"All done, Master Jacob! All done!" says Nanny, tilting her trusty hand-mirror "around the back" so that I may judge her excellent handiwork for myself.

All done, indeed! Spit-spot! And – yes – at last the sun is shining in places it has never shone before!

ALLISON PEARSON: Reach for the designer shades and the Factor 50! Britain has shaken off its chains and the sun is shining bright.

What's more, green shoots are, in the words of the immortal song, "comin' up roses".

Just look at the evidence of joyous national renewal.

The beloved Great British Bake Off has carried off first prize at the National Television Awards.

"Smart" lanes are making our Great British Motorways speedier than ever – with barely a handful of people killed for every extra mile travelled!

National Treasure Carol Vorderman has been spotted buying a splendid new kitchen unit from John Lewis. And everybody knows she would never be doing that unless we had waved goodbye to Europe!

Elsewhere in London, the lovely Carrie Symonds has been seen out and about in a ravishing new dress from top British designer Lorenzo Bellotti. And let's not forget her adored pooch Dilyn, who continues to capture the heart of every true British patriot.

By the way, have you noticed? No one mentions "climate change" any more. Thankfully, now we're out of the EU, it no longer effects us.

And – at long last – that Great British Company, Huawei, has finally taken back control of our all-important networks.

Top former British Prime Minister Winston Churchill would be proud of us.

And you know what?

It's all down to Brexit.

As told to
CRAIG BROWN

ARISTROCRATIC FUGITIVE FROM JUSTICE FINALLY FOUND

MARY BEARD'S INCREDIBLE NEW REVELATION IN LID-LIFTING TV ARTS EXPOSÉ

WERE female nudes painted for the gratification of men?

Other series in the pipeline include:

■ Were Catholics made Popes for the gratification of the church?

■ Were woods shat in for the gratification of bears?

Forgotten Moments In Music History

Lulu's brief career as a librarian

"Have you seen George?"

Mick couldn't hold back the years forever

Daily Chain Mail

LADY MACBETH – 'NO ONE HAS SUFFERED MORE THAN ME'

by Our Political Correspondent
Will 'of-the-people' Shakespeare

IN A heart-breaking interview with the Daily Chain Mail, Lady Macbeth has opened her heart to reveal the pain she has suffered as a result of her husband's controversial political decisions which have culminated in a divided nation and civil war.

"Although I am the victor, I feel very much the victim," she told anyone who would listen. "As a result of this conflict, I have lost friends and family – many of them murdered by my husband – and yet my people accuse me of being a sort of Sarah Vine character, pushing my husband ever-onward in pursuit of power. Nothing could be further from the fiction."

Lady Macbeth's softly spoken Scottish husband, Michael, Thane of Notting Hill, has been accused of "seeing a dagger before him" and using it to stab his rivals in the back at any opportunity.

As a result, Lady Macbeth feels she has been ostracised and when she said to Scottish clan leader David and his wife Sam (The Camerons of That Hut), "When shall we three meet again?" Sam said, "Never's good for me!"

Lady Macbeth continued, "It's all been hubble, bubble, toil and trouble in my life, yet no one feels any sympathy for me. But at least I can say happily, 'Out! Out of the EU! Damned Britain!'

And the deed is done. Even if it wasn't done as quickly as it could have been. Still, at least it's finished and there's nothing to worry about tomorrow and tomorrow and tomorrow."

'Yes, I'm on morning TV' admits homosexual

by Our Entertainment Staff
Sophie Sofa

ONE OF Britain's best-known gays finally came out and admitted that he was a presenter on morning television.

Said the gay man, "It was my guilty secret for years and I thought that no one knew what I did, but now I have to be honest with myself and admit that I am indeed a morning TV presenter."

Colleagues in the gay community were quick to support his decision to reveal all, calling it "brave", "moving", "brave", "heart-warming", "brave", "inspirational" and "did we mention brave?"

The public reacted sympathetically, saying, "It must have been very embarrassing, particularly for his family, to find out what the gay man had been up to all this time."

Others, however, expressed their lack of surprise at the supposedly scandalous revelations.

Said one, "Oh, come off it! We all knew that he liked being on television and, of course, he was attracted to sofas. But in this day and age, it's no big deal."

There is, however, a widespread feeling that the gay man's moving confession will encourage other prominent homosexuals to risk public opprobrium and admit that they are not ashamed to exchange pleasantries with Holly Willoughby and introduce the weather where you are *(cont. p94)*

(cont. p94)

LATE NEWS

Second morning TV host comes out

IN a dramatic on-air revelation, in front of literally dozens of viewers, another high-profile staple of ITV's morning schedule has confessed to the secret he has been living with for years.

"Yes, I'm a moron," said Piers Moron. "I tried to conceal it, but I've been living a lie for decades now, and it's about time that I'm true to myself. I speak assertively as if I know what I'm talking about, but underneath it all, my thoughts are truly moronic."

Mr Moron expressed his hope that his example has opened the floodgates and now many more TV presenters will be happy to admit that they too are morons.

Last night, Phillip Schofield praised his colleague, saying, "Piers has been very brave, and, not surprisingly, a bit moronic."

Susanna Reid wasn't available for comment because Piers wouldn't let her get a word in edgeways.

POETRY CORNER

**In Memoriam
Wing Commander
Paul Farnes**

So. Farewell
Then Paul Farnes,
Last Battle of Britain
"Ace".

Sorry to hear
You bought it,
Aged 101.

But now you
Have once again
Got your wings
And are soaring
Above the clouds.

Bandits at 4 o'clock?
No – they're angels
(One five).

Sadly, this time,
It's over and
Out.

*PS. Say hello to Ginger
for me.*

E.J. Thribb (17½ kills)

News in brief

Chinese lockdown continues

■ Millions of people in Xinjiang are still being held in quarantine after authorities there put the population under a strict lockdown, with all transportation links to the region closed and communication links shut down.

Chinese security services say they are testing anyone for what they have termed the "Muslim" virus. With that in mind, they are holding millions of the local Uighur population in re-education camps, where they are monitored for their ability to shout Communist Party slogans and swear loyalty to China's President Xi Jinping. There are fears that the autonomous beliefs held by the Uighurs could spread to other regions.

CORONAVIRUS GUIDANCE FROM THE CHINESE GOVERNMENT TO HONG KONG RESIDENTS

■ **Facemasks must be worn in public at all times**

■ **Anyone seen wearing a facemask in public will be arrested**

■ **Er...**

■ **That's it.**

"There's no denying Sir Henry's courage, but his choice of steed leaves much to be desired"

NEW CABINET ANNOUNCED

CHANCELLOR OF THE EXCHEQUER | FOREIGN SECRETARY | HOME SECRETARY | DEFENCE SECRETARY

JUSTICE SECRETARY | BUSINESS SECRETARY | HEALTH SECRETARY | INTERNATIONAL TRADE SECRETARY

EDUCATION SECRETARY | ENVIRONMENT SECRETARY | TRANSPORT SECRETARY | WORK & PENSIONS SECRETARY

Allison Pearson's wine column

This week Allison looks only at British wines, on the grounds that they're not foreign

1. Middlesex Merlot
Grown on the fertile banks of the Regent's Canal, this musky delight has notes of shopping trolley and dead tramp. Before Brexit I would probably have turned up my nose at this wine, but now I would highly recommend it. Mmmm. English. Magnifique. Oops!

2. Birmingham Barolo
Grown on the fertile banks of the Brummie Bullring, this fruity treasure has notes of petro-diesel, with a hint of roadkill. Before Brexit I wouldn't have given it shelf room, but now – a whole crate, please. Grazie signore! Whoops!

3. Blue Nuneaton
Grown on the fertile banks of the former gas works, this aromatic treat has notes of toxic rust and asbestos. Before Brexit I wouldn't have given it the time of day, but now I'll happily quaff a bottle before writing this article. Danke schön, mein herr! Oopsie!

4. American Chlorine
Mmm, this is lovely. Not strictly a British wine, this tangy beverage is perfect with chicken. Before Brexit I would have used it to clean the toilet, but now, "line 'em up, buddy"...
(You've had enough, you're fired. Ed)

"Do you have anything which will complement the unrealistic expectations we have of one another?"

snadbott

Historic trade deal with USA in question

AS BRITAIN finally finds itself free to forge new business relationships around the world, there are concerns that a deal with our oldest ally may founder.

The special relationship was under serious strain last night, as negotiators haggled over the terms of a landmark deal. Said one insider at the talks, "The deal was based on an exchange of exports, with hit-and-run driver Anne Sacoolas going to the UK in return for a crate containing His Royal Highness Prince Andrew."

Late last night, negotiations were in the balance. As the Americans stuck to their line of refusing to hand over Sacoolas, the British trade representatives pleaded for them to take Prince Andrew in return for nothing.

Boris Johnson then personally took control of negotiations, thereby guaranteeing that Anne Sacoolas will stay exactly where she is forever.

The Prime Minister later admitted that he had at some point in the negotiations sold America the NHS, adding, "This is a bold, bright new dawn for give and take between our two mighty nations. We give – they take." *(Rotters)*

TRUMP AND NETANYAHU UNVEIL MIDDLE EAST PEACE PLAN

This is something we can build on

Yes, it's called the West Bank

TERROR ON LONDON STREETS

by Our Man Watching Other People's Mobile Phone Footage On Telly At Home **Phil Space**

YET again, the question is Why? Why oh why is it only possible to be wise after the event after the event?

We've seen it all too often before. A surprise event surprising everyone, but then reported as if it were inevitable. **That** was inevitable!

So why didn't we see this piece coming? As we dashed to our keyboards to respond to this entirely predictable incident, which everyone failed to predict, the soul-searching began. Who to blame? The police? They were reasonably wise before the event, but were still caught out. The Government? They're making wise noises now, but where was that wisdom before?

Only one person knew for sure what was going to happen. The extremist with the knife. Why didn't he alert the authorities about what he was intending to do? Oh yes, he did.

So why didn't anyone do anything? Yet again, the question is Why? Why oh why *(cont. p94)*

ON OTHER PAGES

How was this person released to reoffend on the streets?

Questions asked, as Priti Patel pledges again to do something about terrorism, like she did last November. Why did no one stop her?

2020 A.D.

(Anno Dominic)

THE NEW YORK
DAILY ▣ CRUISE
NOVEMBER 1872

CRUISE SHIP ADRIFT AS PORTS CLOSE THEIR DOORS

by Our Maritime Staff **DAVY JONES**

THE popular cruise liner, the Mary Celeste, continues to roam the world's oceans following the mysterious outbreak of a plague.

No one is sure how many holiday makers have been affected by the viral outbreak, but observers are fearing the worst. "The Captain's table has been deserted and the decks,

once busy, with activities like quoits and yoga, are empty."

The last message (in a bottle) from an elderly couple, on what they thought would be "the voyage of a lifetime", simply said "Help".

At present, no ports are allowing the Mary Celeste to dock, out of fear of... *(cont. p94)*

2020 CRUISE SHIP PASSENGER DRESS CODE

| Breakfast | Lunch | Dinner |

LATE NEWS

China finds source of coronavirus outbreak

THE Chinese authorities have been deeply concerned about the spread of information about the coronavirus, and indeed how it got out in the first place.

They have assured the world that they did everything in their power to contain the story and to stop it getting out of China and into the news around the world.

President Xi said, "Mumble, mumble, mumble," and refused to take off his mask.

His spokesman said, "We located the source, the so-called 'truth spreader', and we were going to put him in isolation for a very, very long time. Fortunately, he's now dead, so he can no longer infect anyone with the dangerous facts." *(Rotters)*

Notes&queries

What is a pangolin?

● A pangolin is a seven-stringed medieval instrument similar to the lyre, also called the "Jester's harp". It is believed that Henry VIII wrote *Blue Breeches* on a pangolin, which was his less successful follow-up to *Greensleeves*, and which failed to make "Ye Tudor Chartes", as they were known. This led to Henry dispensing with the services, and indeed the head, of his manager, Simon of Cowell. In more recent times, Sting recorded an entire concept album of tantric pangolin music called *Every String You Break*.
Mr Hugh Wawei, Hubei Province, China

● Mr Wawei is sadly mistaken. Pangolin was a baby narwhal in the hugely successful animated cartoon series *Pingu*. Pingu and Pangolin had frequent adventures together and in one memorable episode met a plasticine Sir David Attenborough (voiced by a pre-*Suits* Meghan Markle),

who emerged from a fishing hole in the ice in order to deliver a message about global warming.
Fay Smarsk, Wuhan, China

● Ms Smarsk is pitifully misinformed, touching though her memories of children's television are. As everyone with a decent education knows, a pangolin is a cross between a palindrome and an anagram. Despite the efforts of literary scholars for over 300 years, there are no known examples in the English language. Ancient Norse, however, abounds with pangolins, as do some of the Mesopotamian languages, including Buttigieg and Klobuchar. I would be delighted to be corrected by any reader who can crack this ancient puzzle.
Karina Virus, the SS Mary Celeste, care of Saga Cruises

● Oh for heaven's sake, as any oriental street foodie knows perfectly well, sweet and sour pangolin is the... *(cont. p94)*

Early handwashing

"Happy birthday to me, happy birthday to me, happy birthday, dear Pilate..."

'IT'S WHAT CAROLINE WOULD HAVE WANTED'

by Our Reality TV Correspondent **Doctor Moreau**

ITV CONFIRMED today that despite calls for Love Island to be axed after former host Caroline Flack's tragic suicide, it would be staying on air as, having consulted widely with its accountants, it is certain this is what she would have wanted.

"We're certain Caroline would want nothing more than for this brutal reality show, where contestants are judged solely on their looks and willingness to have sex with virtual strangers live on TV by a baying mob on social media, to continue in her memory," said an ITV spokesman.

"This is a totally different situation from the suicide which forced The Jeremy Kyle Show off air, as that wasn't one of ITV's biggest shows generating huge amounts of cash.

"It would be highly distasteful to our shareholders for Love Island not to continue as a tribute to Roberta Flack. Sorry, I meant Caroline Flynn. Whatever her name was."

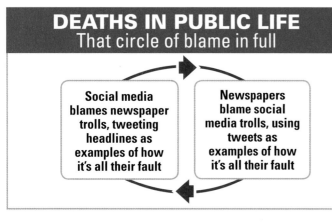

DEATHS IN PUBLIC LIFE
That circle of blame in full

Social media blames newspaper trolls, tweeting headlines as examples of how it's all their fault

Newspapers blame social media trolls, using tweets as examples of how it's all their fault

CORONAVIRUS FACE MASK SHORTAGE SHOCK

Who's laughing now?

AMAZING NEW REVELATION – FAME DOESN'T MAKE YOU HAPPY

IN AN astonishing new discovery this week, all newspapers, television and radio programmes and social media platforms have claimed that being a celebrity might not automatically guarantee happiness.

This breakthrough analysis in the workings of human psychology has managed to fill all available media and many are asking why this phenomenon has never been noticed before.

Said one industry insider, "It's not as though all songs, books, plays and films of the last few centuries have warned us and *(cont. 2094)*

The Eye's Controversial New Columnist

The columnist who gums the edge of news and leaves it soggy

This week I am very angry about the BBC. I am in complete agreement with Dominic Cummings and his goggle-eyed desire to destroy it once and for all. I approve of Mr Cummings: anyone who is that bald and cross about everything can't be wrong, can he?! As you have gathered from myself and my fellow columnists over the years, the BBC is both an over-mighty corporation which has too much influence on everything and a redundant thing that no one watches, and that just proves how insidious it is! Anything that influences everything so much, despite no one watching it, is a sinister thing indeed! This is why it should be reduced in size and stripped of all the useless channels and programmes that are a waste of time, only keeping the things that are obviously important. I have made a list of the things it should keep, and they are as follows: *CBeebies*, *Call the Midwife*, *Eastenders* (because Phil Mitchell reminds me of a younger me) and any wildlife programme which has a tiny baby monkey throwing poo at its parents. Of course, if these are removed by the government, it will be a national scandal and cultural vandalism and I would not hesitate to protest in the strongest *(cont. p94)*

Jersey Royals furious at demotion

by Our Top Potato Correspondent
Tim Chipman, the man who digs up the stories

TOP-ranking potatoes, the Jersey Royals, have been forbidden from using the word Royal to describe their potatoness.

The Jersey Royals had been intending to go it alone as international potato celebrities, using the name Jersey Royals on their website and marketing the Jersey Royal brand on products as varied as potatoes and potatoes. But now they have been banned from cashing in on the royal nomenclature.

Said a friend of the Jersey Royals, "They feel it is very unfair that other potatoes are allowed to trade on their Royal connections.

"They are particularly cross with the King Edward potatoes, who are allowed to exploit their

regal status with no hindrance at all. And what about Duchess potatoes?! It's one rule for one set of potatoes and another rule for another."

Lightly seasoned potato-watchers have observed that the Jersey Royals will now just be called "the Jerseys", and may have trouble selling themselves in the global potato market place. Who is going to want a plain old potato for their after-dinner treat, when they could have a Hollywood celebrity like Mr Potato Head, star of Toy Story 1 potato, 2 potato, 3 potato, 4?

Said one critic, "I wouldn't listen to all this complaining – at the end of the day, the Jersey Royals are just thin-skinned."

ELGIN MARBLES TO BE PART OF BREXIT TALKS?

"I love what you've done with your snakes"

Fears concerning fitting rooms

PLEASE PLEASE PLEASE join my Facebook group NO CHANGE! which names and shames shops that allow men into women's changing rooms. John Lewis is the latest, declaring that 'customers are welcome to use whichever fitting room makes them feel most comfortable'. (Perhaps Edgar the arsonist from their highly problematic Christmas ad will be welcomed in to set fire to us as we dress!) Campaign hero Jean Hatchet put it best in this wonderful tweet: Dear @jlandpartners which changing room do you think a rapist of women would feel 'most comfortable in'?
– Supermum

not bein funny but if all men are rapist's then a rapist will feel most comfortable in the mens room with all the other rapist's? **– Hayley 321**

Yawn! Spare us the faux outrage about 'upskirters' and other anaemic opportunists infiltrating female-only spaces. These part-time peepers are 'voyeurs' in name only, sharing NOTHING in common with that daring band of brothers who perch in precarious 'hides', illicitly install hidden cameras, and risk their liberty to covertly enjoy womankind in her most exalted state: bare and unaware. **– Monkey see**

i went in the female room and there was no birds at all 😞 when i complaned it was

empty they said theres nothing they can do about it 😡 GUTTED **– luke**

of course men like to look at us lady's its only natural 😃 my old man used to love page 3 he said it brightened up his day but even that got band by extremist's 😞 **– Hunny pot**

My husband and I are in our sixties and have many hobbies, including real ale, non-league football, crown green bowls and dogging. You hear stories about pervs who take sneaky pics of bra fittings, but these types run a mile when you invite them in for a proper look! My best experience was in a Birmingham store in the 1980s when the ladies room was full and I tried on 200 quids worth of lingerie in the mens room with the help of a dozen or so willing blokes. When the staff asked me to leave, one of them flashed his CID badge and they left us to it. 😃 Fitting Room Fantasy remains my most popular webcam role-play request to this day! **– Gilfy Gracie**

I am a hirsute plus-size 48-year-old woman who is often mistaken for a man. I feel most comfortable trying on clothes while emptying my bowels, and bring a plastic potty with me for this purpose. Although I always use a curtained cubicle, a few reactionary stores still object. **– Beth**

The cost of screw-in penile implants in Barnet might surprise you. fosbyclinic.com **– bh^*-h2>yc**

EU and Britain lay out their negotiating positions

by Our Brexit Correspondent
Noah Deal

Trade talks to find a post-Brexit trade deal between Europe and the UK have begun in Brussels, with both sides using the opening day to lay out their negotiating position.

"You don't frighten us, you English pig dogs. Go and boil your bottoms, you sons of a silly person. I blow my nose at you. No, now go away or I shall taunt you a second time, you empty-headed animal food trough wiper. I fart in your general direction. Your mother was a hamster and

your father smelt of elderberries," said an EU negotiator.

The British delegation responded with a rousing rendition of *Jerusalem* before spending the rest of the opening morning taunting the German delegates with a chant of "Two World Wars and One World Cup".

PRIME MINISTER'S HAPPY NEWS

It's your Number 10 baby
Is it? I lost count at 8...
And we're getting married
Yes – we can't have another bastard in Downing Street

Exclusive to all newspapers, to accompany boring Boris baby coverage

YES, I'M AN OLD DAD TOO!

PHIL SPACE on becoming a father at 55

MY JAW dropped when she broke the news. "Phil," said my editor, "guess what? I'm going to have a piece by you." "When?" I breathlessly enquired. "By tomorrow lunchtime," she replied.

Joy mixed with panic, as I considered the implications. Wasn't I too old for this sort of thing, having to churn out words about fatherhood at a moment's notice? On the other hand, it would keep me young and, as my editor said, "You've got lead in your pencil, Phil, use it to write 1000 words."

Soon, I was into the familiar routine of sleepless nights, as I kept my much younger partner awake, worrying how I could pad the article out... before the dreaded cry, "It needs changing".

But at the end of the day, it all seemed worth it. As I said to my editor, "I don't care what the cheque's like, as long as it's healthy."

A FAILURE OF DUTY

THE DISGRACEFUL absence of the Prime Minister from the flood zones is completely incomprehensible. It has long been accepted that one of the jobs of the Prime Minister in a time of national crisis is to turn up and be abused by enraged members of the public.

If the current incumbent of this great Office is incapable of registering this simple fact, of donning the Prime Ministerial Hunter Wellington boots and subjecting himself to cries of "Fuck off, Boris!", "Go back to Westminster, you toffee-nosed tosser!" and "This isn't the Brexit we voted for!", then he should seriously consider his position.

It is not enough to send a mere minister to perform this essential function, since there is no comparable pleasure in abusing the Environment Secretary, George Eustice, by shouting "You're useless, Eustice!"

There is even less pleasure in listening to the Prince of Wales tell you that he was right actually about all this environmental stuff, and nobody listened.

There comes a point in every great leader's life when they need to step up to the mark and be told that they are unfit to lead the nation, whilst holding a mop in a large puddle. That moment is now, Boris! And like King Cnut, even if you cannot turn back the tide, you can at least turn up and be called a total Cnut!

That is why we say that Boris Johnson must get out of Downing Street and visit the disaster area known as the Home Office as soon as possible, before *(Is this right? Ed.)*

BIBLICAL TIMES

Friday 6 March 2020

Authorities appeal for calm

BY OUR MAN ON PATMOS, ST JON SNOW (CH. 4)

THE World Heaven Organization (WHO) today refused to categorise recent events as the End of Days. Whilst conceding that there were some causes for concern around the globe, these phenomena did not yet constitute evidence of the Apocalypse.

Said a WHO spokesman, "Yes, we have seen a number of unrelated cataclysmic events including: floods in Shropshire, fires in Australia, plagues of locusts in East Africa, and plagues of, well... plague really, everywhere. But this is in no way definitive proof that God has plans to wipe humanity off the face of the earth because it's all been a horrible mistake."

He continued, "I mean it doesn't look good, admittedly, and I don't feel that well myself. But we've yet to see rivers turn to blood, thunderstorms of frogs, the dead rising or the emergence of The Beast. Although Donald Trump is about to make an upbeat statement about everything being under control."

If any of the issues in the above piece are causing you concern, then please call our helpline by dialling 666.

WHAT WILL THE NUMBER 10 BABY BE CALLED? YOU DECIDE

BOY	GIRL
Dominic	Dominica
Randy	Phibby
Zippy	Mustique
Darius	Priti
Winston	Govia
Spaffy	Brexitella
Pericles	Delia-Telegraphia
Buller	Eugenica
Tory McToryface	Verity
Damien (from the Omen)	Garden-Bridget

Ceci n'est pas une pipe.

"It is what it is"

News in brief

Flooding update

The Conservative Party has been cheered by news that the north of England has been turned completely blue, due to a series of events known as "floods" that have completely swept away all the local defences in the region.

"This really is great news for us," said one Conservative source, speaking from Central London. "We were absolutely convinced there was some sort of massive 'Red Wall' in place that would keep us from making any progress whatsoever, but it turns out that nobody had spent nearly enough money on flood defences in the last ten years and, as a result,there is nothing but blue – well, kind of blue, really it's a sort of murky brown – as far as the eye can see."

When asked if there was any longer-term risk created by half the country being left underwater without any support, the Conservative source explained: "We've done the relevant risk assessment and according to that, we don't have to give a toss about anyone north of Watford for nearly five years."

Boris Johnson MP
● Live   385,000,000 Views

People's Prime Minister's Question Time – Live on Fakebook

0 people **like this**

👍 Like   💬 Comment

Hi there, People's People!
And let's get straight down to answering **your** questions **honestly**, directly and **transparently**. First up is Frank Speaking. What's your question, Frank?

> What are you doing about coronavirus, apart from nothing?

Good question and what I will say is this: **I'M HAVING A BABY**!!!!! Yes, it's true. My beloved Carrie [Check name, Dom!] and I are expecting the pitter patter of journalists rushing to write **glowing** pieces about the Downing Street sprog! I promised **good** news post-Brexit, and here it is! And what could be more feelgood and optimistic than a baby?

It's even **better** than the puppy – no offence, Dom, good idea, but I went one better! So thanks for your congratulations and **good** wishes, Frank. I am sure the whole nation is behind you. Next it's a Miss Lead. And what's your question?

> Are we all going to die?

Cripes! That's one for Dom's "super-forecasters", but unfortunately they've all been sacked for being weird, misfit, racist, eugenicist **lunatics**! (No offence!) But what I can say is that **I'M GETTING MARRIED**. Isn't that great? Next question from an Allison Pearson. Great name! You sound a sensible sort of person...

> Congratulations to you and the lovely Carrie and can I say how gentlemanly and honourable it was of you not to get married to your pregnant mistress before your divorce came through?

Tough question, Allison, and thanks for agreeing to ask it. Yes, my **divorce** is a bit like Brexit – it's done and dusted. Just as I promised. OK, so the decree nisi (which is Latin for "**Hello**, younger woman!") was slightly later than desirable (a good 25 years according to Marina) and the financial settlement was rather more **punitive** than anticipated. But **divorced** I am. Two formerly united parties are now amicably **not** speaking to each other and we're moving forward in a spirit of mutual **animosity** and **recrimination**. It proves to all the doomsters and gloomsters in my family that it **can** be done. I've pulled off what I would suggest is a very, very good deal and sends out a message to the world that, when it comes to negotiations, the

Bozzmeister is not to be **trifled** with. So, we split everything 50/50. Marina got 50% of all our assets and the other half went to Marina. I **did** get to keep the family home – or my **car**, as it was known. As a result, I go into the negotiations with our European partners (soon to be ex-partners) **confident** that I am ready for anything – apart from them employing Marina as chief negotiator, which would be a bit of a **bummer**. Next question from Ivor Flooded Kitchen in Yorkshire...

> Where the bloody hell have you been for the last week? Forget your bloody baby, the waters have broken round here!

Well, Ivor, as it happens I've been concentrating on flood **defences** and the **best** one I've come up with for not showing my face in any of the submerged regions of this great country of ours is that, er, I've been **very**, **very busy** doing very important, high level things, which I can't tell you about, or indeed **remember**. Next – and this is the **last** question – from Mr I. Reader, who says:

> Are you going to pretend there aren't any more questions to answer, like you did last time? There were actually 4,692 questions still to go, weren't there?

Ah, we don't seem to have any more questions, that's a **shame**. So, till next time, this is your **transparent**, open, honest, **accountable**, tennis-playing, country-house loving, wellie-phobic, people's Prime Minister leaving you. Not **you**, Carrie! No need to get hysterical!

👑 Home Office

THE POINTS-BASED IMMIGRATION SYSTEM EXPLAINED IN 10 EASY STEPS

1. Piss off, all of you.
2. Seriously, we mean it, nobody unskilled whatsoever, you're not welcome.
3. Unless we need you very, very briefly around the time of the fruit harvest.
4. But that's it, nobody else unskilled. Seriously, get lost.
5. Except if we're a bit short in the nursing homes, of course.
6. Or the hospitals, actually.
7. Might need a few plumbers or brickies at some point too.
8. Or nannies, come to think of it, someone's going to have to look after all the PM's children.
9. Maybe a few people for the supermarket tills, actually, and to do all the cleaning in case we need anyone zero-hours, bord students are a completely different thing, and we may think of a few exceptions to this which will be put into this clause just in case we've forgotten anything. Taxi drivers! Knew we'd forgotten something.
10. But everyone else: piss off.

"If you don't want to know the scores, look away now"

GOVID-19: THE FACTS

Govid-19 is a malignant and contagious entity that can lay low any Prime Ministers and colleagues who stand too close to it. Here are the symptoms:

1 A sharp stabbing pain in the shoulder blades.

2 A persistent low buzzing in the ear.

3 Hallucinations where the afflicted person believes that he can see pledges of loyalty.

IF YOU FEEL THESE SYMPTOMS, SEE A SPIN-DOCTOR IMMEDIATELY

Gnome Health

Coronavirus: your questions answered

● Can you catch the coronavirus from eating a frozen Italian pizza?

● Can you get the coronavirus from watching old episodes of *The Chinese Detective* on UK Drama?

● If I am in a public restroom where no hand sanitiser is available, should I flush myself down the toilet?

● Should I start wearing a HazMat suit during sex, as my wife got the flu twice last year?

● Is it true that eating nothing but broccoli smothered with marshmallows protects you from contracting the coronavirus?

● Are gimp masks as effective as face masks?

● Is it true that millions of new cases will be discovered every day from now on, all our major cities will be shut down, the army called in to collect bodies and bury them in an enormous plague pit on the Isle of Wight and giant rats will roam the deserted landscape for the rest of time?

ANSWERS
Who knows? Someone in this train carriage just sneezed and I'm far too busy writing out my last will and testament to answer any questions.

"For goodness' sake, Geoff... we're not at the pet-eating stage yet"

Yes Minister

Unseen episode discovered

(Scene: the interior of the Home Office)

Sir Humphrey: And that, Minister, is why the points-based Australian system will not work.

Bernard: In fact, it's more of a point-less system, really.

Sir Humphrey: Oh – very good, Bernard.

(Audience laughs at Oxbridge-educated mandarins indulging in facile but elegant wordplay)

Priti Patel: You're both fucking useless. What are you?

Bernard: We're civil servants, Minister.

Sir Humphrey: Very good again, Bernard.

(Audience laughs even more at charming, self-deprecating, public school-educated bureaucrats)

Priti Patel: You're fucking sacked, is what you are!

(Audience doesn't laugh nervously at new 21st Century ministerial approach)

Sir Humphrey: Minister, might I suggest you're being a little precipitous and perhaps a moment's reflection might be beneficial to all parties concerned.

Priti Patel: Speak fucking English, you twat! That's point one on my immigration control rules.

Bernard: Indeed. But wasn't point two, Minister, that people with no skills at all should not be given jobs in Britain?

Sir Humphrey: Quite so. And are we not looking for the brightest and the best? As opposed to the dimmest and the least able, Minister?

Priti Patel: I don't get your point.

(There is a pause as they both stare at her significantly)

Priti Patel: You're looking at me, aren't you?

Sir Humphrey: No, no, Minister. Heaven forfend.

Priti Patel: You're doubly fucking fired!

Sir Humphrey: Might I enquire on what grounds this peremptory dismissal is based?

Priti Patel: You've been briefing against me, telling the press that MI5 don't trust me and that I don't have enough intelligence to do the job.

Bernard: Intelligence **has** always been a problem for you.

Sir Humphrey: Brilliant, Bernard!

(Audience laughs again with relief at traditional Whitehall-based snobbery)

Priti Patel: Fuck off!

Sir Humphrey: I'm perfectly happy to tender my resignation, but I should warn you that you may regret it...

Priti Patel: So what are you going to do, Sir Fuckface? Sue me?

Sir Humphrey: Guess, Minister!

(Audience dies laughing. Civil Service just dies)

What you won't read in the Guardian

Shameful hypocrisy exposed

Why is Priti Patel under such ferocious attack from newspapers and social media?

It's simple racism, isn't it? Forget all the nonsense about her behaviour and her personality, the **real** reason no one likes Priti Patel is **exactly** the same as the **real** reason no one likes Meghan Markle: she comes from an ethnic minority and no one in Britain can put up with such a figure in public life without resorting to hysterical abuse. That is why this newspaper is solidly behind Meghan Patel and why we will resist "Prexit" at all costs and will take Priti's side in any clash between the elderly, white, racist, sexist, imperialist civil service and the blameless, innocent home secretary who *(That's enough. Ed.)*

A President writes...

Coronavirus

AS A President, I am often asked, "What do you know about the coronavirus?" and the simple answer is: "You've come to the right guy."

People are impressed by how much I know. I probably know more than anybody else, including doctors, about epideedoodaaology, as we experts call it.

So, viruses have been booking plane tickets from Europe to America. Fact! So, I'm not allowing any more viruses to buy any more tickets. Unless they are American viruses. Or British. Or Irish.

Another fact you probably don't know, but I do, is that sleepy Joe Biden's son in Ukraniania was the first American to get the virus, and he spread it to every Democrat in America. Fact!

Many of you reading this may think I've got a touch of the crazies, your President's gone loopy-loo. Maybe he's got the virus. But no, I haven't. 'Cos I don't touch my face, and you know why? 'Cos I don't want my fingers to go orange. Fact!

I told Melania that I'm going to keep my distance. She took this better than expected. And flew straight to Europe.

I'm going to make America ill again. Remember: don't believe what you read in the failing mainstream media and the loser New York Times and the Washing-your-hands Post – it's all Fake Flus.

© A President.

"The fact that you have an opinion is threatening my safe space"

HARVEY WEINSTEIN FOUND GUILTY – #METOO MOVEMENT GROWS

There has been a huge increase in the #MeToo movement, in the wake of Harvey Weinstein's guilty verdict on two counts of rape.

"I always knew Harvey was a monster and a predator," said one Hollywood A-lister who made seven movies with the disgraced movie mogul.

"Me too," said another, who regularly partied with Harvey for the best part of a decade.

"Me too," said another well-known Hollywood star. "I knew he was evil every minute of the five movies we made together."

"Me too," said another Hollywood star, who says he was sickened to his stomach by the mogul on each of the six occasions he travelled to Cannes on Harvey's private jet.

This is a watershed moment for the #MeToo movement in Hollywood.

Unlikely Headlines No 94

Now we look at the fruity women he hung out with

■ FINALLY, the monster Harvey Weinstein has been found guilty of two counts of sexual assault and rape.

Let's look at the GORGEOUS women he's been hanging out with, in our photo supplement "Beauties and the Beast!".

They're all there! Gwyneth Paltrow! Renée Zellweger! Uma Thurman! Keira Knightley! Sienna Miller! Kate Beckinsale!

This newspaper says PHWOAR to all of them and if you need to see photos of the loathsome toad hanging out with some top-class Hollywood totty then you can rest assured we'll be providing more pictures like this at every opportunity we can until (*cont. p94*)

THIS WEEK

RACHEL JOHNSON

Does your brother have a favourite spoon?

I'd rather talk about my own spoons, if that's…

So he *doesn't* have a favourite – is *that* what you are saying?

I am a person in my own right and not just the sister of my brother…

Is that what your brother thinks?

No, but…

As a child growing up…

Carry on…

…did your brother ever hit you with a spoon?

Look, I don't want to talk about my brother's relationship with spoons.

Fair enough. I respect that. Has anything amusing…

Yes…

…ever happened…

Yes…

…to your brother in connection with a spoon?

Just give me the money.

Social distancing – what is the correct distance to keep away from people?

Family and friends	1 metre
Strangers	2 metres
Strangers sniffing	5 metres
Alex Salmond	*(That's enough. Ed.)*

The Eye's Controversial New Columnist

The columnist who refuses to use environmentally friendly nappies

This week I am very angry about this University of Warwick study that states you should ignore babies and let them cry. Speaking as a baby *(see photo)*, I am very much against this attitude. Nobody should ignore me when I cry, as I see it as an issue of free speech. So if my free speech is ignored, it is censorship of the most heinous nature. Thank heavens Toby Young is on hand to set up a benefit gig to highlight the plight of the sadly ignored tantrum-throwing columnist, silenced by the establishment, apart from the columns, books, LBC show and *(cont. p94)*

FreeSpeechUnion.org

You're a tosser

That'll be £49.95

I thought it was **free** speech

Lookalikes

Swede   **Thunberg**

Sir,
    Are they related?
        Best regards,
        PETER LAMMER.

Moriarty   **Cummings**

Sir,
    I recently came across Sidney Paget's 1893 depiction of arch-criminal mastermind Professor Moriarty, and I couldn't help noticing a remarkable resemblance to the PM's Chief Advisor Dominic Cummings. I wonder if by chance the two are related?
    JOHN MORGAN.

Gogo Yubari   **Claudia Winkleman**

Sir,
    Has anyone noticed, as I have, the extraordinary resemblance between Claudia Winkleman from Strictly Come Dancing and Gogo Yubari, the teenage assassin, from Kill Bill.
    Are they, by any chance, related?
    ENA B. WHATMORE.

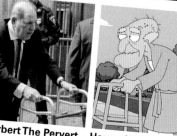

Herbert The Pervert   **Harvey Weinstein**

Sir,
    Seeing a frail Harvey Weinstein at his New York court appearance requiring the assistance of a walker, I wonder if there is any relation to the character Herbert "The Pervert" from American cartoon series, Family Guy? Surely not.
    BEN WEBB.

Andrew Neil   **Yoda**

Sir,
    Noticed has anyone remarkable the resemblance between of the BBC Andrew Neil and Jedi Master legendary Yoda?
    PHILIP CLARKE,
Melbourne.

Partridge   **Williamson**

Sir,
    I was briefly reassured today when I saw that Alan Partridge had taken over the exam grading issue. Sadly, on closer inspection, it transpired Gavin Williamson was still in charge.

    LESLEY QUERIPEL.

Harry Kane   **John Frederick Lewis**

Sir,
    I recently visited the wonderful British Museum and couldn't help wondering whether the English artist John Frederick Lewis [see this 19th Century self-portrait (selfie)] is a distant relative of the English and Spurs footballer Harry [one of our own] Kane.

    DES CONWAY,
Nottingham.

Adele   **Tombliboo**

Sir,
    I hope you have not missed the similarity between Adele's Notting Hill Carnival outfit and the laundry-obsessed denizens of In The Night Garden, known as Tcombliboos. I'd get out more but Iglepiggle has stolen my face mask. Any similarity between the musical styles of Adele and Tombliboos is almost certainly coincidental.

    ADAM KEAN.

Gilbert and George   **Patrick and Chris**

Sir,
    Has anyone noticed, as I have, the extraordinary resemblance between Professor Chris Whitty and Sir Patrick Vallance and distinguished modern artists, Gilbert and George? Are they by any chance related? I think we should be told.
    ENA B. WILSON.

Captain Ramius   **Qasem Soleimani**

Sir,
    Whilst President Trump wanted to kill an enemy of the US and start a little war, was he perhaps after Sean Connery's character in The Hunt For Red October when he bumped off that pesky Iranian bloke?
    MATTHEW JONES.

Pop pop   **Poop poop**

Sir,
    David Hockney or Toad of Toad Hall?
    SHELLEY LAWSON.

Everage   **Moran**

Sir,
    Surely there is something antipodean about Lib Dem leadership candidate Layla Moran?

    JOHN ARNOLD.

The scarecrow   **Rory Stewart**

Sir,
    I think good candidates for your regular Lookalike feature would be Rory Stewart and the scarecrow in the Wizard of Oz. Every time I see the former, I think of the latter.
    GEOFF RENSHAW.

Donald Trump

Kennet pilbox

Sir,
  This Berkshire Kennetside WW2 pillbox reminded me of Donald Trump. I wonder if by chance the two are related?
  ENA B. PEARSON,
Reading.

Rowland   **Wilson**

Sir,
  I see the biographer and novelist AN Wilson has been moonlighting as the front man of Dexy's Midnight Runners. I presume Kevin Rowland's busy researching the Saxe-Coburgs. You in those specs, my thoughts I confess/ Verge on dirty... Too ra loo ra, too raloo rye aye.
  ROWAN PELLING.

Body wash   **Rylan**

Sir,
  While relaxing in my bath I noticed the unnerving similarity between my body wash and a certain celebrity. I wonder whether the two 'Mr Perfects' are related?
  CHRIS KNAPMAN.

Sir,
  While watching the hilarious, sometimes gross and shocking shenanigans in the popular film 'Bridesmaids' recently, I was reminded of a similar, more current, farce. I wonder if, perhaps, they are related?
  NON TAYLOR,
Swansea.

Attorney General   **Rocket man**

Sir,
  Have any of your readers noticed the similarity between US Attorney General William Barr and national treasure Elton John? Are the two related?
  MICHAEL PANTELI,
Hove.

Betty   **Shami**

Sir,
  Has anyone noticed, as I have, the similarity between the 1930s Max Fleischer animated cartoon character, Betty Boop, and the Shadow Attorney General, Baroness Chakrabarti. Are they by any chance related?
  ENA B. ELLINAS.

Stan Laurel   **Pope Francis**

Sir,
  Has anyone noticed, as I have, the extraordinary resemblance between the saintly Stan Laurel and the master of slapstick, Pope Francis? Here's another fine mess you've gotten me into...
  ENA B. SAMUEL,
Burry Port, Wales.

Ben   **Vincent**

Sir,
  There is no record of Vincent van Gogh in The Royal Dutch Cricket Board's history, but I am struck by the resemblance of the England all-rounder and the great artist. I wonder if they are, in any way, related?
  ALEX WILLIAMS.

Moggalike

Sir,
  Has anybody noticed, as I have, that the Leader of the House of Commons appears to be shamelessly aping movie star Burt Reynolds's iconic Cosmopolitan centrefold? A second career beckons, perchance?
  STEPHEN WATTS.

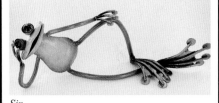

Sir,
  Whilst shopping online, I noticed a strong resemblance between this reclining amphibian and a charming metal frog. Are they the same species?
  JIM MURRELL.

Sir,
  Endangered species: Magnet for the females or lazy, fat alpha male? Which is which?
  CHERYL BURR.

Sir,
  While idly perusing the World's Greatest Gallery of Seductive Radishes online, I couldn't help but notice the resemblance between this twisted vegetable and the Honourable Member for North East Somerset.
  ANDY FLOOD.

DIARY

THE INFLUENCERS

PIERS MORGAN: So where did this so-called coronavirus come from?

The answer is quite literally staring us in the face.

Meghan Markle.

Fact. Just three weeks ago, there was not a single reported case in the UK. Not one. If you don't believe me – ask the experts.

Fact. Last week, Meghan Markle flew back to the UK. And she spent the next few days shaking as many hands and breathing over as many people as she possibly could.

Fact. Meghan Markle is now safely back in Canada. But she has left behind her a deadly trail of literally hundreds of thousands of reported cases of coronavirus.

And it pains me deeply to say that the numbers are rising.

Is this tragic toll of misery really what fresh-faced Prince Harry intended back in 2017 when he first went all gooey-eyed, as the seductive Californian soap star divorcee mercilessly reeled him in?

Personally, I don't believe so. But it's no exaggeration to say that he now finds himself shackled to the serial-killing ambassador for the most deadly disease ever to hit our shores.

And that's a fact.

YOKO ONO @YOKOONO: Just dream dreams, and corona will leave you alone, to dream those dreams in peace.

Corona is not a virus. She only thinks she's a virus because we keep telling her she is. As Corona spreads, love spreads with her. Don't be angry with Corona. Be positive!

MICHAEL PARKINSON: Whatever happened to the great viruses?

From the way the young go on about it, you'd imagine that coronavirus was up there with the all-time greats!

Sorry, but I beg to differ.

In my day, we had smallpox – one of the truly legendary viruses.

Whatever happened to smallpox? It bred many imitators – but none was as memorable as the real thing.

I'll never forget the day I caught rabies off the late, great Sammy Davis Jr.

We were sitting there in the studio, and he was treating me to one of his truly legendary performances, when – wholly impromptu – he bit me on the leg. He just had the most tremendous instinct for these things

Never in my wildest dreams did I ever think I'd contract rabies from one of the greatest entertainers in the history of showbusiness. A great song-and-dance man. A tremendous raconteur. But, above all, a wonderful human being. And I was given the chance to share his very own virus. A magical moment. A moment to treasure.

Smallpox, rabies, Spanish flu, the great plague – frankly, coronavirus has got nothing on them.

I once had the late, great Bob Hope on the show and – I'll never forget – before we went on, he took me to one side and passed the Black Death on to me.

But who remembers Black Death these days? Mention it to the young and and they don't know what the heck you're on about. I had it on the show a couple of times. That's what I call entertainment. For a start, you could sing along with it, and that's not a claim you can make for any of these modern viruses, more's the pity.

SARAH FERGUSON @SARAHTHE DUCHESS: So happy to announce that I have been appointed Brand Ambassador for @coronavirus. Deeply proud and privileged to be helping spread this inspirational new virus!

PETER HITCHENS: If we had never discovered coronavirus, and so had not descended into a constant floundering panic about it, it would be doing far less damage than it already is.

But ever since the days of the pernicious nosy-parker Albert Schweitzer, we can't leave well alone. Whenever a pushy little virus comes along, we greet it with a song and dance.

Let me explain. The government is forcing us to scrub our hands with antiseptic hand sanitiser. This is because it is in league with foreign governments which force the stuff upon us. You only have to taste sanitiser to know that it is vile. I drank a glass the other day and I found it almost as disgusting as champagne, another grossly overrated drink, also favoured by our liberal-left elite.

Inevitably, all this attention is exactly what the wretched little virus wants. We are playing into its hands. But if we ignored it, it would go away.

My own tactic when walking into a public place is to cough and sneeze as much as possible. This is the only way to tell the coronavirus in no uncertain terms that it hasn't a hope of winning. But will the powers-that-be ever advise everyone to follow suit? Not when they're in hock to America and China.

This is Britain today.

LIZ JONES: Thousands dead.
Billions wiped off the economy.
The world in total meltdown.
Why me?

As told to
CRAIG BROWN

CUT-OUT-AND-KEEP GUIDE FOR OFFICE WORKERS WORKING FROM HOME TO PREVENT SPREAD OF VIRUS

- Wake up, shower and come downstairs as usual

- Make a cup of tea and turn on your computer

- Realise you are 45 minutes early for work

- Go back to bed for a half-hour nap

- Wake up at 10am and realise you are an hour late for work

- Turn on the computer and discover the broadband is on the blink

- Make toast and watch two episodes of 'Murder She Wrote'

- Spend 90 minutes on hold, as your broadband provider is experiencing a higher than usual volume

of calls at this time, due to people self-isolating

- Give up and wash your hands again singing any of the following:

Happy Birthday

God Save The Queen

Gels Just Wanna Have Fun

Don't Stand So Close To Me

I Don't Wanna Hold Your Hand

- Er…

- That's it.

THOSE ISOLATIONS IN FULL

Self-isolating Staying at home for a fortnight in case you've got coronavirus

Shelf-isolating Removing all the toilet rolls from supermarkets

Will Self-isolating Sitting alone, writing boring books about your drug history

Wealth-isolating Hiding in the Cayman Islands from HMRC

Elf-isolating Bunking off from your job making toys at the North Pole

Oracle at Delph-isolating Hiding in a cave and pretending you can predict the future

(That's enough. Ed.)

YOUR AUDIO IS BAD, YOU SOUND LIKE A HUMAN!

Boris Johnson

Home   Create

Boris Johnson MP
● Live   385,000,000 Views

People's Prime Minister's Question Time – Still Alive on Fakebook
(no thanks to Nadine! Just kidding, get well soon)

👍 Like   💬 Comment

0 people like this

Hi there, Facebookers... or should I say don't-touch-your-Facebookers?!

Because **this** week it's Serious Statesman Bozza, not Funster Bojo. And the message is **Keep Calm** and **Corona On**! Too flippant, Dom? Yes, you're probably right, what with all the **wrinklies** popping their clogs... so, solemn face and **first** question from Ivor Drycough.

What is the latest government thinking on the coronavirus crisis?

Well, the main message to the nation is **Churchillian**. Can we beat this virus? Oh **yussss**! What's that Dom, the **other** Churchill? Yes, of course. World War Two, Spirit of the Blitz, etc etc. So our position is **clear** – life goes on, except where it doesn't. There is no need to cancel anything, **unless** there is. We will be taking the **right** action at the **right** time. Whatever that is. And not **before**. And not **after**. And by the right action, I mean not the **wrong** action, which would be a mistake. I hope that puts everyone's minds at ease. **Next** question from Mr Ronnie Nose.

Why aren't you doing what all the other countries are doing?

Thanks, Mr Nose, but I can reassure you that I am acting on the advice of **experts** – not the sort of experts that we Tories said we'd had enough of, but good, **proper** experts with degrees and everything. You've probably seen me with a couple of these chaps and they are top-notch, Grade A experts with **suits** and **glasses** and graphs to boot! They've assured me that they can guarantee immunity – for **me** obviously because it's **not** my fault... I'm just doing what

these so-called experts tell me. And **one** thing they've told me is the importance of "social distancing", ie I keep very **close** to them, at no distance at all, in the hope that I will be infected with some credibility. So, Ronnie, I **hope** that reassures you.

No, it doesn't.

Good! Excellent! Glad to calm things down a little. Next question from Will Catchit, who asks:

Are you actually going to do anything useful rather than just wittering on with your boosterish bluster?

Yes, **glad** you asked that, Will. By the time you read this I'll have started my daily Government Information Broadcasts, giving **comprehensive** updates about how the **war** on the virus is going and how we can turn your saucepans into Spitfires, or possibly **ventilators**. Anyway, that way you'll know that your Prime Minister is a **serious** figure taking this crisis **seriously** in a **serious** way... So let's **stomp** on that sombrero and, to continue the Mexican metaphor, let's send Señor Corona back to his snoozy **siesta**, to return mañana... no, hang on, that's not quite **right**, is it? Dom, where are those experts? **Help**!

GLENDA SLAGG

There's no shortage of her, sadly!!!? (Geddit?!)

■ **DANIEL CRAIG?!!** Put it away, Daniel – your torso, I mean!? And do up your flies while you're about it!? Ok, so you looked "ripped", even though you are 94 (subs, check age)!!!! Well, take a tip from Auntie Glenda – you're making a Spectre of yourself and you should say "Dr No" next time they ask you to take your kit off and make a right Casino Royale fool of yourself!!?? Tell you what – THAT picture is the one that should have been postponed and not the rotten old new Bond flick!?! Just saying, no offence!!?!?

■ MMMM! Daniel Craig!!! Ooh – ooh – seven, I'm talkin' about!?!! He's the Buffest Butchest Bond in the biz!!!! And I **spy** (!?!) super-pecs, great abs and his flies are undone!?!!? What more could a red-blooded gal want!?! I think I'm Skyfalling for you, Danny Boy, and in these tough

times, your naked nips offer us all a Quantum of Solace!?!!?! (*This is terrible, keep it up! Ed.*)

■ **WAYNE ROONEY!!?!?!** The new Sunday Times signing has got all us fellow columnists quakin' in our football boots (geddit!?!) Ok, the spudfaced nipper knows everything there is about... well... being a nipper and being spud-faced, but can he write!!?? No!!! But who can??!! Good luck to you, Wayney, and I hope your sensational Sportz column is more successful than your beard!?! (*You're fired. Ed.*)

■ SEEN the new Julian Fellowes ITV drama, Belgravia Abbey?!?? Or is it Upstairs Downton??!!? Who cares???! There's nothing else to do on a Sunday except read Wayne Rooney's exciting new column, commissioned by the excellent editor!?! (*You're hired again. Ed.*)

Byeee!!

Good News

EVENT TO GO AHEAD

AS THE nation's cinemas, theatres, concert halls and football grounds all closed, there was widespread cheer that at least one event would be going ahead as scheduled.

The organisers of the End of the World announced, "The End of the World has been planned for well over 200 years and it'll take more than a pandemic to postpone this long-awaited apocalypse."

They continued, "The End of Days is a great chance to bring people together at a time of great worry and it would be a real shame for people not to enjoy what they have been looking forward to, as promised by the Book of

Revelations, Nostradamus and Ticketmaster."

Late News

● DUE TO unforeseen circumstances, the organisers regret that the End of the World has been cancelled. One of the main performers, Pestilence, has developed a slight cough and is self-isolating. And Death has decided that he will be "reaping from home". Famine has been caught on CCTV at a Tesco Metro stockpiling pasta, baked beans and tinned tuna. Only War is happy to carry on as normal and can be seen in theatres around the world.

British Theatre

BIRCH

LOCKDOWN – A NATION UNITES

Is that an essential activity?

True British Spirit brought out by time of crisis

It has been confirmed that the coronavirus crisis has created a huge source for the great spirit of Britain: shopping your neighbours to the authorities for minor offences.

"All over the country, we're seeing people grassing each other up, complaining on Twitter about bloody joggers or bloody pedestrians, or ringing the fuzz to say that they've seen people going to the shops more than strictly necessary," said one sociologist. "This is a classic British characteristic and it shows exactly the spirit of petty-minded little Hitlerism that helped us win the war."

Another expert said, "In times of crisis there's often an urge for people to work together, and although we have seen some of that, we've seen thousands and thousands of people saying 'Why are there people still going to the bloody park?' while they are literally walking in the park, or 'These stockpilers are disgraceful', as they stagger home from the shops with 168 rolls of toilet paper.

"Then they'll ring the police to complain that the people at number 94 had a friend round for tea yesterday or that they can smell a barbecue coming from the south-west and the local authority should send in the tanks. It's a huge source of national pride to see everyone pulling apart at a time like this."

(PA)

A Statement from Her Majesty the Queen

IN THE LIGHT of recent revelations in court about the involvement of His Royal Highness in unsavoury relationships with women, some of them very young, Her Majesty the Queen has decided that she is going to distance herself from this particular royal acquaintance.

Henceforth, communication between the two royals will be less friendly and despite their well-documented historic close relationship, the Queen will be withdrawing her official cordiality.

Her Majesty would like to

make it clear that she will no longer appear in photographs with this disgraced senior member of the Royal Family, ie Andrew.

Sheikh Mohammed will, of course, be welcome in the Royal Enclosure at Ascot, as usual.

IT'S THE SUN WOT LOST IT!

YES, Your super soaraway Sun has gone completely BUST!

Our old editor made a few expensive BOOBS about phone hacking, our ASSets are worthless, our circulation is on a low CURVE and we're on our last LEGS! BOTTOM line is, folks, we're 68 BIG ONES in debt!

Talk about being in the RED top! We often go on about how we like to BANG CRUMPET, but now we're totally BANG KRUPT! Looks like we'll have to go ON OUR KNEES to Rupert for a bail-out! Let's hope he GIVES US ONE!

Kathy, 23, from Neasden says: "They couldn't even afford to buy me a bikini that fits! Looks like the Sun's shelf life on the

stands will be even shorter than my shelf life as a glamour model!"

We're desperate, folks! If you want an old man to wash your windows for a few quid, write to Trevor Kavanagh, care of the Sun, and he'll do them for a tenner!

Racing from Newmarket

The Sheikh Mohammed bin Rashid Al Maktoum High-Stakes Chase
Those runners in full

👕	His Wife
👕	His Daughter
👕	His Other Daughter
👕	The Bodyguard who slept with his wife
👕	The Queen
👕	ER...
👕	Yes, that's the one
👕	I meant 'er'... as in hesitation
👕	Oh, I see
👕	That's it

AFTER "THE SEVENTH SEAL"

POETRY CORNER

In Memoriam Max von Sydow, screen legend

So. Farewell
Then Max von Sydow,
You played chess
With Death in
The Seventh Seal.

I didn't see
The other six,
But apparently they
Were very good too,
Which is rare
For sequels.

In the film,
Death cheated you,
But eventually
You could not
Cheat death.

You also played
Jesus Christ in
The Greatest Story Ever Told,
So now He can
Give you his notes.

But perhaps your
Greatest role was as
Ming The Merciless
In *Flash Gordon,*
The one in which
Brian Blessed
Famously shouted
"Gordon's Alive".

Sadly, now
Max isn't.

E.J. Thribb (17½ Seals)

"Can you stay inside your home, please, sir?"

Lines on the acquittal of Alex Salmond on all charges of sexual assault

'Twas on the twenty-third day of the third month of the year

That Alex Salmond finally had news to cheer.

After many a month of a trial most fraught,

He was found innocent by an Edinburgh court.

The prosecution contested he tried to have his way

With various lassies, starting with Woman A.

His lawyer argued it was plain to see

That puir Alex was being stitched up by Woman B.

The whole tale, said he, was entirely far-fetched,

Confected by Women, C, D , E, F , G and Aitch.

The defence continued to concede that he was a 'naughty boy'

And the consenting women were bent on a sinister ploy

To smear the good name of the Party's ex-leader,

For reasons that are not entirely plain to this reader.

It was all apparently to do with the Party's civil war

And auld enemies trying to settle a score.

Including yon Krankie-lookalike, Nicola,

Who it turned out could nae have been fickler.

As fingers were pointed at bonnie Ms Sturgeon,

Her problems in government were just beginning to burgeon.

The long-promised Indy Ref Two,

Looked like it was going down the loo.

Mr Salmond was strongly supported by TV station Russia Today,

Though whether this helped I couldnae possibly say.

But the jury were left in no doubt by his accusers

As to what went on with or without his troosers .

But in spite of these goings-on under his kilt

There was no question of his lack of guilt.

And so yon Alex, former leader of the SNP,

Was, to everyone's great surprise, allowed to get off Scot free.

© *William McGonnagal 1867*

Olympics need to be delayed

The World Health Organization has once again called on the IOC and the Japanese government to postpone the Summer Olympics in Tokyo, saying that it would speed up the fight against Covid-19.

"No Olympics in 2020 would mean that the hundreds of labs around the world that are working around the clock to produce new drugs which elite athletes can use without being detected in Tokyo could instead be repurposed to search for a coronavirus vaccine."

ELDERLY CORONAVIRUS RISK SHOCK

I've been self-isolating for years. No one ever comes to visit me anyway!

CONSPIRACY UPDATE

As Britain went into lockdown today, the MSM (Mainstream Media) continued to parrot the approved Government line that the coronavirus was a naturally occurring global pandemic. Thankfully, a courageous online community of radical freethinkers refused to be spoon-fed so-called facts by so-called 'world renowned epidemiologists'.

"Wake up Sheeple – the coronavirus was created in a Wuhan lab by the Chinese military to destroy the West" blogged TRUTHFINDER23456. "WU is short for 'Western Unravelling' and 'HAN' short for 'Harm All Non-Chinese'. Note that the disease has now 'vanished' in China (where an antidote always existed) but ravages Europe and America? The coronavirus is unquestionably a Chinese biological weapon."

However the highly respected TARDISBOY7689 tweeted to his 97 followers that he believed the coronavirus was a sinister plot conducted by 'Star Trek' fans.

"It was actually unleashed just after the current series of Doctor Who ended, so all the other shows would get higher ratings in that time slot and Doctor Who would get cancelled. Coincidence? Anyone notice that Michael Grade and Chairman Xi Jingping are both middle-aged men, and both come from powerful families and both are brutal dictators (other than Michael Grade)?"

"Stop this deep state plot to exterminate the Doctor!"

The heavily followed DEEPSTATELIES43234 tweeted from the basement of his mum's house that he had it on good authority from a friend in M16 that it was being spread by Hand Gel and Toilet paper. "The coronavirus was created by a cartel of supermarkets to create panic buying. In future only wash your hands in your own urine and wipe your bottom with pebbles."

APOLLO11FAKE233556 rubbished that notion, claiming on his Facebook page to have identified the evil genius profiting most from the coronavirus. "His name is Julian Fellowes. In 2010 with the world in financial meltdown and no one leaving their homes, Fellowes launched a period drama on ITV Sunday night at 9pm called 'Downton Abbey' to massive ratings."

"In 2020 with the world in financial meltdown and no one leaving their homes, Fellowes launched a period drama on ITV Sunday night at 9pm called 'Belgravia' to massive ratings. Join the dots guys?!!!. Fellowes orchestrated the financial crisis and unleashed the coronavirus to make himself stinking rich!!! It's all staring you in the face people, if only you'd bother to look!!!"

The mystery continues...

SATNAV WE ARE WHERE WE ARE

Boris Johnson MP
● Live

Address to the Nation from the People's Wartime Prime Minister, Winston Boris de Pfeffel Churchson

385,000,000 Views

👍 Like   💬 Comment

0 people like this

Prime Minister: Greetings! And let me introduce **straightaway** the two experts who are going to help me in this, the **greatest** challenge in our nation's history, namely making **me** look as though I know what I'm doing. To my **right** is **Boffin A**, Professor Whitty.

Vallance: Actually, I'm Sir Patrick Vallance.

Prime Minister: Ah right, or to give you your full title, **Boffin B**. Detail not my strong point. Except **now** of course, when it is. But let me **reassure** the good people of Britain and their loved ones, who may or may not have died yet, that this is **not** the darkest hour.

Whitty: I think it might be, actually.

Prime Minister: Ah, **Boffin B**!

Whitty: No, I'm Boffin A.

Prime Minister: I'm **boffin'** everyone! Just a little joke there to lighten the mood. **Laughter** is the best medicine – well, the **only** medicine at the moment. **First** question, from Laura Koronaberg, from the BBC.

Koronaberg: Actually I'm from my house.

Prime Minister: Yes, good old **BBC,** broadcasting to the nation in its time of need. Vital national service. **Always** liked it. What would we do without it? Your question, Laura?

Koronaberg: Are you sending out mixed messages?

Prime Minister: **Yes** and **no**. For example, it's **very** important for the British people to come together, and then keep their distance. It's **very** important for everyone to get out into the fresh air, whilst staying safely indoors. It's **vital** that old people can go to the supermarket at a set time, and **equally** important that they get someone else to do the shopping for them while they **remain** at home and **don't** open the door to anyone, **even** if they're carrying food! The boffins

are looking a bit worried, but that's boffins for you, always worrying about something or other! Next question, Death Rigby from Sky?

Rigby: It's Beth, not Death.

Prime Minister: Well, let's wait and see what the **boffins** have to say about that.

Rigby: What measures are you actually taking to limit the spread of the virus in this containment phase?

Prime Minister: Very good! **Top** jargon! I must get my head round some of it sometime, probably soon. What's happening is the following... The pubs **won't** shut. An Englishman's right to sup a cheery pint of frothing **Doom Bar** will never be...

Boffin A: Yes, the pubs will definitely shut.

Prime Minister: OK, they **will**, but there'll be no national lockdown. The liberty of every trueborn Anglo-Saxon male – and female, obviously – is to roam freely over hill and dale...

Boffin B: Yes, there will be a total lockdown.

Prime Minister: OK, there **will** be. Apart from in restaurants...

Boffin A: No.

Prime Minister: Cafés?

Boffin B: No.

Prime Minister: Yes, but people can **still** go to work.

Boffin A and B: No, they can't.

Prime Minister: Right, everyone's got to work at **home**, obviously, except key workers, by which I mean, er, really **important** folk like doctors, nurses, the armed forces, supermarket workers, teachers, delivery drivers, cleaners – basically **anyone** on minimum wage who some people quite **wrongly** used to say were expendable and very unimportant.

Boffin A: You appear to have got something right, Prime Minister. Are you feeling OK?

Prime Minister: Never been **better** cough cough next question. Tim Shipsink from the Sunday Times. **Great** paper, good editorial line. **Hurrah** for Bozza! That sort of trenchant analysis. Go for it, Timbo!

Shipsink: A lot of our elderly readers want to know: does Dominic Cummings intend to kill them?

Prime Minister: No, of course not. It's an **appalling** rumour put about by a shoddy newspaper that's spreading like a, I don't know, like a virus or something. Cough cough cough... Dominic where are you going ? **Sorry** everyone, Dominic appears to be running **very** fast out of the door probably going for his permitted hour-long exercise...

Boffin A: What the Prime Minister is trying to say is that herd immunity is not our policy...

Prime Minister: Not anymore, it's not!

Not since that paper from the **eggheads** at Imperial College which said a million people were going to die in the next five minutes.

Boffin B: That's not exactly what it said, Prime Minister.

Prime Minister: It was a ball-pitch figure.

Boffin A: Ball-park.

Prime Minister: You leave the figures of speech to me, Boffins, that's my speciality, it's my **USB**.

Boffin B: USP.

Prime Minister: That's the chappie. **Last** question, from Robert Pestilence of ITV.

Pestilence: Errrrrrrrrr, what I think the entire country wants to knooooooow iiiiiiiiiis: do hairdressers count as key workers?

Prime Minister: At last, a **serious** question. Thanks, Robert. Of course, yes, what would any of us do without someone to trim our barnets?

Boffin A: Hairdressers and barbers will have to close.

Prime Minister: It's all right for **you**, Professor Baldie! Cough cough cough...

Boffin A: You are not even standing two metres away. You look terrible and I don't want you giving it to me.

Prime Minister: OK – that's enough of Professor Brainstorm and Doctor Strangelove, it's time to sign off with some rousing **rhetoric**. We shall fight them on the **beaches** – though we don't want people going to the beaches just because it's **sunny**. We shall fight them on the **Underground** for an inch of space on the reduced service for key workers. We shall **fight** them on the construction sites, for important flats to sell to Chinese businessmen, if there are any left. We shall **defend** this England (and Scotland and Wales and Northern Ireland), this Albion Rovers, who unfortunately can't play at the moment, this **antiseptic** Isle, set in a silver C-virus, we shall **never** surrender and if we do, it's all the **boffins'** fault.

Boffin A and B: What?

Prime Minister: Is it **hot** in here or is it me ? I think I had better go and self isolate...

Boffin A: Too late! Cough cough...

(Armed Police then enter illegal three-person assembly and arrest Prime Minister on grounds of being irresponsible super-spreader and take him away for total lockdown)

POETRY CORNER

In Memoriam The Segway, self-balancing personal transporter device

So. Farewell
Then the Segway.
Once you were the
Future of transport,
But now you are
The past.

"How does this
Thing work?"
That was your
catchphrase.
"Ouch!"
That was another.

Sadly, you have
Reached the end
Of the road.
The wheels have
Come off and you
Are going nowhere.

You were meant
To be foolproof,
But then George W. Bush
Fell off you.

E.J. Thribb (17½ mph maximum)

Lines on the renaming of the baby of Elon Musk

So. Farewell
Then X Æ A-12,
And hello
X Æ A-Xii.

Apparently, your parents
Wisely decided that
Their first choice of
Name was a bit silly.

Æ. J. Thr-1bb (Xvii½)

Lines on the banning of Katie Hopkins from Twitter

So. Farewell
Then Katie Hopkins,
Or Hatie Hopkins,
As you are
Sometimes known.

You are unpleasant,
Superficial,
Malevolent,
Vindictive,
Spiteful
And ignorant.

So why have
You been banned
From Twitter?

E.J. Thribb (17½ followers –
quite a lot for a poet)

IT'S GRIM IN SELF-ISOLATION — KNIFE & PACKER

TOP FEATURES YOU'RE STILL GOING TO READ IN THE PAPERS

An exclusive guide by **Phil Pages** as to what's going to be filling the pages in the coming months of lockdown

 Travel section Where best to go this summer. Should you head for the kitchen, the bathroom, the kitchen again, the magnificent heights of the attic or hit the spacious idyll of the broom cupboard?

 Food section What to eat. Will it be that out-of-date tin of tuna, or the quinoa you bought in a panic? Why not both, topped with a sprinkling of Frosties, and washed down with that bottle of Ouzo that's been sitting at the back of the kitchen cupboard since that holiday in Paxos in 1983?

Fashion section What to wear when the only contact you have with the outside world is sat at your desk on a Zoom conference call. Yes, the no-trouser look is in! But Vogue's Anna Wintour recommends you wear underpants, saying, "Nobody wants to be in a meeting with a guy who's going commando".

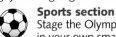 **Sports section** Stage the Olympics in your own small flat with these incredible events: squash, wastepaper basketball, the one-metre dash to the TV remote, sofa hurdle, synchronised shouting, not to mention climbing (up the wall).

 TV section What to watch? Anything. Everything. Over and over again. *(That's enough. Ed.)*

(Actually, that's not nearly enough, we've got months of this. Phil.)

British people turn out not to have a fierce love of liberty after all

After 300 years of telling everyone else how proud they are of their liberty, the people of Britain have revealed that, actually, they don't mind staying at home and doing exactly what they're told, provided there's a good reason for it.

"This is a very exciting development," said one historian who was analysing the findings of a panel of British people patiently sitting at home 23 hours a day.

"Ordinarily, we would have predicted that people would object violently to being forced indoors when the weather's nice, due to the ancient and noble British love of freedom coursing through their veins.

"They would rather die than subject themselves to government diktats about where they can go and with whom they can associate, and despise the drone-like automatons living in other countries who cravenly obey their tyrannical governments.

"It has now emerged that British people quite clearly enjoy sitting quietly indoors watching the news and laughing when they hear that celebrities have the virus."

Government sources confirmed they would definitely not take advantage of this new-found national characteristic when this is all over.

(Rotters)

YOU HAVE REACHED THE END OF NETFLIX. THANK YOU FOR WATCHING.

NETFLIX

grizelda

---

easyJet to demand bailout

by HEATH ROW
Our Aviation Correspondent

A Downing Street spokesman says it had agreed to easyJet's plea for an urgent meeting to discuss a bailout after the airline grounded its entire fleet, but only with strict conditions attached.

1. The easyJet representatives will be charged £40 each if they want to bring a bag/briefcase with them into the meeting.
2. It will be an additional £150 each if they want to sit next to each other.
3. The meeting will take place sixty miles away from where they were told it would take place.

Poet Laureate Attacked

by Our Health and Safety Correspondent
Andy Wash

There were angry scenes in the Lake District when locals turned on celebrity poet, William Wordsworth, for what they considered an irresponsible poem.

Wordsworth, they claimed, deliberately flouted government guidelines by "wandering lonely as a cloud" all over Cumbria.

The poet's excuse that "he was going for his permitted hour's exercise" was dismissed by furious residents.

Said one, "He was quite obviously in a crowd, one might almost say a host, of golden daffodils. Then he bragged about it!"

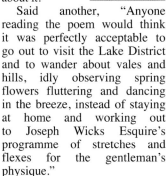

Said another, "Anyone reading the poem would think it was perfectly acceptable to go out to visit the Lake District and to wander about vales and hills, idly observing spring flowers fluttering and dancing in the breeze, instead of staying at home and working out to Joseph Wicks Esquire's programme of stretches and flexes for the gentleman's physique."

Jeremy Corbyn WRITES

HELLO! It's still me again. Again!

Well, it's my last ever column as Leader, but I'm not sure there's any point in Keir Starmer taking over from me. Or anyone! Or any point to the Labour party carrying on, come to that! Because I have not only won the argument (trademark: me), I have now won the whole country!

Yes, Britain is now completely socialist. Toilet rolls are rationed, people are being paid to do nothing and our leaders are conducting their business behind closed doors. I told you it would happen, and here we are! And all it took was the whole population being afraid to leave their homes and the police roaming the streets ready to arrest anyone for defying the government! Just like every other socialist state! Venezuela, eat your heart out!

I am now ready to lead this political Utopia! I've got my little Lenin hat on, and my determined expression. I'm putting my emergency protocols in place (putting my bike in the garage and hanging up my clips). I am now retiring to my garden shed where I will undertake an emergency meeting of COBRA (Cauliflowers, Onions, Broccoli, Radishes and Artichokes), so I can implement a glorious roll-out of crony appointments and punitive measure dressed up as vague notions of the greater good. Just like I did in the Labour party!

So I guess I should thank whoever invented the coronavirus and give them a hug – as long as Len McCluskey is ready with his antiseptic wipes! Cheerio!

What the chancellor proposes borrowing to prop up the economy

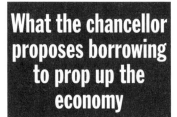

- £300bn from the capital markets
- Every Labour policy from the last election
- Er...
- That's it.

USE OF 'UNPRECEDENTED' AND 'RAMPING UP' RAMPING UP TO UNPRECEDENTED LEVELS

by Our Desperate Correspondent **PHIL SPACE**

IN THESE unprecedented times, the use of the word "unprecedented" is going through an unprecedented level of increase.

Despite the fact that these situations have been precedented, by all the things that preceded them, the one thing that we can guarantee is unprecedented is the number of occasions we have suddenly found ourselves muttering "this is absolutely unprecedented" even as we refer to all the precedents.

Furthermore, the use of the phrase "ramping up" has been ramped up so steeply that if it was a real ramp, it would be an extremely dangerous ramp indeed.

So many things have been ramped up, from the response to the tests to the PPE to the number of pointless press conferences in front of scary-looking podiums with doom-laden messages on them, that now there is a possibility that the entire ramp will have to be ramped down again just so it can be re-vamped (or re-ramped) as once again we ramp up to the second peak of the virus.

LATE NEWS: Grim tally of uses of phrase 'grim tally' ramps up to unprecedented new levels.

That Virus!
GOOD AND BAD NEWS

Massive reductions in CO_2 emissions mean that in the space of a week Britain has reduced its carbon footprint by 98%.

Emissions targets previously thought to have been impossible to achieve before 2050 to defeat climate change have turned out to achievable by next Wednesday just after lunchtime.

Having achieved her climate change goals, Greta Thunberg is finally able to go back to school, only to discover that none of her teachers or school friends are there as it's been shut down.

POETRY CORNER

**In Memoriam
Kenny Rogers, Country
And Western Legend**

So. Farewell
Then Kenny Rogers,
You picked
A fine time
To leave us.

I guess you knew
When to hold 'em
And when to
Fold 'em.

Now, in these
Terrible times,
We are all islands
In the stream...

E.J. Thribb (17½ rpm)

ITV SUPERMARKET SWEEP

2019

2020

ARE 5G MASTS RESPONSIBLE?

by Our Paranoid Correspondent **Hatty Tinfoil**

DESPITE reassurances from the government and scientists, conspiracy theories continue to circulate on the internet claiming that 5G masts are responsible for Eamonn Holmes

"Is it any coincidence that 5G masts are an anagram of 'Eamonn Holmes is an annoying prat' or something like that?" posted TRUTHSEEKR7.

"My sister's boyfriend's cousin has a friend who knows a bloke whose brother-in-law knows a bloke whose nextdoor neighbour's best mate met a bloke in Cyprus last summer who installs 5G masts and he says that every night at midnight at the base of the masts they slaughter the innocent and drink a blood sacrifice so that Eamonn Holmes can make banana bread with Ainsley Harriott on GMTV," posted DEEPSTATUS4567.

"Fifty years ago there was no Eamonn Holmes on the telly and no 5G masts. Need I say more?" posted HOLMESHAMMERTIME2390.

LATE NEWS
Holmes schooling latest

The Government has hailed as a success the programme of 'Holmes Schooling' that has involved the intensive re-education of Eamonn Holmes.

"He's finally taken our word that the coronavirus wasn't created by 5G masts," said a delighted wife. "Now we can move on to convince him that the Royal family aren't baby-eating space lizards."

LOCKDOWN TERM
School news

St Cakes

Lockdown Term begins today. There are just your own children in the home-school. The official uniform is pyjamas. Classes begin at 9am prompt (or later if nobody gets up). Head of Maths is whichever parent got a 'B' at O-Level. Head of English is whichever parent was in the Shakespeare Play in the Fifth Form. Head of PE is Mr Joe Wicks (on loan from St. Youtube's). Domestic science teaching will be shared between Ms Nigella Lawson and Mr Jamie Oliver. Mr I. Pad is in charge of entertainment until further notice. The post of Head of Discipline remains vacant until the nanny situation improves. Games will continue as normal, except they will take place not on Founder's Field but on the sofa: there will be a rotation of Candy Crush, Minecraft and Fifa. Lunch will be whatever's still in the fridge. After lunch there will be a performance of a recorder solo, playing the theme from Harry Potter. Grandparents are invited, if they can figure out how to work Zoom. Parents' evening will now be every evening. Wine to be provided by Messrs Sainsbury and Co. The Headmaster is delighted to announce that in the light of the current emergency, and in consideration of the hardship which he knows parents are enduring, he is going to put the fees up. There will be a 10% increase. This is to cover the cost of his Netflix subscription, and the Rhine Cruise that he and his wife booked, for which he can no longer get a refund. School Motto has been changed from '*Quis Paget Entrat*' to: '*Sumus Omnes Sic In Unum*'.

"So, business as usual"

![Boris Johnson profile] **Boris Johnson MP**
● Live (at time of writing)

Address to the Nation from the People's War Room

385,000,000 Views

👍 Like   💬 Comment

0 people like this

Dominic Raab (sweating profusely): Erm... I'm in charge... No, I am really. I think. Although the Prime Minister is doing very well in hospital and sitting up in bed and responding well to – oh, I've just been told he's in Intensive Care. The situation's grave. It's 50/50. Our thoughts and prayers, particularly mine, go out to him. So, oh no, I really am in charge (sweats more and mops brow). With any luck, I've got it.

Matt Hancock: Thanks, Foreign Secretary, I'll take over now.

Raab: Actually, I'm First Secretary of State.

Hancock: That's what I said, Foreign Secretary. So, as the man who's in charge, I'm very happy to take some questions. Death Rigby from Sky's Falling In News?

Rigby: Just how badly is the Government handling everything?

Hancock: One for you, I think, Dom.

Raab: Mr Cummings isn't here, I'm afraid, he's not well. So, it's over to you, Priti.

Priti Patel: We're doing very well in the fight against Covid-nineteen thousand thirty-four, nine hundred and seventy-four thousand. We're fighting it twenty-four thousand/seven hundred and forty-eight. Isn't that right, Rishi?

Rishi Sunak: It's Dishy, actually. And as Chancellor, I'm very keen for no one to look at any figures too closely, so I'd say yours are about right. Time for another question. Robert Pestilence, ITV? Hopefully your question will be so long there won't be time for any more.

Pestilence: Ahhhhhh, wellllll. Is it right that the UK economy will contract by 35% at a time when unemployment wiiiiiiiiill hit 6 million, causing a laasssssstting recession with a national debt of 94 triiiiiiiillion pounds?

Patel: That's correct. Though I think some of those numbers might not be right.

Sunak: Well, I've done the sums on this and we can balance the books fairly simply, by just getting 99-year-old army veteran Tom Moore to raise the money by doing a few more laps round his garden. If he keeps going till he's 187 and speeds up a bit, I reckon at the current rate of raising £10 million a day, we'll have paid off the debt by the year 3059 – in other words, just after lockdown ends.

Patel: I agree with that four hundred and ninety thousand per cent.

Raab: I haven't said anything for a while and I am in charge, actually. Let's have a question from Laura Koronaberg from the marvellous BBC, which we've always loved.

Koronaberg: Who are you?

Raab: One for you, Matt.

Hancock: Look, what I'm saying is: we will deliver the Personal Protection Equipment. 100,000 masks a minute by tomorrow afternoon. There's no problem with the supply system. It's just the supply system is a bit problematic, so I can't give you any targets that we may or may not reach, but I do have some good news. I have got these special badges to hand out to all care workers.

Koronaberg: How do they protect against the virus?

Hancock: They don't. In fact, they're very dangerous to pin into your PPE apron, as they might tear the plastic. But the good news is there aren't very many of them, because we're having trouble with the supply source. We've got James Dyson working on a pinless badge in Singapore. And the Mercedes F1 team are working on a badge you can take off and put on again very quickly, in 1.8 seconds. And if not, we'll order them all from Turkey or China.

Raab: Can we have another question?

Tim Shipsink: What about these stories in my newspaper that claim that you didn't take the threat seriously and were far too complacent ?

Gove: No we are not worried about those. Nothing to worry about at all. All completely under control. I don't know where you get all these stories from?

Shitstir: I think you do, Michael...

Gove: er... er... Next? The Deadly Mail's Jason Graves...

Graves: What's the Government's strategy now?

Raab: I think the Prime Minister has shown us the way forward. It's very important the public continues to do as we say and not as we do. That means: don't shake hands with everybody, like Boris did; don't go jogging when you're in quarantine, like Mr Gove did; and don't go driving round the country visiting your parents, like Mr Jenrick did.

Graves: I meant a real strategy.

Raab: Yes. We tell journalists to stop asking difficult questions and undermining the national war effort.

Sarah Vine: I agree.

(Suddenly we hear the Hallelujah Chorus from the Messiah, and a familiar figure enters via video-link...)

Boris Johnson: What-ho, folks! I'm **back**!

Vine: Verily, he is risen.

Johnson: Oh, please, please, that's enough of the **Messiah** analogy. But yes, I **have** returned from the dead and I am ready to be your **saviour** and perform **miracles**, apart from healing the sick, which I gather isn't going awfully well, with **one** notable exception! So, can I just **thank** those without whom I would no doubt just **not** be here at all. **These** are the people who made sure that I got out of bed and **returned** to work. And they all come from **immigrant** families. And I'm going to embarrass them by **naming** them. **Priti** Patel, **Dominic** Raab and **Rishi** Sunak. But for their **extraordinary** performances when standing in for me, I would **still** have my feet up, reading "Tintin and the Fuzziewuzzies" and watching "Withchild and I".

Vine: Isn't he great? Hallelujah!

Allison Pearson: No, stop doing him down, Sarah, he's much greater than that!

Raab: That's a bit ungrateful, boss. With us in charge and you doing nothing, your approval ratings have actually gone up.

Patel: Yes, Boris, you're on fifty-one thousand, thirty-four nine-hundred thousand per cent, point two.

(To be continued...)

You are in safe hands... if we can find enough gloves

STAY PROTECT S

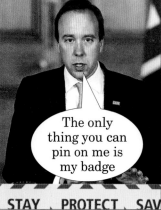

The only thing you can pin on me is my badge

STAY PROTECT SAV

I am one hundred and ninety thousand percent confident in this government

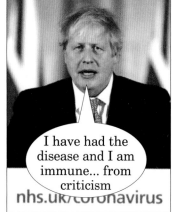

I have had the disease and I am immune... from criticism

nhs.uk/coronavirus

IS THE DEAR LEADER ACTUALLY DEAD?

by Our Man in London
Kim Jong-Very-II

Official media sources are denying the rumour, but speculation is rife that the colourful and charismatic Great Helmsman of this backward country has passed away following an illness.

The state news machine claims that the Beloved Father of the People is still in charge of the government and is fit and well.

But there are many who believe that his ministers are simply too frightened to admit the truth that the Guiding Star of the Party and Nation is no longer with us.

Said one terrified underling, Ali Son Peah Sun, "If it is true that the Great Man who Descended from Heaven is no more, then we could end up with a power vacuum. Will it be his sister Ray-Chel or, even worse, will it be his aged father, the power-mad and hated Stan-Lee? We must all pray for the health of the Peerless Ever Victorious Iron-Willed Commander."

Meanwhile, as the nation spirals out of control, with shortages of food and medicine a growing problem, and police on the streets arresting anyone having a barbecue, the story simply will not die.

KIM ALIVE AFTER BOTCHED HEART OPERATION

Ministers alarmed by dangerously low levels of PPE

by **Magdalen Balliol**

THE government promised urgent action last night to deal with the national shortage of PPE, which is causing grave concern in Whitehall.

"In the old days, there were limitless supplies," said a senior official. "Hugh Gaitskell and Roy Jenkins, Ted Heath and Harold Wilson – all had the know-it-all confidence that comes with an Oxford degree in politics, philosophy and economics.

"More recently, we had William Hague and Peter Mandelson, David Cameron and Ed Balls. Even Theresa May understood the need to maintain stocks of PPE, with Jeremy Hunt and Phil Hammond.

"But now? A bloody classics graduate. And some of his Cabinet didn't even go to Oxford."

Sir Keir Starmer announced last night that Labour would help ease the PPE shortage by rushing supplies of Ed Miliband to the front bench.

The Lib Dems pointed out that their acting leader also had PPE. "Sir Ed Davey – surely you've heard of him?" said a spokeswoman. "No? Oh well."

New graph suggests the number of graphs may have peaked

A NEW graph published today online has given hope that we may have reached "peak graph" and that in the coming days and weeks we may see a flattening of the curve and a gradual reduction in the number of graphs.

The Government, however, sought to dampen down hopes that we could soon be seeing zero graphs within a few weeks, saying that people only had to look at the graph illustrating this press release to see that, while they should diminish over the coming weeks, graphs will sadly be a part of our lives for the foreseeable future.

Notes&queries

We hear a lot about "Furlough" all of a sudden, who or what is a Furlough?
Reverend Byrdde-Flugh

● Come on, Rev, and join the real world! Everybody knows that Furlough were a 1970s' prog-rock band who headlined the legendary Isle of Dogs Festival in 1973 and whose folk-inspired album, *Jesters At the Court of the Corona King*, was number 74 in the charts for over a week. The founder of the group, Dave Furlough, was a bass player from Milton Friedman who joined up with fellow art-school drop-outs to form the Dave Furlough Five which, after musical differences, later became the Dave Furlough One and then eventually simply Furlough. Championed by radio one DJ John Peel, Furlough retired in 1978 and is now a partner in the Haywards Heath solicitors firm of Layoff and Furlough.
Mrs Fluella Simptom,
The Old Swinery, Wilts.

● The good lady is obviously feeling unwell! A Furlough, as any farmer knows, and any Archers fans will be more than aware(!), is the old standard unit of measurement for the optimum distance between 5G masts. Technically, it is equivalent to 25 perches or 32 rods or 78 liddles. These imperial units have

fallen out of favour in recent years, thanks to the dreaded influence of the Metric-Fascists of Brussels, but now it looks like they are going to make a welcome comeback! 5G masts have to be exactly a furlough apart in order to optimise transmission of the Covid-19 virus, ensuring that you catch it much faster than under the antiquated 3G system, which does not have the benefit of Chinese bio-technical know-how!
Professor Hugh Bay,
Porton Down, Barking.

● The Professor is indeed barking if he thinks Furloughs have anything to do with rural communication systems. Furloughs are named after the notorious Victorian social climber Sir Julian Furloughs, who was renowned for his extreme deference to the old aristocracy. The mid-19th Century phrase "tugging your Furlough" has now become obsolete, but was once an obscene reference to the obsequiousness of the portly, top-hatted arriviste.
Ms Bel Gravia, London.
(That's enough. Ed. You are now on Furlough for the next 6 months.)

Answers please:
How many Lembits make an Opik? Should you use Drambuie or uzo in a classic Quarantini? Will lockdown ever end?

"Your first time picking strawberries?"

LOVE IN THE TIME OF CORONA

A Short Story Special

by Dame Sylvie Krin, author of *100 Years of Solitude, Heir of Sorrows, Duchess of Hearts & You're Never Too Old*

THE STORY SO FAR: Cooped up in his 94,000-acre estate in the Highlands, Charles is oneself-isolating with Camilla and several essential key workers, such as the lone piper and the keeper of the Royal Wifi, Old Ghillie McCooper. Now read on…

"**H**ELLO, old friend, how good to see you looking so well." Charles stared at the Zoom thingy, which connected him miraculously with his nearest and dearest. "What have you been up to? I've missed you terribly." 300 miles away at Highgrove, his old friend, the aspidistra in the Titchmarsh Wing of the Royal Conservatory, maintained an enigmatic silence.

"McCooper! This screen whatsit has frozen again. I can't hear anything and nothing's moving."

"That may be because it's a plant, sire," answered the faithful retainer, tactfully, from the array of plugs under the desk, slightly regretting he had retrained from beating the heather for grouse to connecting an ether-cable via the router to the prince's Apple McMac.

"And now I've run out of time!" lamented Charles, as the forty-minute warning flashed on his screen. "Cheerio, old bean, same time tomorrow?" Charles waved at his green companion, but alas it had already logged off.

Suddenly his screen leapt to life once more. "McCooper! What's happening?"

"It's an invitation from the Archewelloff Foundation, sire."

"And who the blazes are they?" asked Charles suspiciously, having already been stung earlier in the week by a Nigerian Prince who seemed to want to give him a million pounds. But then, on screen, a familiar bearded face appeared.

"Watcha, Pops! Hazza here!" Charles smiled with delight as his beloved son Harry or Harry™, as he was now publicly known, loomed large on the screen, in front of a background of the HOLLYWOOD sign. "Really sorry you got the dreaded lurgy. How are ya?"

"Enough small talk," interrupted an American female voice off-camera, "ask him about the money."

"You see, the thing is, Pops, now we've moved to La La Land, no one wants to pay for our protection."

For a moment Charles was puzzled. "Surely you can buy a face mask and some hand sanitiser in California? I'm sure we've got an organic Duchy Nettle and Turmeric range. I mean, it makes your hands a bit yellow, but…"

"No, Your Royal Majestyness," Meghan interjected, her face bobbing in and out of view as she curtseyed to her father-in-law. "Police protection, commensurate with our status as brand leaders in Wellnessphilanthropy, Celebroyalty and Disneyvoiceoverartistery."

Charles felt a sinking feeling, familiar to nearly all parents, as the point of their offspring's call reveals itself. It was less to do with inquiring about one's health and more to do with the health of their bank balance.

Yet again, it was a request to the Bank of Mater and Pater – or specifically Pater, as Step-Mater was singularly unforthcoming when it came to largesse with the doshington. Camilla always had more important causes to support, namely the Marlborough Trust (cigarettes, not Duke) and Beefeaters (gin, not crown-jewel custodians).

Before Charles could even think of the word to describe this appalling state of affairs, another pair of faces appeared on the screen.

"Yo, guys, Wills and Kate here to join the Buck Houseparty!"

"Er, gotta go, Pops," said Harry hastily. "Gwyneth is hosting an online Gloop-group-hug live on Malibu Beach." And with that he vanished into cyberspace.

Charles waved at his son and heir. "Wills, did you see me opening that hospital via my interweb connection?"

"Er, yah, sorry, basically, totes missed that," said Wills, in that unthinkingly self-centred way with which the young so casually dismiss their parents' achievements. "But the good news is we've been smashing it online. George has got more Instagram followers than Zoella, Charlotte's fashion range has just overtaken Posh Beckham's, and Louis has his own YouTube toddler-exercise channel."

"And even better," chipped in Kate, "I've lost more weight."

Charles endeavoured to take this latest blow to his self-esteem with good grace. After all, the younger generation would inevitably be more adept at harnessing the invisible powers of modern technology than their elders.

AT that moment, a Royal Mailonline alert surrounded by crown emojis burst colourfully onto the screen, accompanied by a techno version of the National Anthem. It announced that Her Majesty the Queen, at the age of 93, had gone viral and that her National Emergency covideo-19 remote online cyber-conferencing message to the nation had broken all internet records for downloads, sharing, hits, blogs, podcasts and likes.

(To be continued…)

BRITAIN TO CELEBRATE VE DAY!

by Our History Staff **Will Meetagain**

Yes! The government has decided that now is the time to commemorate the historic achievement of this nation's triumph over Europe.

Virus in Europe Day will mark the moment when the United Kingdom's death toll beat that of the entire continent. This remarkable feat was considered impossible at the start of the war against coronavirus, but thanks to the leadership of the Prime Minister, Johnston Churchill, by May 2020 it had become an incredible reality.

America came in late and will no doubt claim the victory in global figures, but it is Britain standing alone that must take the credit and go down in the history books.

A UK government spokesman said, "This has been achieved by the sheer determination of the leadership to do as little as possible in the early phase of the war and then to react extremely slowly to events as they unfolded."

Under the slogan *Best we Forget*, the nation is being asked to come together and express its joy at what the Prime Minister calls "a success" and which he hopes will be forever remembered in the wrong way.

The grateful public are expected not to take to the streets in large numbers and not to dance in the fountains in Trafalgar Square, or else they will be arrested.

Instead, they will sit at home, waving flags and singing that great wartime hit *We'll meet again on Zoom* by Dame Viral Lynn.

MOORE TRIBUTES POUR IN

by Our Hero Staff **Charity Walker**

THE NATION has taken him to their hearts and yesterday, on his 100th birthday, they were keen to salute the man known simply as Captain Charles Moore.

Moore, an elderly veteran of the *Daily Telegraph,* who saw action in the Great Circulation War, has come to prominence following his extraordinary raising of millions of votes for the Conservative party – by simply going round and round in circles, writing the same piece every day.

Observers cannot believe his stamina and have been keen to pay tribute to his tenacity and bravery. The man who saw action in the campaign against the BBC licence fee has amazed the world.

"You would have thought he would have given up by now," said one fan (Mrs Moore), "but when he starts up, there is no stopping him."

The latest count is that Moore has notched up an astonishing 29 million words about Mrs Thatcher, Boris Johnson, the EU, fox-hunting and the difficulty of sourcing top hats in modern Britain.

There are now calls for him to be given a knighthood by the Queen for his services to the litter-tray industry.

The last word must go to his old friend and former colleague, Simon Hefferlump: "You've got to hand it to Captain Moore-Words-Please, he just goes on and on and on and on and on and on and on and on and *(cont. p94)*

POLICE LOG

Neasden Central Police Station

08.17 hrs Officers gather for a meeting on Zoom from the four corners of the station to help minimise exposure to each other. New campaign 'Stay Indoors Neasden' will be rolled out across the local area today. Officers will be patrolling area to explain social distancing to anyone seen outdoors. To comply with government guidelines, officers have been issued with extra-long handcuffs and all units of Neasden Police Pepper Spray have been attached to selfie sticks.

09.24 hrs 'Stay Indoors Neasden' has met with great success. Thirty-eight people were stopped in the streets by officers and given Enhanced Police Guidance about the danger and irresponsibility of being outside their home. Unfortunately, seven of the people stopped were key workers, six were homeless, and two more were off-duty members of Neasden Police Service. All others, including three in their front garden, one person leaning outside their window, and one walking an insufficiently energetic dog were issued with £60 fines, payable immediately by cash and sanitised by Officer Nobbs using official lemon antiseptic wipes. Elsewhere, officers have placed spikes along all benches in Neasden Park to deter any irresponsible sitting. Station answerphone reveals no reports of social distancing being breached; only a number of incidents of shoplifting and breaking and entering. As these crimes involve people responsibly being indoors, they will be treated as low priority for the duration of the crisis.

10.16 hrs Officers have completed their work in the non-essential aisles of Neasden Tesco, ie all aisles not selling milk, bread and toilet paper, examining shopping baskets for non-essential goods (macaroons, copies of the Guardian, Pink Lady apples, etc). This drew a number of people ino the luxury aisles to protest, who were then threatened with arrest and fined for spending time in non-essential parts of the supermarket.

A return to the station reveals further answerphone allegations of widespread rioting and looting in Greater Neasden, along with multiple reports of spike-related injuries in Neasden Park. The phone has been wiped down and the claims will be assessed from within the station to observe rules on Social Distancing.

"I'm not sure that's going to work, Hugo"

DONT MISS

▸ The coronavirus which looks like Lord Sugar! Experts gasp as microscope reveals uncanny resemblance.

▸ Kourtney Kardashian appeals for "all the people of the world to come together to fight this terrible virus" while twerking in sexy lingerie that leaves nothing to the imagination. VIDEO

▸ Can revealing up to 50 percent more cleavage ward off coronavirus?

▸ Good Morning Britain's Jemima Potts reveals her stepmother's friend's younger sister might have had coronavirus "but luckily not too badly".

▸ Lockdown forces crushed Meghan and Harry to scrap plans for a celebrity-filled bash to celebrate Archie's first birthday as Meghan's dad claims the "mean" Royal couple are "just trying to get out of paying for a birthday cake."

▸ Friends say snubbed Britney Spears was "never sent" invitation to attend baby Archie's first birthday.

▸ Carol Vorderman flaunts her toned physique while enjoying cup of tea during lockdown.

▸ Let's conquer killer virus! Britney Spears puts on brave face in figure-hugging leotard. VIDEO

▸ Ginger Spice dons face mask for trip to Sainsbury's. Former Spice Girl purchased breakfast cereal, bananas, strawberry jam, detergent, fresh vegetables and frozen pizza, reveals fellow shopper.

▸ Self-isolating Bono praises people of the world for their "fortitude and compassion at this time of very real peril".

▸ Expert denies coronavirus was caused by TV's Carol Vorderman eating Malteser in February, but questions remain to be asked.

▸ Onlookers shocked as callous Meghan Markle is spotted grinning in LA park just three days after Italy announces 20,000th corona victim.

▸ "Deeply moved" people of the world thank Bono "from the bottom of our hearts" for Irish star's heartfelt praise.

▸ The 200 most entertaining serial killer series on Netflix to watch during lockdown.

CELEBRITIES IN LOCKDOWN

▸ Let me entertain you! Adorable family hamster, Hammy, nods head almost in time to vintage Robbie Williams track, as coronavirus sadly claims its 20,000th victim.

▸ Lobster supports brave nurses. Smiling crustacean offers thumbs-up to NHS workers. VIDEO

▸ TOWIE'S Kelly Storm donates full colour selfie in IKEA frame to NHS. "It's my way of saying thank you for all your hard work," says tearful Kelly as she unveils new Primark fragrance deal.

▸ Katie Hopkins blasts NHS doctors and nurses for being "bone lazy and just scoffing chocolate and gossiping when they should be working to help others like the rest of us." VIDEO

▸ EastEnders star Dean Gaffney says "family is everything at this time", as he is spotted stocking up on toilet paper and satsumas at local Tesco.

▸ Elizabeth Hurley, 54, puts on very busty display in barely-there Victoria's Secret top as she congratulates NHS staff from her tropical hideaway.

▸ Amanda Holden bravely flaunts toned body while clapping for NHS in skimpy polka dot bikini amid coronavirus pandemic.

▸ Prince Archie "enjoying life under lockdown" in LA home, say friends.

▸ Heartwarming moment pet goldfish Goldie appears to mime to Yellow Submarine, as elderly owner dies of coronavirus. VIDEO

▸ Tiger King's Carole Baskin tipped to star in Julian Fellowes new ITV period drama Corona. "I'm so thrilled for Carole" says Katie Price's former husband Peter Andre.

▸ Prince Archie "depressed, lonely, angry and restless" as friends voice concern.

▸ James Corden piles on the pounds in California lockdown binge.

▸ Former Pussycat Doll Melody Thornton showcases her sensational curves as she washes hands to beat Corona and urges all the people of the world to do the same.

▸ Outraged onlookers condemn coronavirus spotted illegally riding in bicycle lane.

▸ How I Shed Pounds – James Corden tells of triumphant lockdown weight-loss.

▸ Desiree DuLally, 22, spotted going bra-less out walking pet poodle Lukas, 2, in Central Park. VIDEO

▸ Doubts raised by experts as pet dachsund sings Amazing Grace with voice just like Kiri Te Kanawa's.

▸ Attish-WHO! Former Doctor Who star contracts coronavirus.

▸ Gutsy Ann Widdecombe attempts viral T-shirt handstand challenge as she isolates at her home amid coronavirus lockdown. VIDEO

▸ Woman, 39, forgets to wash hands after touching door handle but then luckily remembers. VIDEO

▸ Fears grow as Princess Anne asks for second glass of water.

▸ Love Island's Gayle Bunting puts on a busty display in glamorous selfie while expressing her despair at spilling tea over favourite table cloth during Corvid lockdown.

▸ Former Baywatch star Betsy Pouter shows off trim figure in hospital bed minutes before dying of killer coronavirus.

▸ Victoria Beckham sports new £15,000 Gucci handbag "in support of our NHS".

▸ Former Celebrity Pole-Dance Class Aimee LaDook strips down to bra and undies for sizzling selfie at late mother's online funeral.

▸ Lord Sugar spotted in face-mask on trip to Waitrose, emerges bearing potatoes.

▸ Piers Morgan points finger at self-serving celebrities who pursue publicity by pointing their fingers at their fellow celebrities.

PRESIDENT XI SPEAKS OUT

We have arrested the spread of the virus... and lots of doctors

CLAP! CLAP! CLAP!

Births

IT'S A BOY FOR BORIS!

Deaths

Joe Bloggs, Joanna Bloggs, Joe Bloggs, Joanna Bloggs, Joe Bloggs, Joanna Bloggs, Joe Bloggs, Joanna Bloggs, Joe Bloggs, Joanna Bloggs, Joe Bloggs, Joanna Bloggs, Joe Bloggs, Joanna Bloggs, Joe Bloggs, Joanna Bloggs, Joe Bloggs, Joanna Bloggs, Joe Bloggs, Joanna Bloggs, Joe Bloggs, Joanna Bloggs, Joe Bloggs, Joanna Bloggs, Joe Bloggs, Joanna Bloggs, Joe Bloggs, Joanna Bloggs, Joe Bloggs, Joanna Bloggs, Joe Bloggs, Joanna Bloggs, Joe Bloggs, Joanna Bloggs, Joanna Bloggs, Joe Bloggs, Joanna Bloggs, Joe Bloggs, Joanna Bloggs, Joe Bloggs, Joanna Bloggs, Joe Bloggs, Joanna Bloggs, Joe Bloggs, Joanna Bloggs, Joe Bloggs, Joanna Bloggs, Joe Bloggs, Joanna Bloggs, Joe Bloggs, Joanna Bloggs, Joe Bloggs, Joanna Bloggs, Joe Bloggs, Joanna Bloggs, Joe Bloggs, Joanna Bloggs, Joe Bloggs, Joanna Bloggs, Joe Bloggs, Joanna Bloggs, Joe Bloggs, Joanna Bloggs, Joe Bloggs, Joanna Bloggs, Joe Bloggs, Joanna Bloggs, Joe Bloggs Joanna Bloggs…

The Eye's Controversial New Columnist

The columnist who can still hit you with his bodily fluids from well over two metres

This week I am very angry about people mocking Donald Trump. Here is a man showing his expertise, demonstrating how he has researched the science of the pandemic, and the mainstream media have nothing better to do than mock him, implying that injecting with bleach is somehow "harmful". This kind of poo-pooing inhibits out-of-the-box thinking. To that end, I would like to share with you my own research and how I have discovered a cure for the coronavirus: Lego. I have ingested a few pieces a day from my Lego hospital, just the odd brick, an arm from a nurse and the occasional doctor's smiley head, and I have felt no symptoms of coronavirus whatsoever. Naturally, this research is in its infancy, but the results are astounding. Not only do I feel fit and healthy, I look a great deal better than my parents, who both look increasingly pale and hollow-eyed. Yes, Lego is the key. And if you have a quick look on eBay, you'll find I am selling a great deal of incomplete Lego sets which you are welcome to panic-buy at vastly inflated *(cont. p94)*

A President writes…

AS a leading Epideedoodaa-epideedaymyohmywhatawonderfuldayologist, I am often asked, "How do we cure the virus?"

Simple. So, so simple. So many ways. Sunshine, moonlight, boogie! And that's just four.

But I hear that there are interesting developments with disinfectants. I've seen the ad on TV – bleach kills all known germs. Well Covid's a known germ. Fact! So here's my idea, which may work. It may not. I dunno. I'm not the medical doctor, but it's worth looking at. If it works when you wipe it on the toilet bowl, then why not just drink it? Not the toilet bowl – that would be crazy.

The bleach, I'm talking about. Covid won't know what's hit it. Domestos. Dettol. Lysol. Uric Acid. Sulphuric Acid. We got these new baseball caps we are bringing out with MADD on them: "Make America Drink Disinfectant". Neat, huh?

And what about chlorine? How many chickens have currently reported into hospital with Covid? Huh?! No more than a dozen, I bet. Fact! Why? Cos it works – they're full of chlorine. And, no, I don't have any shares in chlorine.

They're saying more Americans have died from this germ thing than from the Vietnam War. But that's another war we won. Thanks to Agent Orange.

Hey! We should try drinking that as well! I have! How do you think I get this colour? And talking of Vietnam, didn't you love that movie? Where he says "I love the smell of disinfectant in the morning"?!

● *This article got a 94% approval rating from all the Americans who have been admitted to hospital for ingesting household cleaning fluids in the last week.*

"He's doing another interview for TV"

Advertisement

Are you entitled to PPE compensation?

Have you been mis-sold a promise of PPE?

Then your family could be entitled to PPE compensation of £60,000!

YES, £££s could be yours! Well, not yours exactly… because, sadly, you personally won't see a penny of it, due to the promise of PPE that you were mis-sold.

Says TV's Matt Hancock, *"Would you like a 'Care' badge instead?"*

WARNING: This offer is not as good as it sounds

GLENDA SLAGG

Fleet Street's Pique Expert!!!

■ ADELE? Why are you so thin? It doesn't suit you, luv!!! Why can't you be fat like the rest of us?!! You're a terrible role model to gals everywhere for selfishly shedding the pounds and turning into a skinny stick-insect!!! Remember the old saying "It ain't over till the fat lady sings"? Well, now that the THIN lady is singing, it's all over for you!!!!? No offence but Hello!!?!! Someone Like You should know better!!! Geddit???

■ HATS OFF to Adele?!! Or rather Fats Off more like??!? Yes, the Newly Svelte Songstress has shed more pounds than I've shed tears over her heartbreakin' harmonies – and that's a lot!!! I've cried me a river *(That's someone else. Ed. You're fired.)* What a great role model she is – as opposed to a Roly Poly model – encouraging gals everywhere to stop eating all the pies?!!! The weight is Skyfalling off you, darling, and Rumour Has It that you are happier and healthier than ever now that you are not Rolling in the Fat!?? Geddit ??!! *(This is really terrible. You are hired again. Ed.)*

Byeee!!

I'VE HAD 311 'LIKES'

BRITAIN WINS EUROVIRUS CONTEST

by Our Entertainment Staff **Katrina and the Second Wave**

THERE were scenes of jubilation across Europe, as Britain unexpectedly scooped the coveted top prize when all the figures came in.

The United Kingdom topped the charts and scored the highest number of deaths from the virus in Europe.

There was disappointment for the much-fancied Italians, whom the bookies had all backed after an early lead, and the Spanish had also looked like being contenders at one stage. But it was the plucky Brits who triumphed in the end, with their unbeatable entry *Doom Bang a Bang* by Looloo which swept the board.

As the results came in from round Europe, and Norway

scored their traditional "nearly nul deaths", the excitement mounted.

Sweden came up with a different approach and there were hopes that their unconventional number would backfire – but no, it was still far too low to challenge the United Kingdom.

Said one Eurovirus fan, Sir Graham Nortie, "You've got to hand it to the Brits this year – they have come up with a Eurovirus classic. It is catchy, it's infectious and once you've got it in your head, you can't get rid of it!

"It's already a massive hit in the UK and I think it's destined to hang around in the comparative global charts for a very long time!"

FARAGE EXPOSES POLICE STATE

Lockdown is just pants

"I said, you're standing too close!"

Health fad divides opinion

Guys! Anyone here into Perineum Sunning? It's a new health kick, where you drop your strides and point the old Aris at the sky! Apparently, '30 seconds of direct sunlight injection to the anal orifice is equivalent to being outside in the sun all day.' So who's up for making an arse of themselves in a Periscope streaming session to raise money for the NHS?! – **Bogbrush**

Isn't Gentleman's Relish called Patum Perineum? I always thought it was made from anchovies, but this has rather put me off. – **Godfrey**

remember that time i was up the park an i sudly took of my trouser's juss to see wat it felt like? only i dint have any pant's on? wel this other persen done the same an we done a sort of exersise with are botums up in the air. it felt nice but i never new its calld perineum –**hAnsolo**

Bogbrush, the last thing our NHS heroes need is irresponsible idiots turning up with sunburnt anuses! Please stay inside, wash your hands and wipe your bottom. As the National Medical Director said: 'Now is not the time for complacency.' – **Supermum**

When WILL it be time for complacency? This is simply t-t-too tiresome! – **The Plover's Egg**

The gambling community now offers safe indoor opportunities to enjoy everything from online fruit machines to CGI horse racing! Profits from the virtual Grand National were donated to the NHS, and it would be a lovely gesture if, when applauding the frontline health heroes, we had an extra two minutes applause for our wonderful bookies, who keep our spirits up in these challenging times. #getinspired – **In It To Win It**

During my perfectly legal perambulations in a public park, I was accosted by the local Gestapo. I had replaced my usual head-to-toe costume (representing the wagging finger of the nanny state) with a two-metre pink finger extended horizontally from my waist. By spinning around I satirised the ridiculous 'social distancing' diktat. Unfortunately, this led to a misunderstanding with a gentleman who threatened to 'do time' if I went near his daughters, and the police were as usual delighted to have an excuse to arrest me. My new pamphlet exposes the connection between Covid-19, 5G, Bill Gates, Gary Lineker and Professor A.C. Grayling. – **Edwin**

This post has been removed by the moderators. – **Family Man**

Why no word of Mr. Bastaphaya From Birth A Gifted Spiritual Healer? For all problems Mr. Bastaphaya is the answer 7 days guaranteed! Protection against Jealous people, voodoo, Black Magic, Jadoo. COVID 19 IS NEWEST PROTECTION. Government Expert Man useless but always on TV! Why? – **Gladys**

Great stuff guys! – **Bogbrush**

WATER DISCOVERED IN OCEAN

by Our Marine Staff
Sven Seas

SCIENTISTS were amazed last week when they found small amounts of water in the world's oceans, amidst all the plastic.

Said the leader of one expedition, Greta Iceberg, "We scooped up a sample in the middle of the Atlantic, and there, along with the plastic bags, face masks, bottles and nappies, was the unmistakable sign of water. Admittedly the amounts were minuscule, but we put them in our sample jars and drove the Jeep back across the Atlantic."

Scientists fear that if this trend continues, and increasing amounts of H_2O get into the plastic system, then we could all end up ingesting small amounts of water, or micro-water as it's known. This might result in some human beings just about clinging to life for another decade or two.

However, Global Wetting deniers dismissed the claims as alarmist nonsense, with one proclaiming, "I went swimming in the Med this year, and there wasn't a drop of water in all the sparkling, bright blue plastic."

GOVERNMENT'S MIXED MESSAGES

STAY ALERT

It's vital we protect our careers... sorry, carers

STAY ALIVE

We all need to lose a few pounds

How about a trillion?

STAY AHEAD

When will you start learning lessons?

STAY AWAKE

Hooray! Nannies can return to work

Lockdown easing 'guided by experts'

■ As plans began to end the lockdown, Downing Street insisted it would at all times be guided on the speed of lifting restrictions by an expert panel of columnists writing for The Daily Telegraph and the Daily Mail.

"We're guided every step of the way by these self-appointed sages of Fleet Street, who have unrivalled reputations for spouting whatever rubbish their proprietors demand," said a Downing Street spokesman.

"The restrictions the lockdown has placed on the Barclay Brothers and Lord Rothermere's ability to make money have been onerous.

"A clear picture is now emerging of the very real need to make the economic health of the proprietors the key factor guiding our decisions."

Dead people accused of political bias

■ The government yesterday accused those UK citizens who've died of the coronavirus of "shameless political bias".

Said a spokesperson, "These people are dying willy-nilly, clearly trying to prevent the government moving on from the bad headlines generated by this pandemic. One has to ask the question: what are their motives in dying? Who has put them up to it?"

"I certainly think Guido Fawkes should look into the backgrounds of those who've died so far," continued the spokesperson.

"I think they will find that a lot of those who have expired were Labour sympathisers with a clear agenda to make the government look bad.

"A lot of them seem to be in poorer areas, which have primarily voted Labour in the past. The majority of them seem to work in low-paid jobs, like check-out staff, or in care homes which are jobs associated with common people.

"None of them appear to be stockbrokers, disaster capitalists or newspaper columnists, which seems very suspicious."

PLUS: Cabinet Ministers to be banned from appearing on the 'Gogglebox' programme after clear political bias.

LOCKDOWN LATEST

Crucial supplies beginning to run out

by Our Working-from-home Staff
Ray Mote and **Noah Trousers**

As we enter week 94 of Lockdown, there are fears that households are beginning to suffer from a severe shortage.

Said one frantic husband, "We are beginning to run out of the key essentials: patience, humour and, worst of all, conversation."

His wife responded, "You said the exact same thing yesterday! I mean, is that the best you can do? At least listen to a podcast and tell me something I don't already know!"

Relationship counsellors around the country are warning against use of such expressions as "How was your day?" when you both know exactly how it's been.

Couples are feeling the strain, as the joke of "Where do you fancy going for our holidays? How about the Living Room?" is now as well-worn as the carpet they've been chewing.

Said one counsellor, "Jokes about not wearing trousers during Zoom meetings really did seem funny back in March, but now they are being cited in several Zoom meetings with divorce lawyers. Now, if you'll excuse me, it's wine o'clock and time for my 'Quarantini'!"

At this point, the counsellor's partner packed her suitcase and said, "That's it, I'm leaving you. I've been waiting eight weeks for the government to let me out of this living hell. I wonder if Neil Ferguson's free?"

Exclusive to all newspapers

ISN'T THE WEATHER NICE?!?!

YES, it's been another super-warm lovely month of fabulous weather and there's more ahead!!!

The weather has been absolutely fabulous and we can't wait for another full summer of amazing sunshine and no rain!!!

Fingers crossed that it stays like this for ever and ever!!!

On other pages

● Ok, so the rivers are a bit dry and some species are baking to death and the planet is cooking furiously, but at least it's nothing to do with the virus!!!

That Keir Starmer QC 'forensic cross-examination' in full

1. Prime Minister, Would You Not Agree That A Lot Of People Have Died?

2. And The Figures Show That Quite A Lot Of Them Died In Care Homes, Didn't They?

3. And Testing And Equipment Targets Don't Seem To Have Been Met, Do They?

4. Do You Think This Is Something You Should Be Concerned About?

YES, this was the merciless barrage of lawyerly interrogation which dismantled the government's defences and had Boris on the ropes, ready to throw in the towel.

Furious backbenchers accused Starmer of "resorting to dirty tricks" and harked back to a kinder, gentler Prime Minister's Questions when the leader of the Opposition had merely asked questions about bus timetables or allotment licensing, rather than introducing party politics into parliamentary questions.

Said one, Sir Humbert Humbug (Shameless South), "The function of the Opposition is to support the government. The clue is in the name. They are called 'Her Majesty's Loyal Opposition', which means they should be loyal to His Majesty World King Boris."

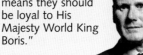

Daily Telegraph Friday 8 May 2020

Small businesses in plea to 'break lockdown'

A large number of small-to-medium businesses are furiously lobbying the government and asking them to end this lockdown before they go bankrupt.

The burglary sector is being hit particularly hard and those in the house-breaking community are desperate for ordinary people to leave their homes as soon as possible.

Said one single-trader burglar, "If only the government would act responsibly, our industry could get back on its feet and I could return to work, putting a pair of silk tights over my head and a bag labelled 'swag' over my shoulder.

"I've had to put all those plans on hold. It's a complete crime."

© *Rotters.*

EYE DATA REPORT
HOW THE NATION HAS BEEN SPENDING ITS TIME

63% of people are better off than before due to all the money they're saving, but **78%** of people are much worse off than before because they've lost their jobs and spent all their savings

56% of people are baking and cooking brilliant, creative, nutritious meals, although **59%** are now only eating crisps and Mars Bars

76% of the nation have put on more than three stone in weight, although **84%** have been exercising more and are in the best shape of their lives

94% of people have been spending more time outside, but not the **112%** of people who have been too terrified to leave their house in the last ten weeks, even if it caught fire

118% of people are enjoying virtual operas and art galleries and museums, but another **135%** are only watching old episodes of Emmerdale and Gogglebox

100% of people are now a bit sick of pub quizzes

Nursery Times
································· Friday, Once-upon-a-time ·································

NEW LOCKDOWN RULES
YOUR QUESTIONS ANSWERED

AS lockdown eases across Nurseryland, there is widespread confusion over what exactly the new regulations mean for ordinary folk.

Jack and Jill write: We are in dire need of a pail of water – are we allowed to go up the hill together to fetch one, or should we go separately? And if we both fall down, and come tumbling within six feet of each other, will we be arrested?

Editor: I have no idea.

Mary Mary writes: I run a gardening centre. I want to reopen but, on the contrary, fear that I shouldn't. I want to sell silver bells and cockleshells, but am worried that my pretty maids in a row breach social distancing guidelines. Should I stay closed?

Editor: I have no idea.

A teddy bear writes: This may come as a big surprise, but I want to go on a picnic down in the woods with a number of my friends. Well, with every bear that ever there was, in fact. And today is the day. Is this legal?

Editor: I have no idea.

A cow writes: I have been planning a flight of a lifetime over the moon. Will I have to be quarantined on the moon, and on my return?

Editor: I have no idea.

The Grand old Duke of York writes: I have 10,000 men. Can I march them up to the top of the hill and then march them down again? Is this an outdoor public gathering and therefore forbidden, or is it permitted exercise within the same household cavalry?

Editor: I have no idea.

An old woman writes: Can I put my shoe on the market? Can I invite people to come and look around the shoe, even though I have so many children there, I don't know what to do?

Editor: I have no idea.

Little Red Riding Hood writes: My grandmother has been self-isolating in a cottage in the forest for months, is it safe for me to go and see her now, or might she be being impersonated by a Big Bad Wolf waiting for me to come and check up on her health issues vis big teeth, big eyes, big ears?

Editor: I have no idea.

A gingerbread man writes: I am a keen runner and I want to run run as fast as I can. Can I drive to the local park? Am I allowed repeated exercise sessions? Can I be confident that the police won't ever catch me?

Editor: I have no idea.

Three Little Pigs write: We are three porcine construction workers, keen to get the economy going by building new houses, and are skilled in the use of various different materials. Is it prudent to build houses of straw and sticks, or should we stick to bricks?

Editor: I have no idea.

We write: Can we go gathering nuts in May, nuts in May, nuts in May?

Editor: I have no idea, no idea, no idea.

What will happen when families finally reunite

"Right, where were we?"

A word of warning. One must allow more than a single day for the reading of Edward Gibbon's 12-volume *Decline and Fall of the Roman Empire*, particularly if one is to absorb all the footnotes.

It would not, I think, be going too far to suggest that Gibbon's surname is a misnomer. The man writes with a precision and grandeur denied the lower orders of primate.

What does the work hold for the biographer and historian? Having re-read it on the last weekend of April, I would say that it is, above all else, about not only the Fall of the Roman Empire, but also its Rise. Yet, at all times it balances the Rise with the Fall, and, conversely, the Fall with the Rise, so that, in the end, it is very much about both the Rise and the Fall of the Roman Empire. Sadly, this is a detail too often forgotten by the more slovenly of the scholarly fraternity.

Shakespeare's great tragedies, among which I refuse to include the lacklustre and boorish *Hamlet*, are, for the most part, just about worth a re-read on an inclement day, even if, contrary to *bien pensant* opinion, they seldom rise above the below-average.

I first encountered Romeo and Juliet at university, where, through no fault of my own, I was soon to be awarded a First. I found it crude in its portrayal of the internal politics of 16th century Verona. Shakespeare's most obvious mistake is to concentrate his attention on two adolescents who have little of interest to say for themselves. He would have been wiser to focus on Prince Escalus, who is, in my view, a man of real heft.

I entertain similar misgivings about *King Lear*. The fellow is not only a bore but a buffoon. The last time I perambulated a blasted heath, I took every reasonable precaution to wrap up well in Mackintosh, jumper, thick woollen socks and seasonal cravat. Those who fail to take such elementary precautions have only themselves to blame. "Blow, winds and crack your cheeks!" But not if you were sufficiently wise to don your sou'wester and Garrick Club scarf before setting out.

I first encountered Proust's *In Search of Lost Time* at the age of six. I read it in translation, which I now regret, but it helped when a decade or so later I tackled it in the original French. Though "A La Recherche du Temps Perdu" does indeed translate, albeit very roughly, as "In Search of Lost Time", it lacks the unmistakably French quality of the original. In due course, I have every intention of reading the books themselves, but not before I have finished re-re-reading Sir Walter's magnificent *Waverley Novels*, all 32 of them, and all in the original English.

A day could be profitably spent reading *Paradise Lost* in its entirety, so as to capture the musical mastery of Milton's verse. Though I have every sympathy with Adam, I would never have got myself into such a pickle, as I prefer my apples in pie form, baked by a halfway-competent cook with a goodly dollop of Finest Devonshire (never Cornish) Cream on the top. For her part, Eve was ill-advised to hob-nob with a serpent. Ordering her gardener to embark on prompt action against the unseemly creature with a sharp-edged spade or fork would have been much the more appropriate course of action.

Andrew Marvell is known for just a couple of poems but repays deeper investigation. Whenever I pick up one of his volumes, I investigate it deeply, and find that it repays. But for those drawn to English poetry, though much of it perfectly readable, warnings are required: the best of Wordsworth and Tennyson is admirable, but large acreages leave much to be desired. Did Wordsworth ever know what he was talking about? It seems increasingly doubtful. "I wandered lonely as a cloud" is simply absurd, for instance, as clouds invariably flock together, like football hooligans, Remoaners, and other undesirables.

And Tennyson's iniquitous *The Charge of the Light Brigade* is, quite simply, a gratuitous insult against those in the hard-pressed high command of the British Army. The "health and safety" brigade might, with the benefit of hindsight, argue that the Light Brigade could have avoided a few bruises by taking a different route that day. But it ill-behoves those in the long-haired-poet smelly-socks brigade, like Tennyson, to act as armchair generals when none of them had any intention of getting their knees dirty. "Theirs not to reason why, Theirs but to do and die". Yes, and what, might one ask, is so wrong with that?

This may be the chance to read George Eliot beyond *Middlemarch*, her characteristically catty and vindictive assault on the well-read Mr Casaubon. Trollope can amuse, but most of his novels are turgid and repetitive of plot. Furthermore, they are turgid and repetitive of plot – not to mention the fact that they are, one regrets to say, turgid and repetitive of plot. But the odd one or two would do little harm, particularly for the female of the species, for whom the act of reading, unsugared by melodrama, may sometimes prove to be an uphill struggle.

Some of Dickens's less well-known novels have enormous charm, but suffer deeply from the author's virtue-signalling "concern" for the underclasses. "Who will buy my sweet red roses?" The answer is simple. Those who want them will buy them for a reasonable price, having evaluated the rest of the market to their own satisfaction. But Dickens was ill-equipped to understand these simple rules of economics, a grave failing in any novelist aspiring to the first division. Incidentally, Trollope can amuse, but most of his novels are turgid and repetitive of plot.

As told to
CRAIG BROWN

COTSWOLDS WOMAN WHO DIDN'T CLAP FOR THE NHS TO BE BURNED AT THE STAKE

by Our Clapping Correspondent
Goody Proctor

RESIDENTS in the picturesque Cotswolds village of Wyntonshire have confirmed today that local resident and mum of three, Deborah Jenson, will be burnt at the stake this weekend, after failing to take part in the weekly 'Clap for the NHS'.

"It was her nextdoor neighbour, Laura at No7, out banging her pots and pans, who first noticed Deborah's no-show," said town councillor Gregory Townsend.

"Laura was horrified, so of course she immediately put the awful news on her local mums' WhatsApp group and then on their Facebook page. The reaction was one of sheer revulsion that a creature of such pure evil as Deborah, who doesn't love the NHS, could live among us decent folk".

The next day, as a mob were daubing "traitor" on the front of her house and smashing in her windows, a tearful Deborah emerged from inside, begging for forgiveness and explaining that she'd been up all night with the youngest being sick and had fully meant to take part in the clapping, but she'd fallen asleep on the sofa. But it was too late for excuses.

Said the councillor, "Deborah's burning at the stake on Sunday will be a massive charity event in aid of local good causes and there'll be a barbeque with tombola, cake stall, and bring-and-buy. Everyone welcome."

EU-phemisms

"We accept Britain's departure in a spirit of togetherness and co-operation for the future"

We'll get you, you bastards

"We can see some positives in this crisis"

We hope no matter how bad things get for Europe, the UK will be worse

JOY AS HONG KONG SLOWLY GETS BACK TO NORMAL

by Our Hong Kong Staff **Ruth Less**

AFTER months of everyone being cooped up inside during lockdown to prevent the spread of the coronavirus, there were finally signs of normal life returning to the streets, as protestors fought running battles with riot police.

"How we've missed the distinctive smell of pepper spray in the air and the sound of rubber bullets whizzing down the streets," said one Hong Kong local.

"It's nice to know that once again people will be ferried in ambulances to hospitals because they have been beaten senseless by the riot police and not because they have contracted the coronavirus."

Meanwhile, Hong Kong's leader, Carrie Lam, has insisted that a draconian new security law to be passed this week will not change the way Hong Kong is governed.

"Hong Kong will continue to be governed from Beijing. There is no change. However, new social distancing measures in the wake of Covid-19 means that anyone displaying symptoms of independent thought will be placed, for their own safety, into a jail cell and isolated for 14 years to stop the spread of democracy, as per WHO guidelines."

Lines written on the sudden resignation of the Scottish Chief Medical Officer

'Twas at the height of the Coronovirus Pandemic

That a scandal occurred involving Scotland's Chief Medic.

Catherine Calderwood was yon foolish lassie's name

And on her own head she brought opprobrium and shame.

For she had embarrassed the Caledonian body political

By actions that were frankly somewhat hypocritical.

For she told the whole nation to stay in their home

And nae through the highlands and islands to roam.

Yet all the while she was packing up her motor car

To drive to her holiday home in Fife – an hour afar!

A trip to her second abode in the coastal town of Earlsferry

Turned out to be for Ms Calderwood, unwise... very, very.

She ignored her own lockdown and found herself papped

By a wily photographer in whose lens she was trapped.

Then Inspector McKnacker came knocking on her door

And declared that her journey was not essential, for sure .

But Catherine Jane Calderwood, FRCOG, FRCPE

Clearly thought "These rules dinnae apply to me!"

When the story broke Ms Sturgeon said she would support her

Even though the CMO hadnae behaved as she oughta,

But then Catherine fessed up to another trip the weekend before

Shamelessly motoring past loch and through glen and o'er moor.

Now nothing could save the hapless Ms Calderwood

From the wrath of the Krankie-lookalike in Holyrood.

"You're fired!" said the First Minister, "for no one will admire us

If we appear two-faced in our advice about combatting yon virus.

For amidst all this global pandemic catastrophe

The one casualty we dinnae want is myself and the SNP."

© *William McGonnagal 1867*

GLENDA SLAGG

She's so toxic she should be in quarantine!!!?!

■ CROWNS OFF to Caring Kate for having the guts to protect her mum from the Snooty Snobs of Tittle Tatler magazine!?!! The inbred insiders say the Elegant Mrs Middleton is NQOCD – meaning Not Quite Our Class Darling! Tell you what, Up-Tight Tatleristas – have you heard of Glenda's pithy acronym? NAFFOFF – it stands for Naff Off!!?! Geddit??!? Carole's got more class in her little finger than you've got toffee in your nose!?!! And that's a lot!?!! So what if she sells party balloons and encouraged her daughters to better themselves??!! It's not a crime in Britain yet!!! Unlike your apology for journalism, which will end up with you lot in court – and then in the Tower for treason, with any luck!!! You reckon Curvy Kate is too thin, do you?!?? Not compared to your articles and your libel defence?!!!! Case closed – like the magazine after five minutes of reading it!!? Geddit?!?!

■ FOR GAWD'S SAKE, Your Royal Duchess of Kateness!?!! Have you gone stark staring bonkers??!! Suing the press? Who do you think you are? Meghan Markle?!?! Is that another of the Royal duties you have taken on from her – along with full-time whingeing about how difficult your job is??!? And so what if the cheeky Tatler said your trolly-dolly Mum is Not Quite First Class but more serving the drinks in Economy??!! Don't get all thin-skinned – you're thin enough as it is!!!! Calling the Toff's Bible sexist and snobbish is not exactly news, is it, darling? Unless you are too middle-class to have ever read it!!!! No, my advice, Ms Middlebrow, is to keep out of court – that's the legal one, not the one at Buckingham Palace that you successfully infiltrated!!?! Ok, so the jealous journos called you and Pippa the Wisteria Sisters (social climbers, geddit??!!?) No need to get all wisterical about it!!? No offence.

■ SHAME ON YOU, Emily Maitlis!! Your rantin' and ravin' on Snoozenight is the final nail in the BBC's coffin!!?! No one is interested in your opinions, love, and just because you stitched up Prince Andrew like a kipper doesn't mean you're suddenly the voice of the entire nation!!??! You may think you are the Beeb's knees (geddit??!!), but we've seen quite enough of your knees in those short skirts, darling – no unsisterly offence meant, Emily, to a fellow female professional!!?! Just saying!??!! In future, can we have more fact-finding and less showboating from Ms Shameless?!!? Now, that would keep me awake in the middle of the newsnight!!! Geddit??!!?

■ SHAME ON YOU, BBC bosses, reprimanding our fearless Emily when all she was doing was telling it like it is!!! A billion Twitter followers can't be wrong, you know!!?! And why is the only casualty in the whole sorry saga of Dominic's Cummings and Goings (Geddit!!!!???) a journalist???? Ironic, no??? Unless you don't care that Truth is the real casualty here?!!? It's Newsnight, for gawd's sake – not NewsNice!!!? How dare the British Cowardly Corporation replace Emily Peerless??! She should be presenting every programme all the time until the government resigns in disgrace!!!!???

■ Elon Musk??!! What a waste of SPACE (Geddit?!!?) You think you're so clever, but it's not exactly rocket science, is it??!? (*Yes it is, Ed.*) Take it from me, Musky, it's one small snooze for man and one giant sleep for mankind!!?!! Space X??? Space Zzzzzzzzzzzzzzz more like?!!!!

Byeee!!

UPDATED DOWNING STREET CORONAVIRUS ADVICE

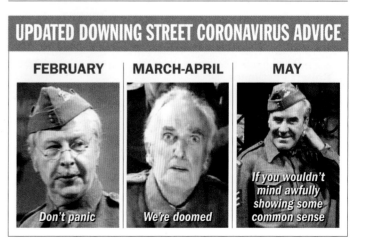

FEBRUARY	MARCH-APRIL	MAY
Don't panic	We're doomed	If you wouldn't mind awfully showing some common sense

Boris Johnson MP
● Live   385,000,000 Views

The Prime Minister's Press Conference, live half an hour late from the Rose Garden of Number Ten Downing Street

👍 Like   💬 Comment

0 people **like this**

(Enter the Prime Minister, smartly dressed in scruffy white shirt and baggy jeans, sitting behind picnic table, as if conducting job interview)

Dominic Cummings: I've been asked to give a statement. So here it is. "I did nothing wrong. The media are to blame. I have no regrets. Now fuck off." Oh no, I was told to cut that last bit. Right, that's it. Any questions? Oh, no, hang on, it's not that bit yet. I've got to read you this very, very long and plausible alibi involving my desperately ill wife, my vulnerable child, a terror threat to my home, my elderly parents and selfless nieces, my tragic loss of eyesight, bluebells, toilet stops, historic landmarks and an invasion by aliens. Oh no, we agreed to drop the aliens as they sounded too plausible. Anyway, on March 27th I did nothing wrong. On March 28th I made the decision to do nothing wrong again. For the next nine days I did nothing wrong. Once or twice during that time period I may have done nothing wrong. I continued to do nothing wrong until April 12th, when we decided it was time to do nothing wrong...

(Cummings continues for nearly an hour, using humble, sincere voice that no one has ever heard before)

Cummings: Right, that's it. End of. Anyone from the media want to defend why they misreported all of this and whipped up public sentiment against me when I did nothing wrong? Laura from the BBC? Still existing, is it?

Laura Koronaberg: Can I just ask: Do you regret doing nothing wrong? And do you think you should apologise?

Cummings: Look, I've answered all this in my statement. It's you who should be apologising to me.

Koronaberg: Sorry.

Cummings: Next! Robert Pestilence. This should fill up the rest of the time.

Robert Pestilence: Mr Cuuuuuuuuuuummings. I have threeeeeee questions. The first is: why do I aaaaaaaask threeeeeee questions? The second is: does it help let you off the hoooooook, because you pick and choooooooooose whichever bit you want to aaaaanswer? And third: does it slooooooooow down the whole interrogaaaaaaaation, so that everyone's forgoooooooootten what the queeeeeeestions even were?

Cummings: Can you repeat that?

Pestilence: No, I've forgotten it all.

Cummings: Next! Deth Rigby, Sky.

Deth Rigby: Have you thought about resignation?

Cummings: Yes. You should all resign. Next? Yes, you at the back, the one who hasn't bothered to brush his hair.

Boris Johnson: Thank you, Prime Minister. Can **I** come on and **answer** some questions now?

Cummings: OK, but don't say anything stupid. I'm off. And don't ask where. It's none of your business.

All: Thank you very much, Prime Minister Cummings. And please do continue to give us off-the-record briefings, which we can faithfully reproduce and attribute to 'Number Ten insider', 'senior Conservative spokesman' and 'friends of Dilyn the dog'.

(Cummings tries to find the exit, but due to his virus-impaired eyesight, ends up in Durham)

Johnson: Time to **move on**, much like Dominic said when he and his wife were **spotted** near the castle on her birthday, er, I mean, on the day when he'd had to test his **eyesight** by driving with his toddler in the back of his car, as **any** father would. And I say that as a **father** of... well, er, a **number** of children. The **exact** number being harder to calculate than the R number, but it's certainly **above** one and **below** a hundred.

Voice off (from Durham): Get on with the bit about me doing nothing wrong.

Johnson: Dominic Cummings is a man of the **highest** integrity, moral probity and **commitment** to selfless national endeavour.

Voice off (from Castle Barnard): Say it like you mean it! I could change my mind and fire you.

Johnson: Oo-err!!! Let's draw a **line** under this whole Cummings **nonsense**. I think the public understand there were **exceptional** circumstances, which make Dominic the **exception** to the rule that he came up with, and I can't say **clearer** than that. So, questions? Let's have a member of the **public**.

Ah, a **vicar**! How blessed is he who **forgives...**

Vicar: This whole Cummings affair is a disgrace! Are you going to give all the other people who were fined for breaking lockdown rules on childcare their money back?

Johnson: **Cripes!** Matt Hancock, would you like to answer that?

Matt Hancock: Hahahaha! Yes, we'll definitely take a look at that.

Voice off (from bluebells): No, you fucking won't.

Hancock: Hahahaha! As I was saying, vicar, we've looked at it and decided it's not worth looking at. Andrew Marrggh, from the Biased Fraudcasting Corporation.

Andrew Marrggh: Why didn't Dominic Cummings stay in London and get childcare from a friend?

Johnson: He couldn't get childcare from a **friend** because he doesn't **have** any friends.

Marrggh: Good point.

Michael Gove: May I say that Dominic and I have a lot in common. Neither of us has any friends and I too have tested my eyes by taking a drive in my car.

Nick Feverarri (London Brexiteer Cabbies News): I mean, that's just not true, is it, Michael?

Gove: Oh dear, this interview's a total car crash, of the kind I might have had, had I taken an imaginary car ride with dodgy eyesight and a small child in the back!

Emily Mateless: And so, yet again, the government proves itself to be a vile peddler of lies, deceit and misinformation, treating the public like fools, as their evil spin-doctor blatantly tramples over his own rules, resulting in the deaths of literally thousands of people who would otherwise have lived happy contented lives with their families, but instead were sentenced to death by...

BBC Announcer: We seem to have some technical issues and Ms Mateless will be replaced by Ms Peppa Pig.

ALASTAIR CAMPBELL FURY AT DOMINIC CUMMINGS

A sneering, unelected adviser dictating policy at No10, who thinks he's above the law...

...who does Cummings think he is, me?

HOW TRACK AND TRACE WORKS ONCE LOCKDOWN ENDS – IN FULL

■ A contact tracer will text or email a person who has tested positive with coronavirus

■ **That person will assume it's some sort of scam and delete the message**

■ The contact tracer will then phone the person

■ **The person will block the caller, assuming the unknown number is one of those automated calls enquiring if they've recently been in a car accident**

■ The contact tracer finally gets through 36 hours later

to the person, who has meanwhile spread the virus widely, to ask who they have been in contact with, so those people can be made to self-isolate for 14 days

■ **The person with coronavirus includes a number of people they don't like in that list, forcing them to go into two-week quarantine**

■ And conveniently forgets to mention Karen from Marketing with whom they're having an affair

■ **Er...**

■ That's it.

ABBA SONGS TO DANCE TO WHEN YOU'RE BREAKING LOCKDOWN

Dancing Queen ♪

Take A Chance On Everybody

Voulez Flu

Durhama Mia

Super Spreader

Name Of The Blame Game

♪ Waterloobreak ♫

S.O.B.

Thank You For The Virus

The Winner Fakes It All ♫

Atchoo! Atchoo! Atchoo! Atchoo! Atchoo! ♪

BuzzFeed

Top Ten things you're most likely to hear in the office

1 We're closing Buzzfeed UK

2 You're fired

3 So clear your desks

4 You'll find a black bin liner in the cleaner's cupboard

5 Give your security pass to Graham at the front desk

6 Sorry there's no leaving drink, but what with lockdown and everything...

7 I'm sure there are plenty of employers in need of your listy skills

8 Try the Mail Online

9 Oh, you have, sorry

10 Would you like to compile a list of ten different names to call the executives at Buzzfeed USA?

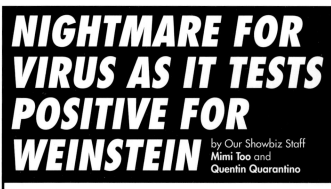

NIGHTMARE FOR VIRUS AS IT TESTS POSITIVE FOR WEINSTEIN

by Our Showbiz Staff **Mimi Too** and **Quentin Quarantino**

THE WORLD of showbiz was united in sympathy, following news that Harvey Weinstein had tested positive for the coronavirus.

Messages on Twitter offered condolences to the virus and hoped that he would get over it soon.

"Stay Well, Virus," tweeted Madonna from the privacy of her bath.

"I'm with you, babe," agreed Gwyneth Paltrow on an Instagram post, showing herself surrounded by anti-viral candles at $999.99 from Gloop. "Bummer!" added Fred Kardashian, the pet gerbil owned by one of the famous family, in a post to his three million followers.

"Thoughts and Prayers be with you Corona, old buddy. You'll come back stronger than ever after your horrific Weinstein experience," said Mike Pence, Vice-President of the United States, on Snapchat. *(That's enough of this piece. Ed.)*

YouGov Survey Reveals: You Are Annoying

A REMARKABLE new survey has revealed that you are very annoying. When surveyed, a staggering **75% of respondents** (your spouse and children) confirmed that, although they had previously suspected you were annoying, the last week in a state of total governmental lockdown had confirmed their suspicions beyond all doubt. The remaining **25% of respondents** confirmed with a strong display of affection that they did not find you annoying, although that is believed to be because you feed them three times a day and take them for walkies.

When asked what could be done to make you less annoying, respondents confirmed that the annoyingness of you is broadly divided into the two categories of **a)** everything you do and **b)** everything you say, including such phrases as "This isn't a holiday, you know, go and do your homework", and "Can anyone help me get Zoom working?"

The survey will be taken several times a day over the next six months, although any expectation that the results will change is seen as highly optimistic.

"This is your final warning, please disperse now..."

THE SUNDAY TIMES
EXTREMELY RICH LIST

James Dyson

Dyson supported Brexit, then left the UK and moved his business to Singapore, while insisting the move was nothing to do with Brexit. That is truly rich.

Jim Ratcliffe

Fabulously rich entry from another Brexit supporter, who insisted Britain held a "decent set of cards" before reportedly moving to Monaco to save billions of pounds in tax.

The Reuben Brothers

Worth £16 billion; still taking money from the government for 750 furloughed staff while living in sunny Monaco. Very rich indeed.

Richard Branson

A staggeringly rich entry from Richard Branson, who spent decades trying to avoid tax and now would like £500 million from the government whose tax he was trying to avoid paying.

Jeff Bezos

One of the world's most extremely rich men, Bezos has made $33 billion during the crisis and is about to end a bonus $2 an hour to his staff. Now THAT is very rich!!!

Rupert Murdoch

[This entry appears to be a mistake. Mr Murdoch is an extremely humble billionaire who is doing everything he can to help the world through its sickness. Please remove immediately. Ed.]

"They're playing 'Follow the Science'"

New shortages revealed by crisis

by Our Financial Staff **Phil Boots**

The public have complained of a nationwide shortage of tiny violins after the Sunday Times revealed that Britain's billionaires "had lost some money" as a result of the pandemic.

This shocking development had sent people flocking to online miniature-musical-instrument-sites to buy minuscule violins, but they were sadly disappointed.

Said one angry customer, "How can I register the scale of my sadness at the plight of these poor billionaires without the help of a tiny violin?"

Another said, "If only the top wealthiest people in the UK had invested in the micro-orchestral market and not in aeroplanes, cars and oil, then they would have made even more money instead of losing a bit."

One financial expert, however, claimed that although it was deeply tragic that these very rich people were not quite as rich now as they were before, they would probably be alright, since they had what are technically known as "Underlying Wealth Conditions", which would protect them against the effects of the virus.

Six people allowed to meet

IN what has been seen as a major step towards a return to normal life, lockdown restrictions in England have been relaxed to allow six people to meet up in the garden.

"For the past two months, playing Zoom quizzes remotely with our friends has been the only thing that has kept us all sane," agreed everyone.

"But, actually getting to spend extended time with them again will remind us just how dull Karen's husband is when he starts going on about his job at the bank, and how

much Barry's wife's laugh gets on your nerves after a bit.

"Then it will be time to fire up the BBQ and, for the first time in months, go through the motions of pretending to enjoy dry, overcooked burgers and undercooked sausages and chicken.

"All of which brings us a step closer to the day when we'll know for sure this pandemic nightmare is over, when we can once again happily cancel plans to see our friends at the last minute because we just can't be bothered.

BEFORE WORK   AT WORK   AFTER WORK

theguardian

Which 'Normal People' character are you?

What lessons can 'Normal People' teach us about surviving lockdown?

'Normal People' – do people go on about it too much?

Is 'Normal People' really about normal people?

Obsessive love. Why is the Guardian so obsessed with 'Normal People'?

How many characters from 'Normal People' now work as Guardian columnists?

Does 'Normal People' really remind everyone of their younger selves, except thinner, more attractive and having sex every half an hour?

Is it possible for us to run an article about, say, growing cauliflowers and not 'Normal People'?

Would Marianne and Connell both have eaten cauliflowers at some point?

Is 'Normal People' the new 'Fleabag'?

ASTONISHING VIDEO GOES VIRAL

by Our US Correspondent **Homer Side**

AN astonishing video showing a black man not being murdered by police has swept across social media and taken America by storm.

The video shows 45-year-old Dexter Jackson, a black chartered accountant from Georgia, going into a grocery store to do his shopping, paying at the till, walking back to his car past a group of white people, driving home after 20 minutes on the freeway without being arrested, walking into his house, eating dinner and then going to bed without being senselessly killed.

The viral video has stunned many Americans with its lack of racist abuse and shocking police brutality.

THE RIOTS
What you will see on the BBC

(We see a huge screen of carnage. HUW EDWARDS, for it is he, is looking very stern.)

Huw Edwards *(with furrowed brow)*: What can you tell us about what's happening there?

Correspondent: Well, Huw, the best way to describe it, and I'm talking BBC guidelines here – a lot of people who obviously passionately believe in what they are doing are clashing with another group of people who obviously passionately believe in what they are doing.

(Huw's brow furrows further)

Huw Edwards: I see. Anything to add to that? Why are they attacking the police, for example?

Correspondent: Well, Huw, naturally, we can't condone people doing bad things, but I'm sure they have their reasons. Fair play to everyone, I say.

Huw Edwards: I notice that the crowd are now attacking you?

Correspondent: Yes. Ow! I don't want to go into which group of people who passionately believe in what they're doing are beating me up, but there are probably several deep-rooted complex issues at the bottom of it.

Huw Edwards: Can you ask them to stop beating you up?

Correspondent: Not really, Huw. Asking them to stop would leave the BBC open to allegations of bias and could flood the duty log with angry viewers.

Huw Edwards: I take your point. Thanks for that.

"I'm here to raise awareness of how aware I am"

'Great Britain' to be removed from all media

by Our TV Staff
Matt Lucas and **David Walliams**

THE long-running comedy series "Great Britain" that has entertained the world for years is to be withdrawn from all platforms forthwith, on the grounds that it is racist, offensive and inappropriate in the modern day.

Said one history professor, "Great Britain was funny back in the day, but times have changed and in 2020 the characters seem very exaggerated and very dated. I'm sure it was all very amusing once, but now nobody wants to see any of this stuff.

"Formerly much-loved characters like Sir Francis Drake, Queen Elizabeth I, William Gladstone, Sir Robert Peel, Lord Nelson, Winston Churchill, etc, with their repetitive and simple catchphrases, have no place in the contemporary world."

The professor concluded, "It is time for Great Britain to be thrown into the sea."

The creators of Great Britain were unavailable for comment.

A President writes…

AS a leading Epideedoodaa-epideeday-myohmy-whata-wonderfuldayplentyofsun-shineheadingmywayepi-deedoodahepideedayologist, I am often asked: "What are you doing about the most deadly threat to America?"

And the answer is simple – I'm closing it down. Yes, it's a terrible, dangerous, viral menace. The most evil contagion to face this nation, ever.

Yes, folks, I'm talking about Twitter. And we know how it works. It's all lies. Except when I'm on it, when it isn't. Fact. And you don't need to check it! I'll go further, if you do check it, you might die. True.

Twitter is trying to ban everything I say. Whatever happened to freedom of tweets?! Look it up! It's the Fourth Amendment. Fact! Even if it isn't. And even worse, you know where Twitter came from? China!

One little tweet escaped from a lab and then before you knew it, the whole world was infected by the viral Twitterbug. They'll deny it, but you know and I know that this is fake news. Unlike the virus, which is fake flus.

So, I'm going to get my smartphone, and I hear this is what you do. Isn't that right, Failing Fauci? You get your smartphone, log on to Twitter and then inject it with bleach. End of Twitter. End of phone. End of story.

Okay, so wanna hear a joke? This one's on Twitter. Which I love. This one's really funny – "The only good democrat is a dead democrat". What do you think of that, Sleepy Joe Biden? Bet you're laughing behind that sad loser mask. Unless you're dead already. Which you might be. I dunno. I'm not saying you are. It's just what people are saying about you. And you hang around a lot of black guys. They're all getting the virus and dying. Just saying.

Might be a connection. Like that guy who had a policeman's knee on his neck for half an hour and then died of the virus. Sad. So sad. But we're doing great on that – most number of deaths in the world now. Beat that, China! Beat that, Twitter!

And you know what the problem was? We were doing too many tests. It was confusing. And we never had the virus before we had the tests. Could be a connection. Just saying. Stop the tests stop the virus.

● *The President's message got a 940% approval rating from members of North Carolina's campaigning group: 'Republicans 4 Really Ram-packed Rallies (and Rifles)'.*

～ GNOMEMART SPECIAL! ～

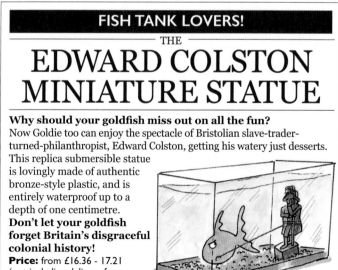

THE ALTERNATIVE VOICE

Dave Spart, Co-Chair of the Neasden "Colossus of Rhodes Must Fall and Burn Harry Potter Now" Action Committee

The spectacle of monuments to the fascist-imperialist-colonialist patriarchy still openly remaining standing in our high streets and public squares is a totally and utterly sickening affront to any right-thinking person and necessitates the immediate removal by force of all outdated relics of our criminal history and a list of offensive statues has been compiled by the democratic will of the people, ie myself, including the fascist Winston Churchill who was worse than the Nazis, the alt-right Admiral Nelson who, amongst other war crimes, committed an act of cultural appropriation by stealing the name of a real hero, ie Nelson Mandela, the British imperialist collaborator Mahatma Gandhi, whose shocking racist views about black people totally invalidate his so-called "peaceful protest movement", which is itself a dated and inappropriate criticism of those who legitimately use force to dismantle the oppressive apparatus of the state... er... er... not to mention the extreme right-wing quasi-reformist William Gladstone and the actual originator of the proto-fascist police state itself, none other than Robert Peel, and not forgetting the most utterly reprehensible statue of all, ie the Paedophile-in-Chief, Hitler Supporter and African Genocide Advocate, Lord Baden-Powell... er... er... only when these symbols of the totalitarian hegemony are consigned to the dustbin of history can we confront our own shameful past and learn the lessons of... er... er... history, the only acceptable and appropriate statues that will be tolerated in the vicinity of Whitehall (to be renamed BAMEhall) are the living statues of Yoda, whose heroic battles against the evil empire of Darth Vader are an inspiration to a new generation of informed and educated citizens who are totally and utterly sick of the spectacle of monuments to (cont. p94)

"Are you going to do this before every bridge night, Roger?"

WHICH FAMOUS BRISTOLIANS SHOULD REPLACE EDWARD COLSTON STATUE?

CHURCHILL SPEAKS OUT

Not our finest hour

Mass rally to save statues

THERE was a huge turnout in Trafalgar Square last night to protest against the removal of statues around the country.

Thousands of angry pigeons collected together in an act of defiance, completely ignoring social distancing and demanding that their public toilets be saved.

"You can't just close every convenience in Britain," said a leading pigeon activist, identified only as Percy, "and expect us to take it on the beak.

"It is part of British tradition for us to defecate on the heads of the supposed great and the good, thus providing a metaphor of the vanity of human endeavour for generations of citizens."

He continued, "How will children learn about the transience of the human condition? It doesn't matter how high you fly in life, you can still be shat upon from a great height."

The police warned that this gathering could increase the spread of disease and advised the pigeons to go home as quickly as they could.

(Rotters)

POETRY CORNER

In Memoriam Ennio Morricone, known as Maestro

So. Farewell
Then Ennio Morricone,
Iconic Italian film
Composer.

You WERE
Spaghetti Westerns
And now you have
Gone West.

The Good, the Bad And the Ugly,
That was your big hit.

All together now
(with whistling,
gun shot, horse
And electric guitar)...

Ay-ee-ah
Wah wah wah
Ay-ee-ah
Wah wah wah.

E.J. Thribb (17½,
the poet with
no first name)

Daily Chain Mail

———— LONDON 1350 ————

PLAGUE PRECAUTIONS END DUE TO BOREDOM

by Our Health Correspondent **Conrad Blackdeath**

Medieval England began to return to normality yesterday as the population ignored the advice of apothecaries and came out of their hovels to resume feudal life.

Said one serf, "We've spent nearly two years painting crosses on our doors and only coming out to bring out our dead. We're sick to death of the Black Death. We want to carry on with our lives, growing failing crops, burning witches, bear baiting and going abroad for a summer Crusade."

Another peasant added, "If you've seen one Plague pit, you've seen them all. They're boring. Let's get the Middle Ages moving again."

The Black Death is believed to have come from China, following Genghis Khan's opening up of the silk road, but there has been growing frustration over the following of science, and the closure of ports due to the advice of so-called "experts".

Said one bubole-ridden sailor, "They don't know whether it's caused by rats or God being annoyed with us for not paying sufficient tithe to the Church, or a mysterious comet in the sky heralding portents of doom. The science says it's unsafe to have open sewers and lack of social distancing, but there's nothing to prove it for sure."

Warnings of a second, third, fourth, fifth and sixth wave of the Plague are also being played down.

Said one seafarer with swellings under his armpits, "It's time to open up the ports and move on – to the new world, hopefully. I'm pretty sure the Black Death won't keep returning for centuries *(cont. 2094)*

TRACE MY CONTACTS? I LIVE WITH 1274 SIBLINGS.

Football to restart in new format

THE proposal that football should be played behind closed doors with no spectators, to avoid dangerous social contact, has met with disapproval from many fans.

They claim that this would entirely ruin their appreciation of the game and they have come up with a radical alternative proposal. That football should be played without any footballers.

This would leave just the fans of the two sides free to get drunk and then pick a fight with each other or the police, who should still be present to ensure the essential nature of the sport.

Said one leading fan, Gary Nutjob, "I mean, no one wants to see empty stadiums – what they want to see is fans like us without our tops on, shouting abuse and getting arrested."

Another fan had an even more radical idea: "Who needs football stadiums full of germs? We could just enjoy ourselves in the open air, say, in Trafalgar square." *(Rotters)*

BLACK LIVES MATTER

STOP CULTURAL APPROPRIATION

"I saw some black people with this slogan and thought it looked cool"

Rugby anthem under scrutiny

Guys, I see the RFU is deliberating on whether 'Swing Low Sweet Chariot' is no longer an appropriate song for the England Rugby brand. I learnt it at prep school in the 1960s with the familiar rude hand gestures (none of which I understood!) but maybe it's time for a rethink. White footballers are taking the knee before matches in solidarity with their black colleagues, and rugby needs a similar empathetic gesture. Instead of spectators at Twickenham wearing red tunics and pith helmets like Stanley Baker and Michael Caine at Rorke's Drift, how about dressing up as their Zulu counterparts? We even have a ready-made replacement song: Haul 'Em Down You Zulu Warrior! – **Bogbrush**

Chief! Chief! Chief! – **Anglia Potatrix**

cunt cunt cunt – **King of the Hill**

Change it to Swing Low Sweet Harriet so Harriet Harperson will sing along 😊 – **Danny Daz**

Why not use Eric Clapton's classic 1975 reggae version of 'Swing Low' to appeal to an urban audience? IIRC his deep appreciation of black music and culture was acknowledged the following year, with the founding of Rock Against Racism. – **Awesome Guys**

I for one welcome this "conversation". Let's have a robust exchange of views of the type that occurred on the Springboks tour in 1969, when the police and the rugby community greeted the anti-apartheid Traitor Peter Hain's rent-a-mob with what the late Bill McLaren used to call "a wee bit of argy-bargy". – **Virgin Sturgeon**

Most traditional rugger songs are older and uglier than Willie John McBride's scrotum, and included what would now be called racism, sexism, rape, coprophilia and sexual torture. No one was ever "offended" by this, or by harmless horseplay such as Ralgex in underpants, dubbin on the wedding tackle, turds in kitbags, urine-quaffing, etc. Worst case scenario was a hairy-arsed prop farting in your face! My old teammates were largely well-adjusted individuals who went on to have careers in the City and the police. – **Zicka Zimba**

Sir Clive Woodward was spot on when he said the key to the issue is education. Well-educated black chaps from the top schools have always played rugger and enjoyed the banter, because they don't have a chip on their shoulder. It reminds me of Price Charles's Asian polo pal, who proudly declared, 'I enjoy being called Sooty!' I hope the RFU's diversity working group will conclude: 'We don't care if you're black, white, or green with purple spots; if you can take a joke, you're in!' – **Pukka Chukka**

I'm not a rugby fan but I painted the words SWING and LOW on my tits and raised £353 for Help for Heroes and the NHS! – **Gilfy Gracie**

Great stuff guys! – **Bogbrush**

FAR-RIGHT PROTESTORS HIT LONDON

Alright, hands up anyone who didn't do GCSE History

MINISTER IN SEXTING SCANDAL

by Our Property Correspondent **Ian Decent-Proposal**

HOUSING Minister Robert Jenrick has admitted to having an improper relationship with porn billionaire, Sir Dirty Desmond, but denies there was anything improper about it.

In a statement issued to a disbelieving House of Commons, Mr Jenuine said, "Sir Dirty showed me something on his mobile phone, which I did not realise was a video of a man making an obscene amount of money. He then suggested I get into bed with him. I did not look at the video, except for a bit, and certainly didn't enjoy the sight of his proposed erection."

The statement continued, "Yes, I did text him afterwards, and I may have said 'Is that a massive donation in your pocket or are you just please to see me?' He did not take advantage of me and I gave my consent willingly. Saying yes, yes, oh yes, yes!"

Sir Dirty, the former proprietor of the TV Channel Filth, and esteemed periodicals including *Big Uns*, *Asian Babes*, and, most disgusting of all, the *Daily Express*, commented, "I was taking money from those Marxists on the local council. They're really disgusting. What's wrong with screwing the public anyway?"

She's Fleet Street's Hot Air Bridge!!!

■ MAXINE PEAKE – arent-chasickofher? She's the leftie luvvie who thinks that as a "Talking Head" (geddit?!!!) her views are of interest to anyone!!! Let me assure you, Mad Maxine, that you're well past your Peake (geddit!!?!) and if we needed a lecture on US police brutality from an angsty actress, we would have given Vanessa Redgrave a call!? No offence, Maxine – loved you as Twinkle in Dinner Ladies, but in those days you were at least trying to be funny!! And someone else was writing the words!! Just saying!!!

■ MAXINE PEAKE! What a diamond! At long last there is a thinking thesp who bothers to find out what's going on in the world (well, Israel anyway)!! Good on you, Max "Talking" Headroom (geddit?!!), it's high time we had more actress activists putting the world to rights – and apologising when they got it wrong and inadvertently caused poor old Rebecca Long-Face to get sacked!!!!! Have we reached Peake Maxine??!! Let's hope not or I'll be Maxine Piqued!!??!!!

■ SO Ian McKellen is to play Hamlet at an unusually advanced age!??!!! Ok, so Sir Ian probably remembers when Shakespeare first wrote the play but so what ?!!! When he plays the scene with the gravedigger, at least he will have one foot in it!!??? Good on you, Gandalf, it shows that you are never too old to play the Mature Student Prince!!?!? "To be 94 or not to be 94, that is the question?" Geddit?!!???

■ GIVE us a break, Old Timer!?! It's you I am talking to, Sir Ian??!!! Shouldn't you be playing Yorick instead of Hamlet!!??? You don't want to make the skull look like a spring chicken in your scenes together, do you?!!?? Try playing something more age appropriate, like Gandalf's Grandad – or, even better, Mick Jagger!??!! (Geddit!??!) "To be or not to be, that is the question" – along with "Where have I put my glasses?", "What did I come into the room for?" and "Who is the Prime Minister ?". Not being ageist, obvs, and no offence, but break a leg – rather than a hip!!!!!????

■ AND talking of taking the Sir Mick??!? What about the Rolling Stones objecting to Trump using their songs at his rallies?!! Tell you what – why doesn't he just play Brown Sugar??!! Sounds perfect for the Pussy-Grabbing President In the All-White House!!??!! No offence to the Octogenarian Troubadours of Testosterone, but just saying your back catalogue from yesteryear might need a revamp!!! Love you Mick, Keef, and the other ones??!!!!

Byeeeeeee !!!

AMAZON SLAVERY BACKLASH

I wish they'd build a statue of Jeff Bezos we could pull down!

NEW HARRY POTTER STORY REVEALED

by Our Harry Potter Staff
Professor Dumblebore

THERE was massive excitement in the wizarding world of Harry Potter after it was revealed there is to be a new instalment in the youthful wizard's adventures, entitled *Harry Potter and the Cauldron of Trolls*.

Harry Potter and the Cauldron of Trolls sees JK Rowling travel to the brutal Troll world of Twitter.

After she whips up a storm of magical proportions by tweeting about menstruation and all-women changing rooms, she finds she is deserted by former friends Daniel Radcliffe, Emma Watson and Eddie Redmayne, who are terrified of falling victim to the Trolls.

Nothing in the Harry Potter world will ever be the same again.

Will JK survive? Or will she be cast into outer darkness by the powerful spell of the Trolls?

"Expelliarmus!" they shout.

"Well, I never thought I'd be burning Harry Potter books"

Facebook ad boycott wipes $6 billion from Zuckerberg fortune

by Our Silicon Valley Correspondent
Jim Crow

Facebook has admitted that Mark Zuckerberg has been stunned, after the growing advertising boycott by companies such as Unilever and Ben and Jerry knocked six billion dollars off his personal worth.

"Of course Mark has been hit hard by this – he's down to his last $78 billion," said a Facebook insider.

"Mark has had to scale back his plans for a holiday home on Mars and put on hold his takeover bid for the Earth, which he had scheduled for 2022.

"Mark's real concern is that if this boycott continues, he might actually have to listen to something Facebook Vice-President and human shield, Sir Nick Clegg, has to say about corporate responsibility."

DIARY

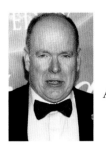

HIS SERENE HIGHNESS PRINCE ALBERT II OF MONACO
Our Prestige Landmarks

I AM honoured to be your guide around the glamorous international landmarks of the Principality of Monaco, where sunshine meets premium-quality sophistication, tradition meets modernity, and a very real concern for the underprivileged meets luxurious fast-tracked streamlining for the world's high-achievers.

Monaco is known throughout the global world as the go-to destination for banking, luxury brands, yachting, elegant gambling opportunities and enlightened tax rates. However, whilst we continue to welcome those of an advanced age, it is our desire to highlight the many high-end facilities we can also offer to a new generation of wealthy young influencers.

LE GRAND THEATRE SIR PHILIP GREEN

In Monaco, we pride ourselves on our age-old appreciation of prestige drama from around the world, and, thanks to a generous donation from an anonymous sponsor, the freshly-renamed Le Grand Theatre Sir Philip Green continues to present a range of exclusive cutting-edge plays and operas. This year, after our hugely successful *Black and White Minstrel Show* we look forward to a revival of *Jesus Christ Superstar*, with iconic Des O'Connor in the title role and international chanteuse Dame Joan Collins as his blessed mother, the Virgin Mary.

How to Get There: From Grand Plaza Hugo Boss, take a sharp right into Boulevard Benito Mussolini. After fifty yards, you will find it off the main square, in the Place Nicholas van Hoogstraten.

GALERIE TINA GREEN

One of my all-time favourite art galleries, this fabulous mecca of world-beating modern and contemporary art continues to occupy a very special place in the hearts of all true Monégasques, offering expertly curated artworks to those in need of both long- and short-term investment strategies.

Galerie Tina Green is currently proud to exhibit Tracey Emin's acclaimed series of installations "Sometimes I Feel So Fucking Real It Like Hurts But Not Always Now I Come To Think Of It", with prices ranging from $81,000-

$3.2 million. Exclusive openings at Galerie Tina Green are acknowledged to attract the cream of the international jet-set. Among the VIPs attending last year's dazzling Jeff Koons opening sponsored by American Express were Peter Andre, Paris Hilton, The Duchess of York, Robert Kilroy-Silk and the Hon Tamara Pringle, iconic heir to the Pringles High-End Crisp fortune.

How to Get There: Head for Avenue Kenneth Noye, then at the Lord Sugar Roundabout take the third exit, signed Boulevard Haw-Haw.

THE MONTE CARLO INTERNATIONAL FESTIVAL OF LUXURY BRANDS

Every year, hundreds of thousands flock to the principality's International Festival of Luxury Brands, which has been running every year in an unbroken line since 2009. Last year, I was delighted when my good friend Princess Camilla of Bourbon-Two Sicilies, glamorous heir to the Bourbon Biscuit fortune, agreed to attend the official opening. The festival takes place every year at the Hotel Grand Palais Weinstein, where luxury VIP penthouse suites start at $27,575-a-night, inclusive of escort. With pavilions devoted to Hermes, Louis Vuitton, Bulgari and Rolex, all tastes are catered for.

Incidentally, I myself always take care to wear my Patek Philippe Tourbillon Perpetual Calendar Platinum watch when I perform my private charitable works in the local hospitals and children's homes. I always find its superb Swiss craftsmanship brings a look of delight to the faces of those perhaps less fortunate than myself.

How to Get There: Traverse the HRH Prince Andrew underpass, then take an immediate left onto Boulevard Silvio Berlusconi. Leaving the Prince Rainier Luxury Casino to your right, drive straight through to the Plaza Francisco Franco and you can't miss it.

FESTIVAL OF INTERNATIONAL STATUARY

There is a lot of excitement about this wonderful new project – destined to become a much-loved part of the Monaco calendar in years to come.

In August, history will take the front row as vintage statues collected from all over the world are exhibited in the verdant surroundings of Le Grand Jardin du Ecclestone Bernard. We premiere with an exclusive collection of ancient statues of some of history's most inspirational movers and shakers, from Bristol UK's premier philanthropreneur Edward Colston to Virginia USA's renowned statesman President Jefferson Davis. We are truly proud to announce that the exhibition will be opened by the celebrated,

multi-award-winning South African sportsman Oscar Pistorius, travel permitting.

How to Get There: Le Grand Jardin du Ecclestone Bernard is situated on Boulevard al Fayed, which can be accessed via Avenue Max Clifford.

CINEMA HISTORIQUE DE MONTE CARLO

My late mother, Her Serene Highness Princess Grace, brought a touch of Hollywood glamour to the Principality when she married my father, His Serene Highness Prince Rainier, in a sparkling wedding attended by many leading members of the international jet-set, including Frank Sinatra, Sam Giancana, Carlo Gambino and Tony "Big Tuna" Accardo.

In honour of her memory, the Cinema Historique de Monte Carlo regularly runs seasons of the classiest movies of all time. This October, we are proud to present "Winner: A Retrospective", featuring the highly-acclaimed films of Michael Winner, including *Death Wish, Death Wish II, Death Wish III, Death Wish IV, Death Wish V* and the consistently under-rated *Death Wish VI*.

All the films will be followed by discussion and Q&A sessions led by Jeremy Clarkson and Nancy Dell'Olio.

How to Get There: Follow Avenue Richard Desmond until you arrive at Place de Karl Lagerfeld. Take the third turning on your right, to Rue de Joe Exotique, and you will see the Cinema Historique straight ahead of you.

THE YACHT CLUB DE MONACO

A favourite port of call for owners and their superyachts (over 40 metres min) and a base for key designers and the major brokers, the Principality of Monaco has always been an exclusive destination. Uniting as it does the most prestigious private yachts in the world under its flag, the Yacht Club occupies prime position in the Luxury Yachting fraternity and is available exclusively for luxury brand product launches and high-end liquidation auctions.

Visit the Yacht Club de Monaco to view the luxury yachts of the future, including the $600 million 181-metre Desirée du Jour megayacht, featuring a choice of luxury bedroom suites to accommodate up to three (3) top-of-the-range silk-veneer helicopters, three ballrooms, a football stadium, and a 8ft-diameter Patek Philippe luxury solid gold watch so large and heavy that it demands to be worn by two men at a time.

How to Get There: Turn left down Rue Myleene Klass, past the Sir James Savile statue, along Boulevard Bernie Madoff and from there direct to the Trump Marina.

As told to

CRAIG BROWN

"Ah, I'll miss the birdsong when the traffic's back"

Yes Minister

Series 94

Foreign Secretary: Now look here, Sir Humphrey, what is all this 'Taking the Knee' nonsense? Sounds to me like it comes from *Game of Thrones*.

Sir Humphrey: A very astute observation, Minister, and one which would play very well with a younger audience.

Foreign Secretary: Do you think so?

Bernard *(sniggering)*: Oh yes, undoubtedly. I think that particular demographic would be most impressed with your detailed knowledge of the customs of King's Landing.

Foreign Secretary: Is that near Dover?

Bernard: Very close. It's certainly on the coast.

Foreign Secretary: So, if I came up with a spontaneous quip along the lines of "the only person I'd take the knee to is the Queen or my wife when I proposed to her", I won't look a complete buffoon and get into hot water with the Twittersphere?

Bernard and Sir Humphrey *(together)*: No, Minister!

(Audience in hysterics at the thought of Raab making idiot of himself and applaud series' creators for coming up with yet another variant on the joke)

Foreign Secretary: Thanks, Bernard. You know, you're a pretty woke sort of a chap.

Bernard: Indeed, Minister, I am a Wokehamist.

(Audience nearly die of laughter at joke about minor public schools delivered by urbane sophisticated ex-Winchester alumnus)

(Enter Dominic Cummings)

Cummings: What have you done now, you prat, Raab?

(Raab takes the knee and begs Cummings for his job)

(Sir Humphrey and Bernard share a knowing look at this latest irony)

Cummings: What are you laughing at, Sir Humphrey? You smug mandarins had better watch it, because a hard rain's going to fall – so get your coat!

Sir Humphrey: Is that threatening-but-obscure remark a reference to the singer-songwriter Dylan?

Bernard: Or perhaps Dilyn the dog?

Sir Humphrey: Very good, Bernard.

Cummings: I've had it with you, Sir Humbug. I hate civil servants – particularly you. We don't want any of your fucking checks and balances!! So fuck off!

Sir Humphrey: Very good, Mr Dummings, but I will require a very large *cheque* and you can pay the *balance* into my account.

Bernard: That's brilliant, Sir Humphrey.

Sir Humphrey: But have you given any thought to my replacement should I depart peaceably and pretend that I haven't been sacked?

Cummings: Yeah, I am getting in someone who won't stand in my way and will do whatever I want. Me! From now on, all I want in every department is Yes-Men.

Sir Humphrey and Bernard *(together)*: Yes, Prime Minister.

(Audience carried out by St John Ambulance, some helpless with laughter, some helpless with Covid due to errors ascribed to Sir Humphrey in endless briefings against him by Cummings)

BOURNEMOUTH BEACH NIGHTMARE

Anyone for a game of catch?

Look, a second wave!

Flu, what a scorcher!

COMPULSORY COVID-19 PRE-HAIRDRESSER RESPONSE FORM

Due to the regulations advising no small talk, all customers must fill in this form and hand it in before having their hair done

WOMEN
☐ Have you been away?
☐ How's the family?
☐ Is Tony/Simon/Phil glad the football's back?
☐ Hot/cold isn't it?

MEN
☐ Have you been away?
☐ How's the family?
☐ Did Marjorie/Desiree/Sandra enjoy the Sewing Bee?
☐ Hot/cold isn't it?

WORLD OF TENNIS

Djokovic reigns supreme in Balkan tournament

THE World Number One tennis player, Coronovak Djokovid, took the title of Champion Superspreader after organising a no-social distancing competition in his hometown of Virus.

Nearly everybody involved caught the tennis bug, including top names in European tennis like: Nastikov, Feva, Swettin, Propersic and Takemonthoff.

Vaccin wasn't invited to take part in any of the matches, nor indeed in the disco dancing afterwards.

Said one spectator, "Once Djokovid takes control, it's game over." Said another, "He's everywhere around the court – in the changing rooms, in the bar, on the taps, and all the door handles." She added, "There's only one word for Coronovak in this kind of form – and that's 'idiot'." (Surely "unbeatable"? Ed.)

Said one tennis expert, Dan Maskall, "It's just bad luck that it was Djokovic. If it had been Federer, we'd have all said 'Poor old Roger, he was only trying to kick-start the sport. Roger, you're such a gent and so well turned-out and charming. Get well soon and love to the twins. Bless'."

the PREMIERSH*TS

THE LONG LAY OFF MEANS A LOT OF THE PLAYERS ARE STILL STRUGGLING WITH MATCH FITNESS...

I KNEW HE SHOULD HAVE WARMED UP BEFORE TAKING THE KNEE!

ARRGH!

DESPERATE BUSINESS

JON & MICK / MODERN TOSS

alright mate, do you wanna buy
my supermarket delivery slot?

Is Steve coming
to this meeting?

yeah he's distancing
from the window

alright, have you
started yet?

yard of ale and a two metre
flute of cider please mate

yeah I overdid it with the toilet rolls
early on so I thought I'd redecorate

blimey what have you bought?

dunno, I just needed
to spend some money

GLAST☉

2020

WHO YOU'LL SEE THIS YEAR

ACOUSTIC STAGE
DAISY AND THE HERD

JOHN PEEL TENT
FLORENCE AND THE MILKING MACHINE

LEFT FIELD
THE FIELD LEFT ALONE

PYRAMID STAGE
EWE 2

STAGE ONE
SHEEP DOGGY DOG

STAGE NUMBER TWOS
PAT COW AND THE COW PATS

THE OTHER STAGE
WILD FLOWERS FEAT. THE BUTTERFLIES

THE PARK STAGE
BRAND NEW COMBINE HARVESTER *(NO WURZELS)*

HEADLINING
SHERYL SCARECROW, DIANA MOSS AND MUD

NEW 'HARDER-HITTING' LITTER CAMPAIGN

Dump your empties, gas canisters, Rizlas, face masks, rubber gloves, wet wipes and shitty toilet paper at whichever beauty spot you find – and the locals will have to clean it up

KEEP BRITAIN GRIMY.

BRITAIN IN SLEEP CRISIS

A COMBINATION of terrible weather, anxiety over job losses and fears about coronavirus have all meant that more and more British people are struggling desperately to sleep each night.

That is why this newspaper will be putting all its efforts into a series designed to help Britain instantly fall into eight hours of uninterrupted slumber, which will include the following pieces:

■ What I, a middle-class journalist, remember about the last time I went to Glastonbury

■ How to recreate Glastonbury in your own home by getting drunk in the garden and not washing for three days

■ What are YOUR top 10 festival memories?

■ Interviews with stars who would be attending Glastonbury, but who are now not doing so

■ Interviews with Glastonbury organisers who were going to be running Glastonbury but now have to do endless interviews about how much better it will be next year

This campaign will run until August, when we will run all the same pieces again but about the Edinburgh Fringe.

THOSE NEW NORMAL PUB NAMES IN FULL

■ The King's Arms-Length

■ The Rose and Corona

■ The Crown and Metre

■ The Non-playing Cricketers

■ The Bird in Hand Sanitiser

■ The Beehave

■ The Spreadout Eagle

■ The Plough Blindly On

■ The Jolly Sensible Sailor

■ The Coach and Hearses
(That's bad taste – Ed.)

■ The Duke of York
(No. that's really bad taste – Ed. You're fired.)

Winston Churchill | **Boris Johnson** | **Dominic Cummings**

PM HAILS DROP IN FIGURES AS CRISIS EASES

by Our Pandemonium Staff
Bernard Castle

FOR the eleventh day running there have been no hostile questions about Dominic Cummings at the Downing Street press conference, the Prime Minister revealed today.

"It is a great step forward," he said, "and I would like to pay a special tribute to the restraint that our brilliant journalists have shown, at what has been a critical moment for all of us. I really believe we can now see light at the end of the tunnel."

The Prime Minister also referred viewers to a graph showing that the number of MPs calling for Cummings to be sacked had remained static at 49, with some experts claiming that the figure might actually have fallen by one or two.

Mr Johnson expressed "warm-hearted thanks to those brilliant MPs who have refrained from joining the protest. We owe them all a tremendous debt of gratitude," he said.

The Prime Minister said he hoped that by the end of this month it would be perfectly safe for Mr Cummings to come out of his house without being attacked by angry protesters, but he warned against over-complacency, urging all parties to be alert and help save the government.

"Feelings could easily flare up again," he said, urging Mr Cummings to wear a mask when appearing in public and to avoid all contact with everybody, apart from himself.

"Is being Prime Minister as much fun as you'd hoped it would be?"

Daily Mail, Friday, July 3, 2020

HOUSE PRICES ABOUT TO RISE/FALL DRAMATICALLY

IN SCENES not seen since the 1960s/1870s/1340s, the British property market is about to take an enormous dive/soar to hitherto un-imaginable heights.

Due to the glut of deceased people's houses on the market/ surge in interest from first-time buyers/total collapse of the employment market/world-ending recession/catastrophic dearth of overseas buyers/ intergenerationally low interest rates/desperate homeowners just itching to sell up, it is clear that the market will soon be worth literally double/half what

it was this time last year.

Furthermore, it is clear that everyone wants to rush into buying inner city flats while they're cheap/get the hell away from any cities and into the countryside. It is expected that the biggest WINNERS will be elderly mansion owners/young flat-owners/first-timers/busy mums of three/buy-to-let landlords and that the biggest LOSERS will be buy-to-let landlords/young flat-owners/first-time buyers/elderly mansion owners.

Estate agents are reporting: any old rubbish that they think people want to hear.

Keir Starmer WRITES

HELLO! It seems a lot of Labour Party members have been taken aback by my 'Night of the Long-Baileys'! "Sir Keir," they say in a respectful tone, "why on earth did you sack your education secretary for innocently re-tweeting an interview with a gobby actress? Isn't that a bit extreme?"

To them I say: You might think so, but just read the text of that interview, and you will understand that I had no choice. It betrayed a bigotry that is shared by a small but vocal minority of Labour members that needs to be pulled out, root and branch, from our party if we are to stand any chance of electoral success at the next General Election.

That prejudice, as we all know, is called anti-Starmetism.

Oh yes, the words in the piece seem innocent enough; a back-handed swipe at people who are only re-joining the party now that Jeremy Corbyn is no longer leader, but within those innocent words are the classic tropes of anti-Starmetism, a prejudice against a tribe of people who wander around looking for a party led by an independently wealthy lawyer who knows how to wear a suit.

Any criticism of these noble people can be construed as anti-Starmetic, and to stop them wandering further afield and pitching their tents with the Lib Dems and their potential leader Layla Moran, we must show that anti-Starmetism has no place in the modern Labour party.

That is why I have taken the courageous step of sacking Rebecca Long-Bailey; it's a risk. I know that taking the step of sacking anyone for any reason means that might make me look like I'm not Prime Ministerial material, but it's a risk I've got to take!

Sincerely, Keir.

① notification: You're fired

Han-z-z-zard

Second Session of Third Debate About 'Which Honourable Members Are More Anti-Racist Than Other Honourable Members?' (2.27pm)

Priti Ghastly *(Highground, East, Con)*: And I am not taking any lessons in racism from the Labour party members opposite because I have got more experience of prejudice and discrimination than they have…

Naz Shahmless *(Righteous, Central, Lab):* I think you'll find that I'm more of a victim than you are and so are all my colleagues on this side of the house. We feel more pain than you do and we don't go around using our experiences to make cheap party points – unlike you Tories!

Priti Ghastly: How dare you! Are you calling me a racist?

Naz Shahmless: How dare you accuse me of calling you a racist? You are gaslighting me!

Priti Ghastly: How dare you accuse me of gaslighting you?

Naz Shahmless: How dare you accuse me of accusing you of gaslighting me… um, what are we talking about?

Priti Ghastly: Whatever it was, I'm just sad that it has come to this.

Naz Shahmless: I am sadder than you are.

Priti Ghastly: No, I think you will find that I am much sadder than you are.

Naz Shahmless: Stop womansplaining!

Speaker: Order! Order me a modern dictionary – I don't know what's going on…

(House Empties)

TV HIGHLIGHTS

The Salisbury Poisonings (BBC1)

Marvellous, nostalgic television, in which the audience can enjoy remembering the old days when you worried about the Russians poisoning your door handle with Novichok, rather than your neighbour touching your door handle and you being infected with *(That's enough nostalgia TV. Ed.)*

LOVE IN THE TIME OF CORONA

A Short Story Special

by Dame Sylvie Krin, author of *100 Years of Solitude, Heir of Sorrows, Duchess of Hearts & You're Never Too Old*

THE STORY SO FAR. Charles and Camilla are back in London, in Claret House, having enjoyed what the royal press have unanimously agreed was "a first-rate pandemic". Now read on…

"**H**AVE you got this right, old thing?" Charles stared bleakly at the new digital Huawei radio which the Chinese Government had so kindly given him for his 70th birthday. "Are you sure there's a Radio Five? I thought it only went up to Four."

Camilla laughed at her elderly yet incredibly fit soulmate's dated knowledge of popular culture. Still, at least he hadn't mentioned the Light Programme.

"Is it the Light Programme? That's where one found the Goons under the blankets after lights out."

"It's Radio Five Live, for heaven's sake. And I'm on in one minute." Camilla grabbed the remote and effortlessly tuned the hostile-state-of-the-art radio to the award-winning drive'n'chat digital platform experience. Out boomed the unmistakable voice of Phil Air.

"Hi, this is Phil Air, bringing you on-the-hour, round-the-clock, up-to-the-minute traffic updates from Britain's deserted roads. First the M94. No tailbacks due to a broken down lorry on the Junction 37b sliproad as yet, but we'll be keeping you informed as and when it doesn't happen."

"What's he blathering on about? What's a tailback? Is it a sort of fish?"

"Shhhh!! It's starting." Camilla turned up the volume, reclined in her wing-backed Parker Bowles armchair and lit up a calming full-strength Tim Rothman's unfiltered Consort Size cigarette.

Charles tried hard to concentrate as the genial radio host Emily Barcode gently probed the Duchess on topical subjects of the day, such as wearing jeans in lockdown and the novelty of using the internet thingie – though he noticed she didn't mention their IT assistant, Auld Ghillie Billie Gates, who had set them up with the Zoomerang device and the Buckingham Houseparty app.

"That's what made lockdown bearable," enthused Camilla across the airwaves.

But had it? Part of Charles thought the new technology had made things a lot worse. He closed his eyes, feigning concentration, as the programme bubbled along like a refreshing Highland burn on the slopes of Ben Stokesy or perhaps the sun-dappled Kelly Brook at Highgrove…

Charles' mind drifted back to the less than satisfactory internet chat with his youngest son, HarryandMeghan™, that morning. It had begun well enough, with Harry informing him that baby Archie had just said his first word and charged 300,000 dollars for it. But then the conversation had

somehow gone awry, as Harry had taken his father to task…

"Look, Pops, Meghan and I have been talking – mostly her, actually – and I don't know if you know this, but the history of Britain is frankly… well, there's only one word for it…"

Charles had an ominous feeling he knew what was coming.

"Appalling," came the familiar Californian twang of Her Royal Wellness, Duchess Meghan of Sparkle.

"I mean, the Empire and the colonies and everything, Pops, it's not as great as you and I think."

Charles sighed. Had they taught Harry nothing at Eton? No, of course not. Apart

from the whereabouts of the Blotto Club on the King's Road and the Third Reich Fancy Dress Novelty Emporium in Royal Slough High Street. It wasn't a great return for all those fees and indeed those extra hours spent with that personal history tutor he'd employed for the boys. What was his name? The grinning chappie who'd walked alone across the Hinduja Kush and become a governor of Iranistan before becoming a MP. Rory Tudor? Or was it Stuart? Or possibly Bremner? Tory Stuart – that was it! His lessons must have covered Britain at some point, surely?

"I mean, the Commonwealth has a lot to answer for, Pops. And to apologise for. It's an outdated historic institution that should be thrown out onto the sidewalk with the trash."

"I couldn't have put it better myself," agreed Meghan™, the co-CEO of the Archewelloff Foundation which was now dedicated since yesterday to the promotion of equal opportunities for the ENJP Community (Everyone Not Just Princesses). Charles had

an awful feeling she was going to bring up the controversial issue of reparations, possibly starting with a large cheque to a philanthropic institution committed to pulling down the statues of all his ancestors.

"Er… I mean, that may be true in a very real sense, though it's not quite that simple and I'm not entirely sure your grandmother would see it that way. Anachronistic institutions may not be a thread that it's wise for the Royal Family to pick at, as it were."

"Check your privilege, Pater," chided the ex-patriot Prince of Bel-Heir from his ranch-style LA mansion, overlooking Laurelandhardy Canyon. "Think about it. Got to go. Megs is doing a voiceover for a new Walt Dismal film *Beauty and the Beastly Royal Family.*"

"**A**BOVE all, I really missed my family." Camilla was still meandering gently through the interview with Ms Barcode, as Charles returned from his reverie to the present. "And I think lockdown taught us all that family really is the most important thing in life."

Charles wasn't entirely sure that this was the message he had taken from the pandemic.

At that moment, the door to the Clive of India Library burst open and there, like the spectre at the feast, was his brother Prince Andrew, still the Duke of York, still Knight of the Garter, still Vice Admiral of the Fleet and still, somehow, the Queen's favourite son.

"She's gone!" Andrew sobbed. And what was that moisture running down his cheeks? It couldn't be sweat, so it must be tears. Charles felt alarmed. He had never seen his cocksure brother so upset. Well, not since failing to play his joker in the 'Falling Off the Wobbly Sausage into a Vat of Foam' round in the epoch-making yet dignified *It's A Royal Knockout!* in 1987.

"She's gone," he repeated, "taken from us! We'll never see her on the throne again."

And before Andrew could explain the context of his remarks, Charles grabbed the nearest sceptre from the wall and an orb from the bowl in the hall, and plucking a crown from the hat rack, was sprinting down the Mall towards Yesminster Abbey. "Long live me! Vivat Caronalingus Rex! Dixit Domino Pizza Express! Zadok Martin the Priest!"

As his voice trailed away into the distance, it was left to Andrew to tell Camilla that his friend Ghislaine Maxwell, who had once jokily sat on the Coronation throne in Buckingham Palace, had been arrested by the FBI. And even worse, she might not be free to take charge of the bridesmaids at the Royal Wedding of his daughter Princess Beetroot to Italian cheese magnate Count Mozzarella…

(To be continued…)

RISHI IN MASSIVE GIVEAWAY

I can't promise to save everyone's jobs

Especially not yours

Government announces £94 zillion billion rescue package for everyone in Britain

The Guardian says: 'It's not enough!'

How typical of the tight-fisted Tories, at a time when the nation is in urgent need of an injection of money, to unleash their Scrooge-like Chancellor, Richi Sunak, to unveil a cynical attack on the poor, disguised as the largest single give-away in human history.

Yes, austerity is back with savage cuts across the board, from hamburgers to chips at a miserly half-price. You're fooling nobody, Ebeneezer Scroogenak!

Why don't you let go of the purse strings, dip into your deep pockets and spare a bob for the Tiny Tims who are struggling to put a foot on the property ladder?

It's all very well cutting stamp duty, why not make houses half price? And why not pay everyone to sit at home doing nothing forever, instead of brutally extending the furlough to a mere six months and offering a cash reward at the end?

Thatcherite to the core. Shame on you, Scrooshi Tightwadnak!

ON OTHER PAGES

■ Isn't it time for a BAME Chancellor? Or maybe Home Secretary? Or is racist Britain not ready for it? p94 *(You're hired. Ed)*

IMPORTANT NOTICE FROM THE CHIEF MEDICAL OFFICER

THE FOLLOWING ARE URGENTLY ASKED TO CONTACT THE GOVERNMENT'S CONTACT TRACING TEAM, AS WE ARE STRUGGLING TO TRACE THEM

They were all in the Dog and Duck in Neasden on Superspreader Saturday, gave their names to the landlord, but now need to isolate for two weeks, due to an utterly unpredictable outbreak of coronavirus in the Snug Bar.

Mr Mickey Mouse

Mr Michael Mouse

Ms Minnie Mouse

Mr Donald Duck

These four friends, who formed a social bubble, are proving very difficult to trace, having appeared in 94 other pubs on the same night.

Also at risk are the following:

Ms Ann Nonymous

Mr Ivor Virus

Messrs Brahms and Liszt

The two European musical gentlemen were spotted playing the pub piano and are of particular concern, due to Interpol registering them as having already died in a previous century. They were also incapable of following the arrow system carefully laid out on the floor. Their health may well be at risk.

TEST MATCH SAVED BY SOUND EFFECTS

CRICKET lovers will have noticed that in the absence of spectators, the television coverage has been enhanced with special sound effects to replicate all the vibrancy of a Test Match atmosphere.

Those sound effects include:

● Yawning

● Snoring

● Umbrellas opening

● Conversations about the bloody weather

● Thunder

● Discussion of Daily Telegraph Cryptic Crossword clue '9 Down'

● Popping of champagne cork at 11am

● Popping of second champagne cork at 11.10

● Annoying Barmy Army song

● Silence as yet another England batsman returns to the pavilion after needlessly throwing away his wicket

● Boos as MCC Members refuse to take part in Mexican wave

● Cheers as drunk streaker removes Y-fronts and evades overweight steward

● Crowd agreement that the 10.3 overs were a jolly good day's cricket

---

Split-ups on the rise since lockdown

by Our Relationship Staff
Di Vorce and **Dee Creenisi**

The pressures of over 100 days of lockdown have had a huge impact on relationships, putting them under the magnifying glass as never before.

Said one counsellor, "It's provided an opportunity for partners to see each other at their very worst and reveal their true natures, warts and all."

Nowhere has this been more evident than in the sad case of a union that has lasted through thick and thin for a number of centuries, but now looks set to founder.

Said an irate Scotland, "I've totally had it with England. There's no excuse for its behaviour. It's selfish, thoughtless, chaotic, greedy, stupid and, above all, arrogant. We came very close to breaking up a few years back, but managed to stick together for the sake of the quids."

England, meanwhile, responded with a shrug, saying, "Scotland needs me. It would be nothing without me."

"See what I have to put up with?!" retorted the Highland nation, packing its bags. "It's over between us. There's no going back. I fancy a fresh start. I love EU!"

100 BEST WALLS TO BE GOING UP

OLD DAVID FROST   NEW DAVID FROST

Hello, good evening and welcome. Super to see you!

Goodbye, good riddance and get lost. Super to leave EU !

NEW PANDEMIC GOVERNMENT GUIDE

Care Home

Don't Care Home

Isn't the BBC terrible?

by Our Media correspondent
Matt Moore-of-this-please

An exclusive poll of Times editors has revealed that the BBC is a tired, lazy, dreary, bloated corporation, staffed by a load of tedious drones who make their money sucking from the cash cow of the British public and offering them nothing but contempt in return.

Nobody watches any of their shows, which is just as well because they are bland and badly made, and they are all ridiculous snowflakes who are more concerned with political correctness than making decent telly, and their radio content is drab and pathetic compared with young, thrusting new stations like, oh, what was it, I could have sworn there was a new radio station on the air somewhere, what's its name again? Oh, that's it, Times Radio, which *(cont. for 94 years)*

Keir Starmer WRITES

HELLO! This week I have undertaken to set an example to my party and sign up for unconscious bias training.

I did it because every one of us in political life should be watchful for prejudice against those who are "different".

I have been accused in the past of having an unconscious bias against those of, shall I say, a "darker" colour then me!

I think you know who I'm talking about – those deep red Corbynistas: members of a tightly knit culture who go to festivals a lot, wear strange clothes (t-shirts with a picture of an old man on the front???) and generally loiter around the streets looking like they're up to something.

Having undertaken that unconscious bias training, I am pleased to say I passed with flying colours!

The people conducting the tests have told me that I have no hint of unconscious bias against Corbynistas, and that my bias is completely and totally 100 percent conscious!

I can't wait to tell them the good news!

Sincerely, Keir.

"Do say if you'd rather play Scrabble without the added crowd noise"

K.J.Lamb

JOHNNY DEPP REVELATIONS

You've been acting very strangely

Well, it's a career

EYE POLL

SHOULD MICHAEL GOVE WEAR A MASK?

You decide

FOR Gove is known to be dangerous and it would be safer if he was covered up whenever he appeared in public so you can't hear what he is saying.

AGAINST The British people should rely on their common sense and be aware that Michael Gove is likely to be spouting nonsense and that they should keep their distance.

AT LAST, GOOD NEWS FOR BRITAIN!

By our Good News staff
Joy Unconfined

HAPPY days are here again, and the nation can once more put a smile on its face. Yes – two celebrities are slagging each other off in court, and we can report all of it!

As bleary Britons staggered out of the pub, they were greeted with the joyous news that Johnny Depp and Amber Heard were hurling mud at each other in a juicy libel action of the type we haven't seen for years.

It's got everything: sex, drugs, microwaved dogs, amputated fingers, cocaine for breakfast, pints of whisky, turds in beds.

Who's telling the truth? Who cares? Will Johnny Depp win his libel action? Who gives a monkey's? Will the Sun lose? No, it can't – it's reprinting all this wonderful, glorious, top-quality filth!

And let's be honest, all that really matters is that Amber Heard is incredibly fruity. As is her sister. And even her lawyer, to be honest! And that's not all! Johnny Depp is a genuine A-1 Nutjob!

What could be better than that?!

From Land's End to John O'Groats, ordinary people are on their doorsteps, banging their saucepans and applauding the Hollywood A-List ex-couple who single-handedly knocked coronavirus off the front pages!

Captain Johnny Sparrow, and Amber Never-Heard-of-you, WE SALUTE YOU!

GAME OF THRONES

Is Andrew next in line?

No, they'll arrest Jeffrey first, then me, then him

Nursery Times

Friday, Once-upon-a-time

CRUELLA DE VIL FURIOUS AT 'GHISLAINE MAXWELL' COMPARISON

by Our Legal Staff **Paedo Pan**

THE heiress and dog lover Cruella de Vil has reacted angrily to suggestions in the media that she is some sort of "Ghislaine Maxwell" figure.

Friends of Cruella (Jasper and Horace) said last night, "Ms de Vil is a respectable collector of dalmations for couture purposes and it is unfair to link her with the sort of activities of which Ms Maxwell has been accused."

The friends, who are very close to the society hostess, continued, "Just because Cruella has a Christian name that sounds a bit like cruel and a surname that could possibly spell out Devil, people

mistakenly assume that she must be in some way be a bad person.

"Can we get this straight? She may have met some dalmations a long time ago, but she has never actively captured them nor attempted to turn them into coats."

Ms de Vil is considering legal action for the insinuation that she and Ms Maxwell are in any way similar, although Ms de Vil could not be contacted, due to the fact that she is in hiding after pictures emerged of her with a hundred and one different dalmations, which she claimed may have been faked by Walt Disney in an attempt to (*cont. p101*)

'We had no idea,' claims everyone buying tops for £4

EVERYONE who's spent years buying unbelievably cheap clothing has made it clear that they had no idea whatsoever they were produced by modern slave labour.

"It comes as a complete surprise to me," said one shopper. "I have happily been paying roughly £2 for every new item of clothing I've bought, and I'm just shocked to hear that this sort of price comes as a result of paying people extremely tiny wages,

and widespread fraud and tax evasion by the companies involved. It just seemed likely that £2 was a fair price to pay."

"It's just terrible," said another. "I'm used to hearing about low wages, but it's far worse when it's happening in Leicester. From now on, I'm only going to buy my £1.99 hoodies and jeans if I can make absolutely sure they were made thousands of miles away, so I don't have to consider it."

The Daily Rishigraph

(formerly the Daily Borisgraph)

Friday, July 17, 2020

Massive spending spree to be paid for with massive tax cuts

by Our Economics Correspondent
Tony Broke

THERE was fresh joy across the nation today as it was confirmed that the hundreds of billions of pounds Chancellor Rishi Sunak had given away in an unprecedented spending spree would be paid for with massive tax cuts.

Most expert economists say that chancellors faced with a deficit of £300bn for the fiscal year should look to steady the markets to prevent Britain's

credit rating being downgraded, by prudently raising taxes, but as this paper has said many times, we've had quite enough of experts saying things we don't want to hear.

In this paper's opinion, only a politician who can walk on water, like Chancellor Rishi Sunak, could both increase spending and slash taxes to balance the books, by shrinking the deficit to a mere £450bn next year!

Rishi really is a miracle worker.

BEZOS RICHER THAN QATAR!

by Our Economics Staff **Rich List**

YES, it's true! Amazon supremo Jeff Bezos, the world's richest man, is $13bn richer than he was yesterday, bringing his wealth to $94 gazillion, which officially makes him even richer than the Gulf State of Qatar.

The news has excited the world of football as, instead of the controversial choice of Qatar, Jeff Bezos could now host the 2022 World Cup.

Said one fan, "Bezos is a far more sensible venue for an International Football Tournament, as his body temperature of 37 degrees is far cooler than the desert furnace that is Qatar."

He continued, "Another advantage is that if we have a

World Cup Prime the whole competition can be delivered by tomorrow afternoon latest."

However, critics were quick to point out that if England were to win it, and not be in at the crucial moment, the Cup itself would be handed to a neighbour, Wales.

Said one pundit, "Whatever happens, whether the stadiums are ultimately built in Bezos or Qatar, it will be a triumph for slave labour."

LATE NEWS

■ Amazon's huge profits due to people's reluctance to behave normally. Said Jeff Bezos, "I, for instance, am very reluctant to pay any tax."

SNIFF! BOO HOO!

BOO HOO!

BOO HOO! SNIFF!...

"THE SOUND OF THESE CLOTHING WORKERS INSPIRED OUR COMPANY NAME"

KEY

🔍 Boris Johnson | Home | Create

Boris Johnson MP
● Live   385,000,000 Views

People's Prime Minister's Question Time – Live on Fakebook

👍 Like   💬 Comment

0 people **like this**

Greetings, Comrades! I mean, Friends.

And by **friends**, I mean people I've never met and certainly **haven't** taken any money from. So, in the interests of **transparency**, this being a proper democratic **accountable** country, let's have a question from a free citizen of this **great** country of ours, Ollie Garch. What's your question, Ollie?

> Would you like some money?

Sorry, I didn't hear that. **Next** question. It's Ivan Enormussczek from **Godalming**. How can I help, Ivan?

> I would like to play you at tennis and also to destabilise the West?

Well, one of those is a **bit** tricky, as my knees are a bit **dodgy** at the moment. No, we don't like **this** question either, do we, Dom? Let's hear from another **British** subject, Igor Rallotovdoshz...

> Are you going to ignore the findings of the Russia Report?

Good question. **Wilfred** is **very** well. He's got a **fine** head of hair and he said his first word yesterday: "**Cripes**!". Chip off the old bloc, but not the **Communist** one, obviously.

> Have you read the report?

As it happens, I **haven't** looked at it. It's best **not** to look at these things or you find out something **unpleasant**. But just to be clear, the important thing is: the Russians have **no** influence in Britain or my name's **not** Boris Nogudenov. So let's not waste **any** more time on **trifling** matters such as how much the Russians may or may **not** have influenced the election and how much **money** they may or may **not** have given to the Conservative party and **why** I sat on this report for nearly a year and was very **cross** when Grayling couldn't even get himself voted as chairman in a **rigged** election – it would **never** happen in Russia, as Vladimir told me.

THOSE AMAZING REPORTS IN FULL

Russian Report: Putin trying to interfere in British public life.

Pope Report: Pontiff triying to interfere in Catholicism.

Toilet Report: Russian bear shitting in British wood.

On other pages
■ Why Did Boris Sit On Toilet? Report **94**

Government's Brilliant Idea to Combine the 'Eat Out To Help Out' Message and the Anti-Obesity Campaign

---

FURIOUS REACTION TO RUSSIAN BREXIT VOTE-MEDDLING CLAIMS

by Our Moscow Correspondent **Olly Garck**

SENIOR politicians at the time of the Brexit referendum have rejected suggestions that Russian interference was crucial in determining the result, pointing instead to their own incompetence.

"To suggest the Brexit Referendum result was down to anything other than the fact I'm a lazy third-rate politician is terribly insulting," former Prime Minister David Cameron told reporters.

"Entitled, complacent and woefully out of touch with voters, I didn't need Russia's help to screw it up. I was more than capable of plunging Britain into untold chaos on my own."

The former Labour leader Jeremy Corbyn insisted he too deserved credit for being a woefully incompetent politician.

"Sure, David Cameron was crap, but even he didn't take a holiday during the Referendum campaign like I did. Just look at the payment those former Labour employees were awarded this week and my petulant response set a new benchmark for woeful."

"No amount of enquiries will find that I did anything to influence the Brexit vote."

SNP FURY
The former SNP leader Alex Salmond also rejected suggestions in the report that Russia had interfered in the Scottish Referendum vote.

"As I've said time and time again on my *Russia Today* chat show, there is no obvious link between the Kremlin and Scottish politics."

"I can assure you that these stories of my links with Russia are completely unfounded"

EXCLUSIVE TO GNOME FILM

NO TIME TO DIE
Movie Preview

(Int. Blofeld lair. Blofeld at desk stroking cat on his lap. Bond enters)

Blofeld *(for it is he)*: Ah, Mr Bond, I was expecting you... er... about eighteen months ago, when I carried out my evil plan to destabilise the West.

Bond: Yes, we decided at MI6 we couldn't really be bothered investigating what you were up to. By not investigating your evil plan it meant there was no evidence there was an evil plan in the first place, so everyone could rest a lot easier.

Blofeld: Surely the construction of my vast under-sea lair set alarm bells ringing for the security services?

Bond: Not really. London is full of dodgy, mega-wealthy oligarchs funneling cash though vast vanity projects. Who are we to say that, like them, you also didn't go from being Putin's hairdresser to a billionaire in the space of a month, totally legally?

Blofeld: MI6 is sounding awfully complacent these days, Mr Bond. But if you're not investigating my evil plans, why are you here?

Bond: Just reminding you that your tennis game with the Prime Minister, which you successfully bid for at that Tory party fundraiser, is this afternoon.

(They both laugh and clink glasses. Silhouetted naked ladies jump into swimming pool as Bond theme plays)

SITUATIONS VACANT

BAR STAFF Owing to over 73,000 applicants for the position of bar worker (£9 per hour), we have had to be more discerning in order to weed out any time-wasters.

The successful applicant will have to have a PhD in Languages (for talking to our drunken clients), a PhD in maths (for short-changing our drunken clients) and a PhD in Physics (for chucking out our drunken clients when they complain they've been short- changed).

A PhD in philosophy is also essential for when the bar closes down next week due to the virus, so that the successful applicant takes it well.

PRIME MINISTER JOHNSON'S DISSOLUTE HONOURS IN FULL

Lord Johnson of Johnson & Johnson Jo Johnson is elevated to the peerage by his brother for services to annoying their father Stanley, who gets nothing, and embarrassing Jo's wife, Amelia Gentleman, who will henceforth be called Lady Gentleman, which amusingly sounds like a public toilet.

Lord Luvaduk of Two-Beards The former Evgeny Luvvieduk is granted a Press Barony, and in addition is awarded the order of the KGB for services to lowering standards at the *Evening Standard*.

Lord Snooty of Torygraph The former Charles Moore is elevated to the Upper Chamber for services to the silk-top hat industry and for his heroic refusal to pay his TV licence.

Sir Philip Mayfly The former First Husband is knighted for his services to the refuse industry, specifically putting the bins out in the Westminster area.

Lord Beefy of Botham For services to political debate and keeping Boris "in", when it looked like he was going to be "out".

Lord Hushpuppy of Clark's The former Ken Clarke has been ironically elevated to the peerage as a thank you for making Brexit so popular by his smug and lackadaisical opposition.

Other peerages include:

Lord Crony

Lord Cronier

Lord Croniest

Coronavirus update

■ THERE was widespread relief today that all those suggestions when the country went into lockdown that people would use the time learning languages, getting fit, baking banana bread, reacquainting themselves with nature and crafting were proved to be bollocks, when new figures revealed we actually just watched loads and loads more television.

Lines written on the Historic Journey of the Prime Minister North of the Border

'Twas in the terrible year of Covid-19

That in the Orkney Islands Boris Johnson was seen,

A rarer sight than the monster of Loch Ness,

A sure sign that the Union was in a terrible mess.

Boris tried to reassure the good Caledonian folk

That his commitment to Scotland was not just a joke.

Unfortunately he was photographed holding up some crabs,

Leading to unsavoury sexual humour in the red-top "tabs".

He then tried to woo the canny Scots with shedloads of money,

Which at least was more effective than trying to be funny.

And he avoided any chance of independence-related trouble

By staying well clear of the fearsome lookalike Krankie double.

Yon Ms Sturgeon, however, could not have been happier

Than when Boris promised that the Cabinet would more often come up here,

For the sight in Bonnie Scotland of the Old Etonian Brexiteer

Could only bring to the SNP faithful great comfort and cheer.

For the net result of all the Prime Minister's tub-thumping ballyhoo

Was to hasten the arrival of Indyref 2!

© *William McGonnagal 1867*

The Mail
ON SUNDAY

EXCLUSIVE

Because even his own newspapers wouldn't print this stuff

Lord Luvaduk, formerly Evgeny Luvvieduk, writes a trenchant attack on the bigotry and intolerance that has blighted his life

BRITAIN looks like a tolerant country, but just beneath the surface of fairness and equality lies a corrosive vein of prejudice.

For years I have been a victim of this discrimination which has blighted my professional and personal life. I am talking about the hatred of beards. You may not choose to believe this, but blatant beardism exists throughout British society.

At every level and in every walk of life, people are subtly hostile to those of us who have beards. How often have I heard someone behind my back saying, "What a silly beard!" or "Why has Beardie put another stupid picture of himself in the Evening Standard sporting a ridiculous beard?"

This sustained campaign of verbal aggression is clearly designed to indicate that people with beards are not to be taken seriously and do not deserve the respect afforded to the non-bearded community.

Even when people with beards are elevated to the highest positions in the land, the beardophobia continues. "Lord Beardie of Goatee" I hear the shaven beard-bigots sneer.

Surely it is now time for the Prime Minister to set an example and appoint someone with a beard to be in charge of, say, the Theatre, meeting famous actors and having his photo taken with them.

Perhaps this bearded person could be given the title "Theatre Czar", which would match his beard perfectly.

© *Lord Luvaduk, 2020.*

Ken Pyne

CUSTOMERS DISMAY AT PIZZA EXPRESS CLOSURES

Advertisement

Gnome Tel presents

NOW THAT'S WHAT I CALL ANNOYING!

YES! It's the hot summer cd that will be playing in all the empty bars and discos across the Mediterranean!

WITH ALL YOUR FAVOURITE SUMMERTIME HITS!

Fever Espania!

Hey-Macorona!

Agadoom!

Ain't No Cure For The Summertime Flus!

Queasy Like Sunday Morning!

The Plane in Spain Stays Mainly on the Tarmac

AND MANY MORE!

JUST £29.99

CALL NIGEL FARAGE (A CAB)

It's your boss on line seven...

Why don't you go back to where you came from?

We must get the children back to school, for their sakes
by All Parents Everywhere

As parents, we only want the best for our children. And to me, it's very obvious that, for the sake of young people everywhere – put that down, darling, Mummy's trying to write an article – that we make sure our precious children can – no, put it down, it's a circular saw, give me that this instant – that they can definitely go back to school on the first of September, and not a day later.

For months we have – darling, don't drink that, that's floor cleaner – we have been coping magnificently as parents with the – be QUIET, you little maniacs, I can't hear myself THINK – with the terribly worrying prospect of our children's education suffering, but the fact is – YOU HORRIBLE BABY, TAKE THOSE PEBBLES OUT OF YOUR MOUTH THIS INSTANT – the fact is that for their sakes and their sakes alone they must be taken away and put in a school for five days a week, so they can resume their vital education.

I will miss them terribly, of course, but – *your mother is going to be very, very angry unless you all shut up right now* – but we will simply have to cope. In fact – thinking about it now, there is a strong argument for "catch-up" time, whereby – I WILL COUNT TO THREE. THIS IS YOUR LAST WARNING TO STOP THROWING THAT INDOORS – whereby the government actually pays us and takes our children away for seven days a week for the next year. For their own good, of course.

Pooh

POETRY CORNER

Lines on the decision to allow pupils to drop the poetry option in their GCSEs

So. Farewell
Then Poetry.

This sad decision
Has neither reason
Nor rhyme.

It is a crime
By 'Ofqual',
Whose very name
Lacks poetry.

Why simply prose?
No one knows.

But it gets worse,
For this could spell
The end of verse
As we know it
And from now on
Everything will be
Blank.

    E.J. Thribb (17½ lines)

What is the poet attempting to convey by the above lines, known as a threnody, and what poetic devices does he employ to advance his argument? Answers in a bin.

University Mathematics Finals

QUESTION 94

If there are 120,000 students from China paying an inflated fee to be at university in the UK and if, due to the worsening political relationship between the two countries, none of them come back:

A How many universities will go bust?

B How stupid were they to get into this position?

C How much grovelling will the UK's Prime Minister have to do?

QUESTION 95

If a Vice-Chancellor earns, on average, £450,000 per annum, with a fully funded pension, by stuffing his university full of Chinese students and then overcharging them, how much will he or she care when the whole scam goes tits up?

A Not much.

B Less than that.

C See ya – wouldn't want to be ya!

QUESTION 96

If China incarcerates a million Uyghur people, how many different convincing explanations will the Chinese Ambassador give on The Andrew Marr Show?

CLUE:
The number is less than one.

Who should replace Dame Jenni Murray as the presenter of Woman's Hour?
You choose the new occupant of Radio 4's hottest feminist hot-seat...

Dame Edna		Grayson Perry		Eddie Izzard		Emma Watson				JK Rowling

Dame Edna · Mrs Brown · Grayson Perry · RuPaul · Eddie Izzard · Eddie Redmayne · Emma Watson · JK Rowling

Numéro 94

Le Migrant Crisis Dans Le Channel

La Home Secretaire, Madame Jolie Patel est dans un top-niveau meeting avec sa counterpart, Le Minister of the interior, Gerard Depardieu (*surement Gerald Darmanin? Editeur*)

Madame Patel: C'est un disaster! Vous Frenchies are not doing nearly assez pour stem le tide des immigrants!

Darmanin: Mais non! Nous sommes being très helpful…

Patel: Helpful aux immigrants by doing rien!!

Darmanin: Non. Non. Non! Nous wouldn't aider les pauvres refugees across La Manche juste because de Brexit!! Pas du tout!! Hahahaha.

Patel: Chaque jour thirty thousand hundred million et vingt-sept immigrants dans les speedboats arrivent sur les plages de Kent! Et le Navy Français tournent un oeil blind!!!

Darmanin: Non, je suis comme votre hero Admiral Nelson "Je see no ships!!" Hahahahaha.

Patel: Are vous taking le piss?

Darmanin: Non. Je suis taking le money. Trente million s'il vous plaît, en Euros naturellement, pour cesser le flood des migrants!!

Patel: Zut alors! C'est blackmail!

Darmanin: Nous avons vous over un barrel! Et pas un gun barrel parce que le British navy modern consiste de one dinghy de rubber!!! Hahaha.

Patel: If vous pensez that je will give in sans un fight…

Darmanin: Oui?

Patel: Puis vous êtes… completely right!!

Darmanin: Bravo, Madame Jolie! Vive l'entente not très cordiale!!!

"Did you pack this boat yourself, sir?"

Vaccine article not quite ready to go

by Our Virus Staff
Piers Review

There was huge excitement last night, when early indications suggested that a vaccine article had reached the stage where it could be rolled out across the newspaper.

The science editor was being cautious, whilst the editor was hailing it as a major breakthrough in the fight against depressingly negative Covid stories, and was undeterred by the fact that it had only been tested on some intern guinea pigs (Sanjeev and Mel from the University of Neasden's Media Studies' course).

"The early signs that they weren't falling asleep by paragraph two were promising," said the editor, "but there's still a long way to go – another 10,000 words, to be precise."

According to another expert in the field, the features editor, "The article could be more effective if combined with a photograph of Liz Hurley in her lockdown bikini enthusing about a possible extension of herd immunity via the vaccine."

Sources close to the editor say that he is trying not to get over-excited, but has ordered 90 million versions of the article, just in case it works and sells a few newspapers.

SOUTH COAST INVASION – A WARNING

THE government has received information that a desperate horde of tens of thousands of people is currently travelling to the beaches of Britain's south coast.

Many of these people have led cramped and horrible lives so far. Almost all of them are escaping after months of incarceration, and are determined to do whatever it takes to get onto the beaches at Bournemouth, Brighton and Hastings, where they will spend the entire day dropping litter and eating ice-creams and filling the car parks and generally ruining the whole place for everyone who lives there.

If you see these people, known as "tourists", please REPORT THEM to the authorities immediately, and remember:

1 They are very under-prepared Most of them will have nothing but the clothes they stand up in, having said to each other, "It's a bit hot, shall we go to the beach today?" They will not hesitate to clear the shelves of the local mini-mart. Many of them will be suffering terribly from the effects of the sun, from only drinking 16 cans of Stella Artois, and from the effects of the beach kebab they've just bought.

2 They don't understand our way of life These people are largely from far-off places like "London" and, as a result, have no ethical standards at all. Try to remember that they are really not like us and make allowances for that. At the same time:

3 Show compassion These people are just looking for a better life, and have deluded themselves into thinking they'll have a nice time at the beach along with all 500,000 other people who've had the same idea. At the same time:

4 Deport them Britain's beaches are no place for holidaymakers and they should all be put on boats and sent to France, so the French can deal with them screaming "deux beers, please" instead.

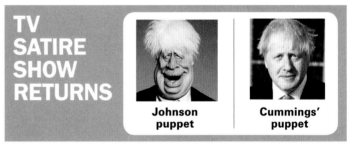

TV SATIRE SHOW RETURNS

Johnson puppet

Cummings' puppet

Liverpool fans gather to celebrate title

by Our Football Staff
M.T. Stadium

At last, they've done it! The wait is over and the title is theirs!

Said one Liverpool supporter, hugging his friends in a packed car park outside Anfield, "Yesssssssss! Winning the title of 'Stupidest Football Fans' is a dream come true. It's been too long since we've been the stupidest – all these years we've had to watch other fans claim the title, but now it's ours again."

There was a late scare when Leeds fans tried to snatch the title away from Liverpool at the last minute, but Klopp's heroes were not to be denied.

Said another stupid fan, after kissing ten other stupid fans, "I'm over the moon," adding with a cough, "although, come tomorrow, I may be even sicker than a parrot."

LATE NEWS

■ Leeds United victory bus route confirmed:

Starts Leeds United's Elland Road Stadium

Ends Leeds General Infirmary

DIARY

GUARDIAN ONLINE

Forget any false sense of security, we'll sadly all be dead by 2022 / Even the most optimistic experts acknowledge that Covid-19 will kill us all by Christmas, says Guardian columnist Pam Denic. And that's terrible news for the future of regional theatre.

It is time to remove Beatrix Potter from our public libraries / There's no place for homophobic white supremacists Tiggy-Winkle, Tittlemouse and Puddle-Duck in 21st century society, says Afua Hirsch.

What does a bin full of rubbish tell us about modern Britain? / I opened the lid of the bin expecting to find a treasure-trove. Instead, I found paper and plastic items that had been termed "rubbish" and chucked away with no thought for their feelings.

The sun may be out now, but past experience tells us it'll have gone in by midnight / We kid ourselves when we claim that the sun is shining. History teaches us that Boris Johnson won't tolerate anything free for long, says Polly Toynbee.

Sherwood Forest: yet another outpost of British hypocrisy / Robin Hood's men had no right to be merry, argues Guardian columnist Maureen Glum. With no female representation, their merriness looks more like a peculiarly vicious brand of green-booted sexist triumphalism.

A tale of two hands / On the one hand, you have five fingers. Or, strictly speaking, four fingers and a thumb. On the other hand, you have the same number, unless, of course, through accident or design, you are digitally impaired, in which case you may have fewer, or none at all. On the other hand, which is to say, on the first hand, you may also possess a below average number of fingers. So what exactly is my point? asks Will Hutton.

Why do the producers of BBC Question Time persist in giving Tories a mouthpiece? / The BBC's much-touted home of "democratic debate" is nothing of the sort, says Guardian columnist Owen Jones – not while unashamed Tories are still welcomed in with open arms.

What sort of country tolerates garden gnomes? / To factory-produce scornful replicas of the short community and then abandon them outdoors in sub-zero temperatures is nothing short of genocidal.

Why are the Covid 19 figures continuing to rise? / If history teaches us anything, it teaches us that coronavirus is spread by senior Tories.

The Home Secretary is a beacon of hypocrisy / What gives Priti Patel the right to think like a white person? asks Afua Hirsch.

When a budgerigar dies in West Malling, we all know who to blame / At the weekend, my elderly mother's adored budgerigar perished unexpectedly. Chirruping one minute, dead the next. Enough is enough. How long can Boris Johnson continue to get away with it? asks Maureen Glum.

My mask has been forced to wear a mask / Yesterday, I noticed that my protective mask was wearing a mask to protect itself from the abuse of the anti-mask campaigners. I blame Dominic Cummings, says Naomi Livid.

As a woman, I have suffered enough / Being forced to go on BBC Question Time to defend my hard-won opinions is yet another example of modern slavery, argues Rebecca Long-Bailey.

The time has come to take down all statues of Nelson Mandela / Evidence continues to emerge that the self-proclaimed freedom fighter failed to support BAME in anything but the most perfunctory fashion, reports full-time activist Vin Dictive.

Cancel culture is the only way to preserve free speech / By failing to silence those we disagree with we allow ourselves to become slaves to imperialism, argues Owen Jones.

Dilyn wreaks of sexist, racist hypocrisy / Boris Johnson's terrier is a white, male Jack Russell, bred to grab innocent foxes by the throat and savage them to death without mercy. What does this tell us about the Prime Minister? asks Polly Toynbee.

So your local panto has been cancelled? Good riddance / Widow Twankey remains a figure of fun to the reactionary cis panto-going patriarchy. The jeers that greet this elderly transgender icon whenever she appears on stage represents bullying at its most hateful.

Let's hear it for underpersons / To describe the poor and downtrodden as "underdogs" is truly revolting. For pity's sake, they are not dogs: they are people, says Mark Sollum.

Why I will no longer read Penguin authors / Krill, fish, squid and other forms of sea life are being slaughtered for food by penguins. Yet the infamous imprint still refuses to change its name.

The muzzling of the Eskimo voice / Eskimo mime troupes are cruelly under-represented in the Old Vic's current theatre season, says Simon Goody. So what is the solution?

Time to put an end to prejudice against the Inuit / For employing the hateful term "E**imo" of the indigenous circumpolar peoples, Simon Goody is demanding to be cancelled, argues Bel Virtue. And his use of the Nazi term "solution" is beyond contempt.

An End to Hate Speech / We all know the weasel word "indigenous" is a phrase employed by apologists for racism, argues Afua Hirsch. And that's why the poisonous hate-speech of Bel Virtue must be stopped.

Let's not stifle debate about the need to stifle debate / Is it time to stifle the debate about whether we should broaden the debate about stifling the debate? argues Jeff Grouting.

As told to
CRAIG BROWN

ROYAL RIFT EXPOSED

CARRIE ON CAMPING!

The Proms – is it time to end this ridiculous annual tradition?

by Our Culture War Correspondent
Hewell Britannia

YET again, we see the same ridiculous ceremony on the horizon, one which has been happening every year for what feels like forever.

This risible annual tradition involves absurd pageantry, pointless choreographed nonsense and the deliberate whipping-up of jingoism and flag-waving patriotism. It's old-fashioned, offensive, and I, for one, think it is time we brought it to a close.

I am referring, of course, to the "Annual British argument over whether *Land of Hope and Glory* and *Rule, Britannia* are acceptable songs for the last night of the Proms".

It is embarrassing to see so many national figures (Nigel Farage, Nick Timothy, Toby Young, James O'Brien) humiliating themselves on a matter this pathetically inconsequential. But year after year, they get their costumes on and strike up the same old tunes, including "These songs are dogwhistle racism and should be banned", "This is the fascist left crushing our proud island history", and "The Brussels bureaucrats can't stand our good old-fashioned British pride in our country".

They are tired tunes, the audiences are increasingly exhausted by being exhorted to sing along, and they don't even sound good.

"Ah well, if we have to quarantine, we have to quarantine"

UK adds UK to quarantine list

AFTER a worrying spike in cases across the United Kingdom, the UK government has decided to include the UK in its list of sanctioned countries.

Anyone taking a so-called "Staycation" in the UK will have to quarantine for 14 days on their return from the UK to their UK home.

This includes anyone taking holidays in their own home, which may have the unfortunate result of their never coming out again.

The Foreign Secretary, Mr Dominic Raab, insisted that these strict measures were entirely necessary, and that whatever the UK government said in its defence, he had been forced to act.

Mr Raab, who was addressing reporters from outside his home, then realised that he would have to quarantine himself for a minimum of two weeks and ran back inside.

The Prime Minister had previously suggested building an air bridge between the UK and the Covid-ridden UK, but negotiations with himself had foundered. *(Rotters)*

Dominic Cummings: The first Question for the Prime Minister comes from a Miss Tree...

> Where are you?

> Hello...? Anyone there?

> Why won't you answer?

Cummings: He's not here, he's gone to Scotland, you can't talk to him.

> Is that the reason he went to Scotland?

Cummings: Fuck off.

Steve Bannon 'charged with fraud'

by *Our US Correspondent*
John Locke-Himup

FORMER senior White House official Steve Bannon was arrested today by federal prosecutors who charged him with defrauding the American people.

"The charge is 'fraud by passing off Donald Trump as a President who'd stand up for the little guy and protect American jobs by building a border wall that Mexico would pay for'," said a New York prosecutor in sunglasses, yesterday.

"None of it was true. From the get-go, the Trump presidency was simply a money-making Ponzi scheme for Bannon and his co-conspirators, the Republican party, to line their pockets by defrauding gullible rednecks in dumb hats out of

their hard-earned votes.

"Once Trump was in office, the extent of Bannon's fraud quickly became apparent, with tax cuts for the rich and Mexico refusing to pay a penny for Trump's dumb wall."

Steve Bannon says these charges are so outrageous that he wishes he'd thought of them, as then he could have bought a second private jet and yacht.

BACK TO OFFICE MONDAY!

BEFORE

AFTER

THERE WERE incredible scenes nationwide on Monday morning, the day Boris Johnson decreed was the day people should finally stop working from home and return to their offices.

"Once empty and deserted streets were instead deserted and empty, tube and train stations in Central London, which for months have seen barely any commuters, instead saw hardly any commuters," said a delighted Downing Street spokesman.

"When the Prime Minister talks, people listen. Then they roll over and enjoy the extra hour in bed that working from home gives them."

Speaking from his glorious lakeside country mansion Chevening in Kent, where he is currently working, the Prime Minister said it was time for the hustle and bustle of city life to resume, saying he was bewildered as to why an entire country that his government has scared witless for the last four months about leaving the house was not jumping at the chance to get back into the office.

"Who wouldn't want to swap the safety of their home-working environment for crowded trains and cramped offices, where the virus spreads most easily?" burbled the messy-haired *(cont. p94)*

(cont. p94)

EXCLUSIVE TO ALL NEWSPAPERS

GET BACK TO WORK!

WHAT is the matter with lazy Lockdown Britain? The country has had quite enough of lying around doing nothing and it is now high time that this national Slackdown stopped!

We say come on you lot! Stop loafing around at home and get back into the office. And get back on those trains. And get back on that underground! And get a newspaper on the way. Or two. Go on. Buy some newspapers. Please.

GOVERNMENT LEVELLING UP IN ACTION

MARCH to APRIL
Coronavirus mostly in London

JULY to AUGUST
Coronavirus mostly in the North

—PILBROW—

Compulsory face masks

Massive black hole 'thought to be too big to exist' discovered

A GIGANTIC black hole in the UK's finances has been detected which experts think is actually too massive for current economic thinking.

The origins of the giant financial black hole, so large that it can clearly be seen with the naked eye by anyone in Britain wishing to look, was generated by the merging of two existing colossal black holes coming together: one caused by the parlous state of the UK economy before the Covid-19 pandemic began, and the other by the catastrophic economic conditions since the outbreak started.

An economic astro-physicist, who wishes to remain anonymous, commented, "This is totally unprecedented – a newly merged monster financial black hole is actually beyond the comprehension of everyone at the moment.

"Treasury analysts have been saying it is 150 times bigger than the sun. We expect this news to cause a huge shockwave that will probably be quietly buried in the financial pages of the more upmarket newspapers." He then issued a warning, "It remains to be seen whether any light at the end of the tunnel will be emitted from this type of black hole."

The Sunday Tudvrgraph

Friday, August 28, 1620

Shakespeare may have been bisexual

by Our Farcical Correspondent
Mal Volio

A new study by eminent Shakespeare scholars has revealed that, far from being a heterosexual, married man, William Shaxpere, the "Bard of Avon", may in fact have been bisexual. *[Have we really got nothing except this olde chestnut? Ed.]*

A revolutionary new study of the 11,594 sonnets written by Shackspare has revealed that, if you read the poems very, very closely indeed, quite a lot of them are actually love poems to a man. The sonnets 269, "I fancy thee though thou art a bloke" and

853, "I don't know how to make this any more obvious, I like the lads and lasses both" have been thought to give extra credence to this extraordinary new theory. *(Haven't we been pretty confident about this since about 1609? Ed.)*

Either way, it is thought that Shagsparr will now be critically reappraised. One of the professors behind the study said, "The nice thing is that we now know this for a fact and we won't have to repeat the story endlessly for the next four hundred years just because there isn't much news on in August."

PANTO NEWS

■ THIS year's Neasden Playhouse production of *Puss in Boots* has been cancelled, as the lead actor has developed Covid. News got out when *Puss in Boots* was seen in Boots buying paracetamol and a Covid thermometer.

When asked if he had developed the virus, Puss said, "Oh, no, I haven't," to which the rest of the cast replied, "Oh, yes, you have!", forcing him to isolate for two weeks in an empty theatre.

It is hoped that Puss will survive the feline strain of cornavirus, due to the fact that he has nine lives.

Embittered fellow thespian, King Rat, said, "Knowing Puss, the bastard will probably land on his feet. Bless him. Love him to bits."

A-Levels Downgrade Fear

by Our Education Staff
Will Disappoint

THERE are concerns that this year will see an effective lowering of the height that the fruity girls jump when they get their results and are photographed on the front of the Daily Telegraph.

Due to lockdown and the closure of schools, teachers have had to make predictions about how high the fruity girls will jump and, in almost all cases, they have overestimated the distances from the ground.

Now OFFGROUND, the regulatory board for leaping schoolgirls, has threatened to downgrade the leaping figures to fit in with previous years' averages.

Said one furious schoolgirl, "I was going to be over the moon with an A* but now I have been brought down to earth with a B."

Man condemned

by Our Exotic Lunchtime Correspondent **Sue Shee**

DOWNING STREET has condemned Gordon Dexter of Weston-super-Mare after he made his own sandwich for lunch for the third day running, accusing him of wanting everyone who works at Pret to lose their jobs.

"How dare Gordon selfishly make his own sandwich for lunch whilst working from home when he could be spending £4.75 on a Pret crayfish and rocket baguette or £8.70 on a crudités platter comprising of some carrot sticks, celery and hummus," said a furious Downing Street spokesman.

"Gordon's probably closed down another five Pret branches in Central London this morning, the selfish bastard."

"It's the economy with the truth, stupid"

BRITAIN'S SCHOOLTEACHERS
An Apology

IN RECENT weeks, we may have given the impression that we felt that Britain's schoolteachers were in some way impeding the return of pupils to full-time education, due to them being members of a feckless, self-serving profession whose judgement could not be trusted. Headlines such as 'Please Sir, Let Me Into School', 'That's Enough HOME Work, Miss!' and 'Dunce's Cap For Useless, Lazy Teachers' may have led readers to believe that we considered the nation's teachers were not qualified to decide on our children's futures.

However, in the light of the recent exam grade fiasco, we now realise that there was not a jot or tittle of truth in the above, and that on the contrary, the teachers are unsung heroes, whose hard-work, dedication and commitment to their pupils makes them the only possible arbiters of their exam results.

Today's headline, 'A Star For All Teachers Everywhere!' should correct any previous erroneous inference drawn by readers. We would like to apologise for any confusion caused by our coverage of educational issues and may have to apologise again if the lazy bastards hide behind the coronavirus and, along with their left-wing union chums, refuse to throw open the school gates in September to get my screaming children out of the bloody house.

Notes&queries

We hear a lot about Ofqual nowadays, what exactly is it?

(Asks Mr Michael Downgrade)

⬤ Ofqual, as my Northern granny used to tell me, is offal of a slightly lower quality, which is therefore cheaper and was used in working-class recipes such as Faggot Pudding, Haggis Rolls, and Black Sausage Soup. Many is the time Nan would say to me, " 'Appen this Ofqual is disgusting! But it is what it is. No use complaining, pet." Nowadays of course we realise that if you complain about Ofqual and the sour taste it leaves in your mouth, you can sometimes get a better alternative.
Miss A Level

⬤ Miss A Level is sadly misinformed. The Offqual (note spelling), is a cricket shot, now not much used, but which used to be very popular in county cricket. The shot was used towards the end of the day, as the light began to fail. It required the batsman to complete an off-drive to the boundary for four, and then to claim that it was in fact a six. Many an intimidated umpire fell for the Offqual, allowing

individuals to record inflated scores. Wisden records Wessex scoring a record 716 runs, including upwards of 35 Offquals, in a single afternoon against Rutland, resulting in the permanent abolition of Wessex as a county cricket team.
Mr GCSE Pass

⬤ Not only is Mr Pass boring, but he would have done better to pass on this one! The Ofqual, as anyone who studied anything at school would know, was the South American civilisation which preceded the Aztecs but far outshone them in terms of Astrology, Poetry, Mathematics, Metal Work and Media Studies. The Ofqual believed in sacrificing teenagers, and throwing them on the scrapheap to propitiate their cruel Gods, Algo and Rithm. This turned out to be a short-sighted policy which led to the end of their civilisation. There is an excellent short paper on them by myself. Which you will find on the following website: *freeessaysforGCSE. org*
Ms PH Dee (no relation to Miss Dee)

Answers please:
What is an uptick?
Is Taylor Swift?
Why has Peter Hitchens grown a beard?

EDUCATION SECRETARY GAVIN WILLIAMSON IN NEW SHOCK

I've been awarded a CBE

That's now been downgraded to a DUD

'A' Level Politics Exam Paper 2020
IN FULL

1 Is it a good idea for a political party to really annoy everyone between the ages of 16 and 18 when you will need at least some of them to vote for you at the next election?

'A' Level Maths Exam Paper 2020
IN FULL

1 Can you fool 100% of a given population for 100% of the time?
Show workings.

Dante's Infurlough

PRESIDENT TRUMP'S CAMPAIGN SPEECH IN FULL

"Hi everyone. C'mon get those masks off! What are you afraid of? Oh yeah – the Chinese virus. Put them on again! I wanna talk to you about an even bigger threat to America, much worse than a virus, much worse than China, much deadlier than death... and that's Sleepy Joe Biden. Fact!

If Joe Biden becomes President, America will shut down, the economy will nose-dive and there will be riots, oh hang on, that's now – let's start again.

Joe Biden is too old to be President, the guy's in his seventies for God's sake. You want an old guy running the country? You want someone who's clearly got dementia making the big decisions? You gotta be kidding. And I'll tell you something else, the guy's got a reputation for being gropey around women. Fact!

Creepy Joe Biden I call him! Sleepy and Creepy! But it's worse, the guy's dodgy on race.

That's why he picked a black woman to try and cover it up. And you know what? She's not even American. She was only born here. Like Obama. Just saying. Since when did being born here make you an American?... What's that? 1791? It's in the Constitution?!

Thanks, guy in a suit. You're fired. Along with the useless Dr Fauci. We don't need facts at a time like this. Fact! So, Sleepy Creepy Weepy Joe can't even string a together sentence of words. Fact!

The more I hear about how unfit for office Biden is, the more worried I get that he'll be President! Typical low Democrat trick putting up a useless candidate who might win – come back Crooked Hillary! Unlock her up! And don't forget – put your votes for me in the mail before I go postal and close it down. It's all rigged. Unless I win – in which case it isn't.

God Help America!"

School news

• • • • • • • • • • • • • • • • • • • •

St Cakes

Bubble Term begins today. Or tomorrow. Or Wednesday. Or never. Please check school website for details. There are 354 boys and girls in the school, and 423 in the Nightingale Sanatorium (formerly the School Sports Hall). AJB Wheezer is Head of Covid's. The school outfitter is Mr Hazmat's on the otherwise closed High Street. Socially distanced arrivals will commence at 8.30am and finish at 1.30pm. Socially distanced departures will commence at 1.30pm and finish at 8.30pm. Despite what you may have read, the school trip to the Algarve is very definitely on. Face masks in house colours must be worn at all times. There is to be no running in the corridors, unless you know someone has tested positive. Lockdowns commence on September 19th. Despite what you may have read, the school trip to the Algarve is very definitely cancelled. Exams will be taken with a pinch of salt and grades assessed by pupils. The Bursar would like parents to know that the fact that the term is likely to be cut short will result in a change in the fee structure. Fees will go up. Despite what you may have read, the school trip to the Algarve is very definitely on. Please check website for updates, although please check updates for updated updates. Term ends this afternoon. Welcome.

FRIENDS OF MEGHAN TO REMAIN ANONYMOUS

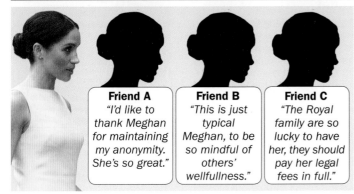

Friend A
"I'd like to thank Meghan for maintaining my anonymity. She's so great."

Friend B
"This is just typical Meghan, to be so mindful of others' wellfullness."

Friend C
"The Royal family are so lucky to have her, they should pay her legal fees in full."

THAT HISTORIC BIDEN CAMPAIGN SPEECH IN FULL

"Hope, dreams, joy... I'm not Trump, light, love, friendship, I'm not Trump... compassion, family, community, I'm not Trump... I'm not Trump, I'm not Trump, I'm not Trump, I'm not Trump, I'm not Trump, I'm not Trump..."
(Continues not being Trump for 50 more mins)

OBAMA SHOCK

America needs a President who is eloquent, engaged and inspiring... but unfortunately I'm not running, so vote for Biden

---

'STRICTLY' IN TV FIRST

by Our Showbiz Staff **Tess Daleymail**

IN what has been hailed as a major breakthrough for popular entertainment, the BBC's *Strictly Come Dancing* flagship and ratings behemoth is to feature a "No-Sex" couple.

This extraordinary innovation involves a heterosexual couple who don't end up having sex with each other.

Said presenter Claudia Winkelfringe, "It's never been tried before and people have said that the British public aren't ready for it. But the programme makers feel that society has moved on sufficiently for our viewers to accept a celebrity and a professional dancer who don't jump into bed with each other half-way through rehearsals".

Traditionalists warn that this could lead to a drop in ratings, and that eliminating the much-loved "Curse of Strictly" removes an essential component of Saturday night television and Sunday morning tabloid newspapers.

ME AND MY SPOON

THIS WEEK

DIDO HARDING

Do you have a favourite spoon?
Well, no. I'm interested in all spoons and...

What about a wooden spoon?
No, not particularly.

Like the one you were awarded for customer service at TalkTalk?
No.

Or would you rather not TalkTalk about that?
That's not very funny.

Is the wooden spoon a metaphor for your performance in all of your jobs?
I don't know what you mean.

Or do you think a silver spoon would be a more appropriate metaphor for the way you get given top jobs with no discernable qualifications other than being a Tory Baroness, and the wife of a Tory MP?
This is very unfair.

Yes, that's what everyone says.
Can you ask me a sensible spoon question, please? I'm a very busy woman.

Is the NHS going to run out of plastic spoons now that you're in charge?
No, we have a world-beating spoon delivery implementation policy.

So that's a 'yes' then. Has anything amusing ever happened to you in connection with a spoon?
I once lost a spoon and couldn't find it.

So you were unable to track and trace it?
If you can't be serious about spoons, I'm walking out of this interview, and into another plum job.

NEXT WEEK: *Brian Cox, Me and My Apple.*

CONSPIRACY UPDATE
TRAFALGAR SQUARE SPECIAL

Now that we are all back from our annual festival I trust I speak for everyone (except the anarchists) and say a good time was had by all!

Our 'no mask' gathering turned out to be a great success and we certainly brought some new and interesting people into our fold! Such as:

ENGERLANDFORTHEINGLISH69 who tweeted:
"The reason that the guvoment wants us to were masks is we wont no who is black or not so we wont no wichshops to burn down."

Well yes, haha, that is an interesting theory that I've not heard before!

To which his friend with the British Union of Fascists flag in his avatar, PAKISGOHOME replied:
"It is all a plot so that efnicks can use masks too hide from Piti Patel but there not fooling us. Come on Priti, send them Pakkis home.!"

Very, um, interesting.

On the other hand, thankfully, we have regular contributor and devoted conspiracy fan DEATHTOZION3542 who put this on his Facebook page:
"I believe masks are designed to slowly suffocate the gentile peoples of the world. Jews, with their naturally larger noses, will survive and further dominate the planet with their Zionist scheming."

Thanks for that DEATHTOZION3542. A little bit of sanity there!

And sticking with sanity, SHEEPLE5678 put this on his website:
"The Virus doesn't exist. Bill Gates invented it to not exist. The only people to die from it didn't exist. The only way to stop Bill Gates controlling our minds through the virus which doesn't exist is to smear our bodies in marmite, cheese sauce and swarfega and wrap ourselves in bacofoil."

Finally we have devoted nutcase and conspiracy chairman P. Corbyn, who has uncovered a sinister plot arising from his £10,000 fine for demonstrating in Trafalgar Square without permission.
He thinks the government was actually behind his fine, as it says 'HM Government' on the paperwork.

Well done, Piers! I think you're onto something there!

EYE COMPETITION
BRITAIN'S WORST PIERS – YOU DECIDE!

Birnbeck **Morgan** **Corbyn**

Channel 4's 'Me and My Penis' disappoints

THE controller of Channel 4 was last night embarrassed by the poor performance of its new cockumentary series *Me and My Penis*.

The much-heralded show broadcast the first image of an erect penis on terrestrial television, and was expected to get a rise out of its viewers, with its frank honesty and taboo-breaking realism, but instead it turned out to be a flop.

"Size of audience isn't everything," said Channel Phwoarr boss Ian Katz, "and ours is a perfectly normal, average size of viewership for this type of documentary." He then added, "And this has never happened to me before."

Critics have suggested other reasons for the flaccid ratings' performance of *Me and My Penis*. Said one, "It's almost as if people who wanted to see an erect penis have found somewhere else on the internet where it's possible to see one."

Mr Katz has been told not to worry about what happened, as it's perfectly normal for a controller his age to experience a disappointing performance in the TV bedroom department. He may well have been tired and under a lot of stress, as he tried desperately to get some viewers for his rotten programmes.

'After he left office, Dave and I went through a rough patch,' says Britain

by Our Political Staff
Samantha Cameron

IN a shock revelation, the United Kingdom has admitted that after the Brexit vote and David Cameron's subsequent resignation as Prime Minister its relationship with the former PM deteriorated significantly, to the point where it wondered if it ever wanted to see him again.

Said the UK, "I was really cross with him, he messed everything up. I blamed him for everything that went wrong. And looking back on it all now, I realise I was 100 percent right."

Mr Cameron had previously said in his memoir that he regretted nothing, that it wasn't his fault, and if the United Kingdom found it annoying when he walked off humming a stupid ditty as their relationship fell apart, that wasn't his problem. And nor was anything else.

When asked whether he'd patched things up with the UK, Mr Cameron was unavailable for comment because he'd been locked in his shepherd's hut by his wife.

Adele 'accused of cultural appropriation'

by Our Music Staff
Bantu Knots

Adele has been widely criticised after sharing a picture of herself on her Instagram, and accused of "cultural appropriation" by skinny women.

"How dare Adele show off a flat belly in a bra top and skintight trousers?" asked one horrified size six woman.

"That is the traditional costume of my people, skinny bitches – women who have dedicated their entire lives to extreme dieting.

"Adele is supposed to be the fat friend who makes us feel superior because we'd never succumb to the temptation of eating a cream cake. I am so disgusted to see her trying to pass herself off as 'skinny'... I might be sick right now. So that's a silver lining, at least."

"Adele needs to go back to being plump and dressed in huge, voluminous kaftans, so that we can admire her talent but also laugh behind her back at what a porker she is," said another extremely angry, skinny woman, half-heartedly eating quinoa.

Film review

Tenet

A ground-breaking Christopher Nolan film, in which time seems to be going backwards and forwards simultaneously. Or is it? Or is it just that you're so terribly bored of this year that it feels like time is going backwards, partly because you're watching a film which is 150 minutes long and doesn't make any sense, like all bloody Christopher Nolan films, and you've been told you have to wear a mask throughout?

Boris Johnson MP
● Live   385,000,000 Views

Prime Minister's Back to Work People's Prime Minister's Question Time Live on Fakebook

👍 Like   💬 Comment

0 people **like this**

▶

(MUSIC: 'RULE, BRITANNIA!' PLAYS VERY LOUDLY)

Boris (singing): **Rule**, Britannia, Britannia rule the **waves**, apart from the bit in the Channel **full** of Froggy fishermen and migrants, obviously, Britons **never** never never shall be **slaves**, unless you work for **Boohoo** or **Amazon** or **Deliveroo** or **Uber** or **Sports Direct** or, in my case, **Dominic Cummings. Rule**, Britannia! Britannia rule the **second** wave!

(MUSIC SWIFTLY CHANGES TO 'LAND OF HOPE AND GLORY')

Boris (singing): **Land** of Groping Tory!

(MUSIC FADES)

Boris: **Whoops**! I'm afraid that's sub

judice! But let me **first** say: It's **great** to be back! Everyone's back at work and by "everyone" I mean virtually no one apart from **me**. So we're getting Britain **moving**, mostly from the **bedroom** to the kitchen table. But **Parliament**'s back! **Government**'s back! **I'm** back! And **Covid**'s back! No no, it **isn't**.

Cummings: Just fucking get on with it.

Boris: We've got to save Britain's economy. And there's only **one** way to do that. We've come up with a new **slogan**. (READS OUT FROM PIECE OF PAPER HANDED TO HIM BY CUMMINGS) "**Wash** hands, **Cover** face, **Make** space." And that means: "**Wash** hands of responsibility, **cover** face in shame when it doesn't work out, and **make** space for new member of Cabinet when I sack Williamson." **Snappy**, eh? So, the first question comes from Mrs Patience Waring-Thynne, a life-long Tory supporter!

> You've had a disastrous summer, full of U-turns. Is Autumn going to be worse?

Boris: Let me answer that very **directly**. I think the **main** thing to say is that Keir Starmer is a member of the **IRA** and I'm **not** going to take lessons from someone who is well-known to be a sleeper for **Hezbollah** and was Colonel Gaddafi's **personal** bodyguard. Does that answer your question?

> Why do you always ignore the question and answer something completely different?

Boris: Thank you and I'm glad you brought up the **BBC**, who have behaved despicably by denying every Englishman his right to stand on the white cliffs of Dover on the Last Night of the Proms and sing that fine old British hymn, which you wouldn't find an **anti-Semite** like Keir Starmer singing, viz '**Jerusalem**'. Next question. It's from a **lawyer**. Oh-oh! Am I behind with the paternity payments again? **Not** that I have any. And it's **none** of anybody's business if I do. Or **don't**. Hello, it's Sir Keir Starmer.

> Prime Minister, why do you just tell complete lies about me, when even a basic study of Wikipedia would tell you that my record on terrorism, anti-Semitism and even the Last Night of the Proms is the opposite to what you're claiming?

Boris: This is **typical** of you, m'learned friend, showing off your **fancy** grasp of the detail and your **high-falutin'** determination to read the brief, rather than just **winging** it with good old British **bombast** and **bluster**. Pah! Take that, your **wigged** m'ludship!

> I wasn't a judge, I was Director of Public Prosecutions.

Boris: Boring, boring! **Yawno**! Time for me to take the dog for a **jog** and my personal trainer for a **shit** in the park. Or is it the **other** way round? Details, details...

Fears for office workers

■ Bosses up and down the country have expressed concern that the longer employees continue to work from home, the more they'll start to enjoy their lives.

"Without that three-hour grinding commute on a crowded train that breaks down outside Crewe at least once a week and eight hours in a small cubicle under harsh lighting, there is a real chance these workers will start to enjoy the same quality of life that we enjoy," said concerned bosses.

"Freed from all that work stress about productivity and promotions, they'll be able to be around to watch their children grow up, spend quality time with their spouse and generally feel that life is worth living. It's horrific."

POETRY CORNER

In Memoriam Robert Trump, younger brother of Donald

So. Farewell
Then the wrong Trump.

        E.J. Thribb (71½)

"I'm cycling to work"

An open letter from the BBC to the Daily Telegraph

Dear Daily Telegraph,

It really pains me to say this because the old Telegraph used to be such a favourite in our house and, to be honest, it was a national institution.

It was famous for its impartial news reporting, its lively sports coverage, its easy crossword and its fascinating stories on page three about randy vicars, but in recent years it's become nothing more than a vehicle for right-wing propaganda.

It used to have dissenting voices and not every piece was about "how great Brexit is" and "what a marvellous job Boris Johnson is doing".

What about the 50% of the population who don't share this view? Don't they get a say? No. All you offer us, I'm afraid, are the same old faces: Charles Moore, Allison Pearson, Janet Daley – or "Janet Daley Telegraph!", as I call her.

It's boring! Come on Daily Telegraph! You can't expect us to pay our £2.50 a day for what I call "The Daily Torygraph!" if you don't occasionally run a double-page spread by a member of the Socialist Workers Party.

I can't help thinking that your falling ratings and increasing unpopularity may have something to do with you being detached from the reality of most people in this country and living in an elitist suburban bubble...
(continues for 94 paragraphs)

The Daily Timesgraph

Friday 11 September 2020

THIS newspaper condemns in the strongest possible terms the disgusting behaviour of Extinction Rebellion protestors in blocking the roads to our printing presses, disrupting the production of our Saturday edition.

This is an unabashed attack on the free press, an attempt to silence a media organisation simply because you do not agree with its politics.

Their repulsive antics meant that thousands of our loyal readers at the weekend were unable to read hundreds of columns all calling for the defunding of the BBC because we are sick of the Beeb ramming its woke political agenda down our necks.

It is a scandal that Extinction Rebellion have attempted to shut down real debate and censor freedom of expression. Now, like never before, we must unite to defend the freedoms that make this nation great.

On other pages
▨ Why we must curtail the right to protest immediately ▨ And the right to large gatherings of anyone who might start protesting, just in case ▨ And we must immediately designate protestors who affect our sales as TERRORISTS and send them to the TOWER OF LONDON and *(That's not nearly enough. Keep going. Ed.)*

EXTINCTION REBELLION PROTESTS

"There is no doubt that the climate has changed. Last time we held a protest, it was warm and friendly and tolerant. This time, it is dramatically cooler and, to be honest, pretty frosty, and we are worried about being frozen out."

Top BBC staff to be told to 'keep political views to themselves'

by Our Broadcasting Staff
Phil Twitter

Senior BBC employees will no longer be able to express their political opinions, under new guidelines issued by the incoming Direc-tory General, Tim Davie.

This is thought to be a thinly veiled attack on highly paid top BBC employee Tim Davie, who has a history of expressing his right-wing beliefs in speeches going back as far as yesterday, when he made it perfectly clear that he was a Conservative

sympathiser. Said Tim Davie, "The impartiality of the BBC is called into question when people like Tim Davie, whom we all know used to be a local Tory candidate and deputy chairman of his local Conservative party, uses his position at the BBC to promote his own personal political agenda."

Gary Lineker tweeted, "Tim used to sell Pepsi for a living, which is fine, but if only he had sold crisps instead, he would be entitled to say whatever he liked."

SAYS

THE criminal actions of the loony left terrorists have stopped your soaraway Sun from reaching your doorstep this morning. If this carries on, the entire British way of life will soon be a distant mammary *(surely "memory"? Ed)*. These are just some of the scary things that will happen if so-called Extinction Rebellion get their way:

1. Paper boys to lose their jobs, turn to drug-dealing and starve to death along with their families.

2. Tramps to freeze to death without their vital tabloid blankets to keep them warm in the heatwave.

3. Fish and chips will cease to exist without their essential recycled-newspaper

packaging, leading to the collapse of British fishing industry, the end of potato farming in the UK and the mass unemployment of pea mushers in Britain's hard-hit regions.

4. Death of all Britain's cats, as all-important litter tray lining is impossible to find and constipated cats tragically explode all over the country. These ER moggy murderers will have this on their conscience.

5. Also hamsters, gerbils and guinea pigs.

6. A plague of wasps to descend on defenceless population, who have been left with no copies of yesterday's newspaper with which to defend themselves.

This is the Sun-less world that the self-appointed destroyers of the free press would like you to live in. We say "Stop them now before we lose any money." *(Surely " the essential liberties inherent in our great democracy?" Ed.)*

LIZ TRUSS PUSHES FOR STILTON DEAL WITH JAPAN

Why are you so obsessed with cheese?

I'm crackers!

Left-wing satirists to be curbed

THE incoming BBC Director General has pledged to curb the all-powerful left-wing BBC satirists who propelled Jeremy Corbyn to victory at the last election.

"Right though 2018 and 2019, these all-powerful leftie jokesters made quips about how badly the Tories were handling Brexit and, as a result, the entire country was brainwashed into voting Corbyn and his socialist government into power.

"What chance did Boris Johnson have of winning a huge 80-seat majority when, just weeks before the vote took place, a comedian on Radio 4's *The News Quiz* got a round of applause by saying Boris was screwing the entire country?"

Trump's Favourite Military Films

Fort Apache
Loser US Cavalry waste energy riding to rescue of other losers besieged by the loser Apaches who should have been building casinos on their reservations. Starring John Wayne as Captain Loser and Henry Fonda as Colonel Sucker.

Saving Private Ryan
Bunch of losers land on beach on D-Day and instead of bravely putting up luxury hotel and spa facility, go on pointless quest to recue loser soldier whose three loser brothers are already dead. Tom Hanks plays Captain Loser with Matt Damon as Private Sucker.

The Great Escape
Loser prisoners in World War Two waste a lot of energy trying to escape, instead of bravely enjoying themselves in the camp playing golf. Starring chief loser Steve McQueen as Captain Loser, the Cooler Loser, who can't even get a motorcycle over a barbed wire fence and some other British losers who deservedly get shot.

(That's enough films. Ed.)

CLEAR GOVERNMENT CORONAVIRUS ADVICE AS WE ENTER AUTUMN

Resume commuting by train and working in the office to revive the moribund economy whilst avoiding public transport and packed enclosed spaces such as offices to stem the rising number of covid cases *(cont. 2094)*

U.S. ELECTION: TRUMP RUNS RIOT

Anyone who says I'm stoking up violence...

...should be shot

Is Russia meddling in the Russian election?

THERE were fears last night that the Kremlin was trying to interfere with the results of the next Russian election.

Suspicions were raised when there was an assassination attempt on the Leader of the Opposition, who was poisoned with a cup of tea before getting on a plane.

Said one observer, "I don't want to be paranoid, but when the Leader of the Opposition is nearly murdered in Russia, you do tend to think that there may be some link to the incumbent President. But don't tell anyone I said that."

The Kremlin announced that they were not involved, as they're far too busy developing a new vaccine for coronavirus which can be administered via a cup of tea, usually before going on an aeroplane.

"This vaccine, provisionally named 'Novichokovid', kills the virus dead, by killing the person carrying it. We are now looking for more volunteers, preferably members of the Opposition, who would like to perform their patriotic duty," said a spokesman, adding, "We wish the late Mr Navalny a speedy recovery." *(Rotters)*

THAT HIGH-TECH GOVERNMENT METHOD USED TO WORK OUT FOREIGN QUARANTINES, EXAM RESULTS AND LOCAL LOCKDOWNS

'OVEN-READY' BREXIT DEAL LATEST

Chancellor announces brilliant new scheme

by Our Economic Staff **Hugh Pay**

The popular chancellor, Rishi Sunshinesoutofhisbackside, has come up with yet another vote-winning, crowd-pleasing solution to the economic crash caused by the coronavirus pandemic.

Yes, the man that gave us "Eat Out to Help Out" has now dreamed up an even more mouth-watering treat for next year. With the catchy slogan "Fork Out to Help Out", the public will be offered a deal in which they pay out half of their income to the Treasury on Mondays, Tuesdays and Wednesdays. And Thursdays, Fridays, Saturdays and Sundays. The fabulous new scheme even includes bank holidays!

Rishi's deal means that you get to keep an amazing 50 percent of your salary, while the other 50 percent goes straight into paying for all that stuff you thought Rishi was giving you for nothing in 2020.

It's bound to be a huge hit, certainly on most people's wallets, and will make Rishi an absolute shoo-in to be prime minister when Boris gets blamed for all the tax increases. Yummy!

PHIL SPACE ASKS: 'IS IT HARDER TO CONCENTRATE AFTER LOCKDOWN?'

IT'S the question we're all asking. Has it become more difficult to focus after our national four-month incarceration? Have we in effect lost our ability to apply ourselves to the matter in hand? Have we become... Oh, they're releasing Mulan on Disney Plus. Wow, $29?! That's a lot of money. Wonder what it is in pounds? I might google that. Oh, is there a Champions League game on tonight? So there is. Now that dog on TikTok is funny, though I read a good conspiracy theory linking it to the Chinese and Beirut. I wonder how much it costs to fly to Spain... Who is that Tory MP? Has Twitter named him? I don't think I can eat any more hummus. Owen Jones looks about eleven. Shall I buy another face mask? I could get one with dinosaurs on it. No, I like gherkins, but they just don't like me. That reminds me, I'd better ring my mum. Oh, and another thing – I've got to write a piece for my editor. What was it about again?

A YEAR OF PRIVATE EYE-SOLATION...

"Maybe it's time to ease off on the Joe Wicks a little, Cyril"

"It's like Piccadilly Circus down there"

"How am I coping? OK... you know... catching up on my reading... learning a new language"

The Man in the Ironed Mask

*"That's not a superhero outfit – **this** is a superhero outfit"*

"Hold on! This isn't a conference call, it's the family collage"

"Are you sure you won't let me cut your hair?"

Face masks to be worn in situations when social distancing is not possible

"I also have a backtracking app which tells me the government's position"

"Can you at least put a hat on, so we know you're there?"

"We have, according to the revised projection of the adjusted figures, something more or less approaching no idea"

"I haven't seen them since the start of lockdown, so I thought I'd Zoom"

"Do you need to borrow my bikini wax?"

"Of course people will remember you were bald before the lockdown, Barry"